The Critical Librarianship and Pedagogy Symposium

Reflections, Revisions, and New Works

edited by
Yvonne Mery
and Anthony Sanchez

Association of College and Research Libraries
A division of the American Library Association
Chicago, Illinois 2023

The paper used in this publication meets the minimum requirements of American National Standard for Information Sciences–Permanence of Paper for Printed Library Materials, ANSI Z39.48-1992. ∞

Library of Congress Control Number: 2023941058

Printed in the United States of America.

27 26 25 24 23 5 4 3 2 1

Contents

INTRODUCTION

Walking the Long Road

Transforming Library Spaces for Liberation

Yvonne Mery and Anthony Sanchez

Background

Perhaps you sense it already—academic librarianship is due for a major paradigm shift. Job requirements are changing, work-life balance expectations are shifting, and researchers are using libraries differently. Supporting social justice movements and empathic approaches to counter the disinformation, hatred, and violence in our world through community building and mutual understanding is more urgent than ever. Moreover, the existential threats to the library profession, such as dwindling budgets, rising costs from major publishers, and the shifting nature of information and truth in the twenty-first century, continue to rise. Educators in the field are at odds between the care and support of the student body and the demanding needs of the administration and proving value in the academy. Librarians are still delving into this very fray, however, with new ideas about community, feminism, education, and social change. These collected chapters are an attempt to capture the essence of that spirit with works from new and familiar voices in the field.

The works presented here expand on past presentations given at the Critical Librarianship and Pedagogy Symposium (CLAPS) held biennially at the University of Arizona Libraries (UAL) since 2016. CLAPS is a collaborative effort of UAL staff and has traditionally been a free event that aims to bring together educators and students to discuss issues related to critical pedagogy. The focus of CLAPS has and continues to be information literacy and instruction, but past presentations have covered a wide range of librarianship practices, including the peer-review process, hiring practices, makerspaces, and cataloging. An impetus for releasing this book was to allow more library practitioners to learn about CLAPS and get to know the types of issues CLAPS addresses.

Learning Outcomes

This anthology will provide readers with a toolkit for critical library pedagogy that recognizes how knowledge is created within historical and deeply politicized contexts. Authors working in library or disciplinary teaching fields explore intersections between information literacy and critical pedagogy. We presuppose a reader's awareness that critical pedagogy recognizes that our education system is shaped by hegemonic political and economic forces, often to the detriment of politically and culturally marginalized students. Through this recognition of the systemic oppression of students (and therefore all peoples), critical librarianship and pedagogy seek transformation of the education system, and ultimately people's liberation, as a praxis.[1] Authors provide current thinking, as well as assessment and reflection, on their practices of teaching students how to recognize and critique the oppressive power structures inherent in educational systems. The work done by librarians is analyzed in a way that reveals the socioeconomic frameworks that drive the costs of our labor.

Topics explored include the advent of neoliberalism in higher education, social justice, white fragility, supporting neurodivergence in education, and disability-rights activism. Furthermore, keeping in mind that "your theory determines what you want to do in terms of helping people grow,"[2] works use lenses such as queer, intersectional, feminist, and critical race theory to examine subjects. Also featured are authors' experiences and practices for sustainable teaching, facilitating dialogue in the classroom, and using tools such as user experience or empathic design. It was imperative to us, as editors of this collection, that the voices in this book be a more expansive representation of librarianship, and in particular of those practicing critical librarianship. Contributors come from a variety of institutions, including universities, community colleges, medical libraries, and special collections. Many are reference and instruction librarians, but there are also scholarly communication librarians, disciplinary professors, and graduate students. Contributors also represent a diversity of race, genders, and sexual orientations. We hope that readers will be inspired to develop their own praxes for incorporating critical pedagogy theory into their practices as educators—both within the library and in higher education in general.

Organization

The book explores five main themes: Critical Pedagogies in the Classroom, Feminist Library Practices, the Labor of Librarianship, Practices of Care, and Community Archives. Each section is outlined below.

Critical Pedagogies In The Classroom

FACILITATION SKILLS FOR CRITICAL LIBRARY INSTRUCTION, BY AMY GILGAN

Gilgan examines how facilitation skills can be used in critical information literacy instruction. Specifically, the author discusses how intergroup dialogue pedagogy and multipartial mediation have informed their library instruction. Although these techniques often require multiple sessions to implement and develop, Gilgan includes tips for how to apply them to one-shot library sessions.

ANTI-ABLEISM IN LIBRARY INSTRUCTION: CONSIDERATIONS FOR NEURODIVERGENT STUDENTS, BY PAIGE CROWL AND ELIZABETH CAROL NOVOSEL

By challenging and countering ableism in the classroom, authors provide an expansive overview of key concepts, such as invisible disabilities and ableism, related to disability and neurodivergence in the context of higher education. The authors compare and contrast the medical and social models of disability and also outline challenges faced by disabled students, providing an accessible overview of Universal Design for Learning (UDL) for all librarians and concluding with practical applications of UDL for library instruction.

INFORMATION STUDIES FOR SOCIAL JUSTICE: PRAXIS IN AN UNDERGRADUATE COURSE, BY LUA GREGORY AND SHANA HIGGINS

This work recounts the experiences and approaches to weaving student discussion and media production on social justice movements of academic librarians for their undergraduate library studies course. Zinesters will rejoice as Gregory and Higgins analyze their students' artistic and intellectual expressions in their final semester project to support their teaching praxis that "growing into one's voice is to become empowered." This chapter is an exciting exploration of how students create community in the classroom, engage with social justice issues, define their own voices, and contribute to the arc for social justice.

Feminist Library Practices

WHAT IS AUTHORITY? A FEMINIST INVESTIGATION OF PERSONAL EXPERIENCE AS KNOWLEDGE IN STUDENT RESEARCH AND WRITING, BY MARTINIQUE HALLERDUFF AND HANNAH CARLTON

Feminist pedagogy and the ACRL *Framework for Information Literacy for Higher Education* both challenge traditional ideas of authority, including encouraging students to use their personal experiences as authoritative sources. In this chapter, the authors discuss a research study they conducted that looked at how students use their personal experiences as forms of knowledge in their writing. The authors also discuss how teaching librarians can encourage students to view their personal experiences as authoritative and use them in their academic research papers.

SITUATED DATA: FEMINIST EPISTEMOLOGY AND DATA CURATION, BY SCOUT CALVERT

Calvert discusses a framework for data curation that is more critical and objective and is informed by feminist epistemology. This new framework, which she calls "situated data," looks at data sharing as a critical part of library practice and one that will allow for fairer and more just views of the world. Calvert also discusses how this new framework can be easily implemented by library practitioners and can also be used for collection development, cataloging, and classification. Calvert also provided a thorough discussion of feminist epistemology and the philosophy of science.

The Labor of Librarianship

ACTING "AS IF": CRITICAL PEDAGOGY, EMPOWERMENT, AND LABOR, BY RAFIA MIRZA, KAREN NICHOLSON, AND MAURA SEALE

Here the authors offer a perspective on some of the shortcomings of critical library pedagogy in the library classroom. They argue that critical library pedagogy, when mainstreamed into institutions with all their pitfalls, positions the instructor in a role of power that takes the teeth out of its liberatory and subversive potential. They consider how to reimagine the application of critical library pedagogy in higher education to create a more just environment for both librarians and students, moving beyond a classroom that feels as if it is a safe space but is really not.

BEYOND SUSTAINABILITY AND SELF-CARE, BY VERONICA ARELLANO DOUGLAS, EMILY DEAL, AND CAROLINA HERNANDEZ

Current self-care models often place the burden of self-care on librarians, and the structures in place in current library teaching programs lead to overworked and overwhelmed librarians. In this chapter, the authors explore engaged pedagogy and how it can help teaching librarians become better teachers as they care for themselves and their students. The authors discuss why teaching librarians should consider not only what their students need but also what they themselves need to thrive as teachers.

Practices of Care

ACADEMIC LIBRARY LABOR AS COMMUNITY CARE WORK, BY SIÂN EVANS AND AMANDA MEEKS

Discussing the role of empathy in labor, Evans and Meeks assert the potential for academic libraries to become loving, caring, radical spaces. The authors examine their experiences working in academic institutions, community organizing with grassroots organizations, and creative practices in an exploration of the library's radical potential, offering frameworks for understanding care work and thoughtfully conveying the urgency of enacting change within libraries in the context of the COVID-19 pandemic.

A PRACTICE OF CONNECTION: APPLYING RELATIONAL-CULTURAL THEORY TO LIBRARIANSHIP, BY ANASTASIA CHIU, VERONICA ARELLANO DOUGLAS, JOANNA GADSBY, ALANA KUMBIER AND LALITHA NATARAJ

This chapter uses the authors' personal stories to examine how they have implemented relational-cultural theory in their professional lives. Each story looks at a different aspect of academic librarianship, including working with teaching faculty, onboarding as a new employee, conducting workplace relationships, consulting with faculty on scholarly communication issues, and building empathy and connection in the classroom. These stories show how relational-cultural theory can help us see how our work affects all of those around us, including ourselves.

Community Archives

COMMUNITY-BASED ARCHIVES AND THEIR PEDAGOGIES, BY JAMIE A. LEE, KRISTEN SUAGEE-BEAUDUY (CHEROKEE NATION), AND SAMANTHA MONTES

The authors introduce their qualitative research about community-based archives (CBAs), sharing meaningful first-person descriptions of what CBAs mean to those who create them. The authors explore the depths of naming practices in the archives and their potential for empowering underrepresented communities and building new historical narratives that challenge the status quo. They challenge the reader to think of fingerweaving as a metaphor and method for understanding how the archives might be created in a way that represents those traditionally pushed to the margins. Their chapter is a call to action for teachers and archivists who want to apply lessons learned from CBAs to shift the paradigm.

Acknowledgments

The editors wish to also recognize and give thanks to the many contributors to this work. Their hard work and perseverance, through what has arguably been one of the most difficult and tumultuous times in our collective lives, is a testament to the strength of educators everywhere who struggle for social change in the face of adversity.

Notes

1. Paulo Freire, *Pedagogy of the Oppressed*, 30th Anniversary ed., trans. Myra Bergman Ramos (New York: Bloomsbury Academic, 2012), 54–55.
2. Myles Horton and Paulo Freire, *We Make the Road by Walking*, ed. Brenda Bell, John Gaventa, and John Peters (Philadelphia: Temple University Press, 1990), 100.

Bibliography

Freire, Paulo. *Pedagogy of the Oppressed*, 30th anniversary ed. Translated by Myra Bergman Ramos. New York: Bloomsbury Academic, 2012.

Horton, Myles, and Paulo Freire. *We Make the Road by Walking: Conversations on Education and Social Change*. Edited by Brenda Bell, John Gaventa, and John Peters. Philadelphia: Temple University Press, 1990.

PART I

Critical Pedagogies in the Classroom

CHAPTER 1

Facilitation Skills for Critical Library Instruction

Amy Gilgan

Introduction

Critical library instruction draws from the dialogic pedagogy of Paulo Freire. Rather than engaging in a banking model of education in which the teacher transmits knowledge to the students from a place of authority, Freire advocates for learning spaces in which teachers and students learn together through dialogue.[1] The library instruction I have done as a facilitator and mediator has been informed by intergroup dialogue (IGD) pedagogy and multipartial mediation.

IGD is a critical practice in that it is a "conscientious effort to examine how individual and group life are embedded within a structural system of inequality and privilege, and to connect that analytical understanding to action."[2] Originating from the University of Michigan in the 1980s, the IGD model draws from the dialogic work of John Dewey, Myles Horton, and Paulo Freire.[3] IGD is dialogic in that it focuses on using communication to build relationships within and across

social identities.[4] IGD is a scaffolded four-stage model in which participants build community norms and communication skills, engage with social identity, apply communication skills to conversations about power, and strategize next steps for building solidarity to take action.

In order to support building relationships between privileged and marginalized groups, IGD utilizes the mediation framework of multipartiality. In contrast to neutrality, multipartial mediation expects, acknowledges, and unpacks power dynamics while creating a space for all parties to participate.[5] Without an analysis of power, both mediation and dialogue can reinforce oppressive power dynamics.[6] In this chapter, I will explore how the principles of multipartial mediation and IGD can be applied to critical library instruction. I will examine how each of the four stages of IGD have influenced my teaching as well as offering practical facilitation tips from each stage. IGD was designed to be practiced over several weeks with a cohort, and I recognize that many academic librarians do not have the option of meeting several times with a class. As a result, this chapter will include facilitation tips that can be applied to one-shot library instruction. Although one-shot sessions do not have the necessary relational scaffolding to engage deeply in the stages of IGD, there are transferable skills to be learned from all four stages. In order to explain how multipartiality influences IGD facilitation, I will provide a brief overview of multipartial mediation.

Multipartiality

Much like librarianship, neutrality is often cited as a core value of mainstream Western mediation.[7] In the 1980s, Janet Rifkin and Sara Cobb analyzed hundreds of recorded community mediation sessions at the University of Massachusetts. Their research revealed that the participant who spoke first in joint mediation sessions was favored 80 percent of the time by the agreements reached.[8] The participants who spoke second often found themselves responding to the first party's narrative, which resulted in the second party not getting the chance to share their full story. This research revealed the ways in which mediators have the power to privilege one story over another through the way they conduct the mediation process. Based on their interviews with mediators, Rifkin and Cobb identified neutrality as mediators being impartial to the content and equidistant in their relationships to the participants.[9] Mediators try to maintain equidistance by treating parties equally and engaging in procedural symmetry. This symmetry is often enacted by giving both parties in a dispute the same amount of time to tell their stories.

Procedural symmetry fails to take into account how dominant cultural narratives operate in mediation. In social justice education, the dominant narrative (also known as the master narrative) refers to the hegemonic norms we are all socialized into that privilege certain social groups.[10] The dominant narrative is more familiar to the mediators, who are disproportionately white, and requires less explanation.[11] When participants from historically marginalized groups share nondominant counternarratives, they may need more time to translate their experience to the mediator, particularly when the mediator holds privileged identities.[12] In other words, it takes less time for a participant to convey a story in line with the dominant narrative than it does for a participant whose story reflects a counternarrative. Given the disparity in the amount of time and effort it takes to share a counternarrative, giving both parties the same amount of time to share their stories privileges the dominant narrative.

In contrast to neutrality, multipartiality recognizes different storytelling needs within a system of power imbalances. It recognizes that within mediation and society as a whole, there are stories that are privileged and stories that are more likely to be suppressed. Multipartial mediation acknowledges systemic oppression and supports both parties' storytelling needs by creating a space where counternarratives can surface and dominant narratives can be unpacked. Leah Wing and Deepika Marya offer a training program in social justice mediation (SJM) in which they provide a model for conducting multipartial mediation.[13] Having completed both the SJM training and mainstream Western mediation training, I was struck by the procedural differences. Mainstream community mediation models in the United States emphasize joint sessions in which both parties are present, whereas SJM utilizes a caucus model in which the mediators meet with each party separately. Once the stories have been gathered and transmitted by the mediators, the parties in an SJM session can decide if they'd like to meet jointly at the end. The goal of SJM is to support all the participants in telling their stories while recognizing that power is operating in the process. Because mediation happens in the context of both conflict and power, the mediators in the SJM model support the storytelling needs of each participant by meeting with them individually to gather their stories. This allows the mediators to be multipartial (i.e., support all participants) because they can be present with the participants' stories and responses without having to manage the power differentials between parties in a joint session. The utilization of caucuses in SJM allows the mediators to invite counternarratives that could be silenced in a joint session.

In IGD, multipartiality is applied as a frame for supporting all participants while unpacking the power dynamics and surfacing counternarratives. Unlike mediation, the IGD curriculum builds relationships and power analysis over several weeks. IGD acts in service of multipartiality through scaffolded relationship building and utilizing strategies like racial affinity groups and journaling so that all participants can share their stories.[14] Although the strategies of supporting multipartiality differ in IGD and mediation, the principle of supporting the growth of all participants while addressing privilege and oppression remains the same. IGD facilitators are not neutral; they recognize the dominant narrative of white supremacy and other oppressions. The facilitators are multipartial in that they are supporting both privileged and oppressed identities as they come to terms with both the counter and dominant narratives, and work toward coalition building. When the dominant narrative surfaces in IGD, the facilitator seeks to "name it and surface or reveal the way it works and its implications" rather than shut the conversation down.[15]

Neutrality in libraries not only perpetuates power imbalances, but also obscures the oppression that libraries actively engage in.[16] The library discourse on neutrality suggests that being anything other than neutral would leave some students unsupported. As Chiu, Ettarh, and Ferritti write, "Framing neutrality as a 'debate' works to polarize the profession, constructing the issue as black and white (for or against) and without nuance."[17] Multipartiality provides a nuanced framework for engaging all students while unpacking power and oppression. Depending on the context and the depth of the relationships, operating multipartially will require different tactics. When I am teaching a one-shot library session, I do not have the level of trust that I experience when facilitating a six-week dialogue. In a classroom context without relationship scaffolding, multipartiality can become a guiding principle. I can ask myself the following questions:

- How will I hold the humanity of everyone in the room while addressing power dynamics?
- How can I create space for counternarratives in this session?
- What opportunities do I have to invite students to unpack the dominant narrative?
- What boundaries need to be in place?

Planning the Dialogue

When planning a dialogue that will take place over the course of several weeks, I try to learn about the context I will be facilitating in. If an institution is requesting IGD, it is important to know if it's in response to a specific event and whether attendance is voluntary. IGD works best when participants choose to participate as it relies on consent, trust, and relationship building. Once the context is established, take time to learn about the social identities of the participants, their familiarity with social justice concepts, and their aspirations for the dialogue. The organization I facilitate with, Rise for Racial Justice, gathers this information ahead of time through the registration form.[18] This information helps us determine the content and activities.

Considerations for Dialogic Activities in Library Instruction

The majority of library instruction I do is in the context of one or two sessions where I am visiting another faculty member's class. In IGD, the process of establishing trust and community aspirations is often referred to as "building the container."[19] In one-shot library instruction, the librarian is walking into someone else's container, often without knowing much about the demographics of the group and classroom culture. IGD is scaffolded and moves from low-risk to high-risk activities, so one should not expect the same depth of sharing in a one-shot library session.

When planning a dialogic activity, consider not only the learning outcomes, but also the pedagogical principles that you are using to guide it. Based on the principles identified in *Teaching for Diversity and Social Justice*,[20] D. Scott Tharp suggests five pedagogical principles: facilitate knowledge development and behavioral awareness, build on student expertise, help students explore their positionality within systems, engage students emotionally and cognitively, and create an inclusive environment.[21] Your pedagogical principles may vary, but the point is to name them and let them guide the activities you choose and how you do them. The goal is to make sure your activities map to either a learning outcome or a pedagogical principle. For example, imagine an activity where students are placed into small groups to discuss the purpose of citing sources and then each group is invited to share a summary of their discussion with the whole class. The outcome of this activity is to identify the purpose of citation, and the pedagogical principle is to build on student expertise. When inviting small-group and class discussions, consider whether or not the format and content of the discussions you're planning map to any of your pedagogical principles.

Stage 1: Building Relationships

In the first session of a multi-week dialogue, IGD focuses on building relationships through activities like low-risk icebreakers and pair-share warm-ups. It is during this stage that the group will create norms and aspirations for how they want to learn together. Facilitators might lead participants through mindful listening activities that help participants practice how to relate to one another in the space.

Building Relationships in Library Instruction

In a one-shot library session, I try to build connection with the students by asking a check-in question at the beginning of class. Low-risk check-in questions invite students to engage emotionally without the expectation of sharing deeply. I am writing this chapter in the context of the COVID-19 worldwide pandemic, and I have been teaching mostly online for the past year. I wanted to find a way to acknowledge the emotions in the room while recognizing that students might not want to share and are not consenting to a deep conversation on trauma. Currently, I open all my classes by acknowledging the pandemic's impact and thanking the students for the work they do in their communities. I then invite them to share—on a virtual bulletin board, such as Google Slides or Jamboard—something they will do today to take care of themselves. Other check-ins could include asking students to name something they are excited about or a word that describes how they are feeling. This brief check-in invites the emotions into the room in a way that is rightsized for a one-off workshop.

Even in the one-shot, there is often an opportunity to build rapport through a low-risk discussion or activity. Before moving into a class discussion, offer students the chance to discuss questions in pairs or small groups. Students are more likely to participate in class discussions if they have had a chance to warm up. According to facilitator Eva Jo Myers, asking students to share out in a large group without starting with a small-group discussion is like asking an opera singer to perform without a vocal warm-up.[22] I have found that when I structure a small-group discussion at the beginning of class, students engage faster and ask more questions. After a brief check-in question, I often put the students into small groups with the prompt "What's the hardest part of finding research?" When I'm teaching in person, it's easier for me to notice when a group is not engaged. In an online setting, one can track engagement by asking each group to have a recorder who adds notes on their conversation to Google Slides (or some other technology the facilitator can see).[23] If I place the students into breakout groups and I notice that a group is not engaging with Google Slides, that can be an indicator that they need some support or clarification on the prompt. After each group reports back to the class on key points from their small-group discussion, there is an opportunity for a large-group discussion. Although I plan activities for each one-shot, sometimes the class discussion leads us to discuss an aspect of research that I had not anticipated.

Stage 2: Exploring Social Identity

In IGD, participants are invited to explore how they internally experience their social identities and how those identities impact how they move through society. By social identity, I am referring to identities that are imposed and reinforced through society—such as race, gender, class. In addition to readings on identity, participants may be asked to map out their identities or the social identities they think about. Cultural Chest, a common activity at this stage, involves inviting participants to share an object that reflects one of their social identities.[24] Affinity groups based on social identity may also be introduced at this stage, particularly as the participants start to grapple with how their identities are situated in a system of power and privilege. The goal of this stage is to get participants to reflect and discuss their social identities in relation to a larger system of power.

Social Identity in Library Instruction

While the typical library one-shot doesn't have the relational scaffolding necessary to go deeply into social identity, it is important to understand how the social identities of the students, teacher, and librarian are operating in the space. I identify as a white, nonbinary, queer person from a working-class background. As a white teacher and facilitator, I strive to be conscious of the space I'm taking up and the narratives I am amplifying during a library session. If I have a relationship with the faculty member, we can strategize about who introduces an activity based on our social identities. IGD is practiced with a co-facilitator with a different social identity. The co-facilitation relationship requires having honest conversations about the facilitators' social identities and how they may impact the dialogue. Moreover, the interaction between the co-facilitators can model intergroup cooperation and coalition building.[25] While teaching a one-shot differs from co-facilitating a dialogue, there may be opportunities to check in with the faculty member about how both our social identities may impact the session.

Of course, co-facilitation may not be an option in a one-shot. In addition to reflecting on how my social identity is impacting the session, I track the patterns of participation. If I am hearing the same few students speak up, I will invite folks who haven't shared yet to speak. If this still doesn't change the dynamic, I will solicit different forms of participation, such as Post-it Notes during an in-person class or a virtual equivalent like Padlet or Google Jamboard. Depending on the power dynamics in the class, discussion could be a barrier or place of harm. In IGD, the facilitator could name the patterns they are seeing (e.g., members of a privileged group dominating the conversation) and invite the group to dialogue on the dynamic.[26] Even if I do not have the container to facilitate that conversation in a one-shot, it's important for me to notice differences in participation and to solicit feedback.

Stage 3: Practicing Dialogue with Challenging Topics

In stage 3 of IGD, participants practice dialoging on challenging topics involving dynamics of power and oppression. Some dialogues focus on current controversies involving race, gender, sexuality, and other social identities. When I co-facilitate with Rise or at my university, the challenging topic involves identifying racism within institutional policies, procedures, and class curriculum. IGD is scaffolded so that by the time the participants arrive at this stage, they have built trust and examined their social identities in the context of systemic power. The depth and level of risk participants may achieve when discussing oppression is much greater in a container that has been built over several weeks or months. While I do not approach a one-shot expecting to have hard conversations about oppression, even low-stakes activities can become challenging. There's always an element of unpredictability when inviting discussion. As a result, I've found my experience with IGD facilitation prepares me for tense moments in library one-shots.

Navigating Activators in Library Instruction

Both IGD and mediation emphasize reflecting on one's activators. In social justice education, the term *triggers* is used to name stimuli that induce an automatic emotional response.[27] I prefer to use the term *activators*, as outlined in the SEEDS Community Resolution Center curriculum,[28] because *trigger* can imply a trauma response, and not all activation rises to that level. First, reflect on the ways you are likely to get activated in a conversation (e.g., someone says something racist, sexist, etc.). Then, reflect on what happens in your body when you are activated. Do you feel tension somewhere in your body? Does your voice change? Try to identify your physical symptoms of activation. Being aware of these physical symptoms can clue you into your activation before you are consciously aware of it. If you're working with a co-facilitator, discuss your activators with them. Let them know what physical signs to look for and how you'd like them to respond if you are activated. You can also establish subtle, nonverbal cues to communicate when one of you needs the other to step in. This is another area where co-facilitating with someone with different social identities can be very helpful. For example, you could ask your co-facilitator to step in when you have been the target of a microaggression.

In cases where I don't have a co-facilitator, I still find it helpful to reflect on my activators and strategize about how to respond. Once I recognize the physical signs in my body, I can take action to calm my nervous system. For me, that could mean deep breathing, feeling the ground with my feet, taking a drink of water, or slowing down my speech. I know that when I'm activated I tend to speak faster, so slowing down my speech helps me calm down. In a workshop I attended on navigating activators as a facilitator, Micia Mosely suggested that assuming the best intentions of the participant can be a self-preservation strategy that allows the facilitator to slow down and make a strategic choice about how to respond.[29] While I do not endorse assuming best intentions in all situations, the key is to find a way to pause when activated before responding. Another strategy is to ask questions and reflect back what the participant has said in order to create space to have an intentional response as a facilitator.[30] Even in situations where I'm not activated, I may be genuinely surprised by something someone says in discussion and not know how to respond. Summarizing and verbalizing what I heard the participant say gives me time to internally process their statement while providing them a chance to clarify.

I have also found the mindful listening, summarizing, reflecting, and questioning skills in both IGD and mediation to be helpful when a faculty member is activated around a one-shot. In one situation, I had a one-shot request to support an assignment that could result in the students appropriating a cultural experience that is not their own. Through a discussion with the faculty member prior to class, we were able to work out some changes to the assignment and a supporting library session that would not invite cultural appropriation. The discussion was challenging as the faculty member was emotionally invested in the assignment. When I initially shared my concerns about the assignment with the faculty member, they doubled down on their commitment to it. When I shifted to rephrasing what the faculty member had said, I was able to ask them questions that helped them explore the possible unintended outcomes of the original assignment.

Dialogic Library Activities as a Challenging Topic

It can be challenging to integrate group discussion into library sessions with faculty members who prefer lecture-based instruction. I try to mitigate this issue by giving the faculty member a brief overview of the session ahead of time. If the faculty member is looking for a lecture and demo, instructional videos may be more effective than synchronous class sessions. I have had a conflict with a faculty member who did not appreciate my use of group discussion and activities. In this case, I took on a one-shot with short notice and I did not provide an overview of the library session ahead of time. The incident reminded me of the importance of front-loading possible activities and my teaching style in advance.

Stage 4: Alliance Building and Action Planning

In the final stage of IGD, participants start to strategize about how they can work together to create change. At this stage, participants can be invited to consider their sphere of control (where they can make immediate changes) and their sphere of influence (where they can use their influence to create change with others).[31] I find naming the sphere of control and influence especially helpful when working with white participants who lack a supervisory position in an organization and do not immediately recognize the influence they have as a result of their racial privilege. When I co-facilitate an introductory racial literacy series with Rise or at my university, the participants are asked in the final session to strategize about how they can address some of the racist policies and practices they identified in the previous sessions.

The participants are not only coming up with interventions, but are also forming potential coalitions to enact them. Although this stage is not achievable in a single library session, it is important to contextualize dialogue as a skill for engaging in anti-racist work. The dialogue itself should not be mistaken for systemic change.

One of the challenges of IGD in higher education is that institutions can try to co-opt it in order to avoid institutional change and accountability. IGD provides tools for engaging in anti-racist work and is intended to be paired with action. In the face of an impending KKK rally in Charlottesville in 2017, the University of Virginia Library hosted a "Welcoming and Inclusive Space" in the library.[32] The library planned to host a "Day of Reflective Conversation" a month later, and the program was canceled due to the white supremacist violence at the Unite the Right rally.[33] Dialogue is a tool for change, but it is not the most effective tool for all contexts. Sometimes the harm is so great and those in power are so resistant to change that making demands or engaging in direct action is the most effective strategy for institutional change. In those instances, one may be called to act as an advocate for change rather than trying to be in dialogue with those in power committing violence. Dialogue and advocacy are both useful strategies in certain contexts, and the critical practitioner must reflect on what strategy they are using and why.

Growing as a Facilitator

This chapter contains some tips and observations on the transferability of IGD skills to library instruction, but is not intended as a manual. If you'd like to learn IGD facilitation, the first step is to experience the IGD process as a participant. As an academic librarian, I understand the temptation of wanting to intellectually learn a facilitation modality without experiencing it first. The first time I encountered an intergroup dialogue, I came into it thinking that I would be a sponge absorbing everything that the BIPOC participants had to offer. I did not initially understand that dialogue is relational practice that requires all participants to be vulnerable and honest. I entered the dialogue as a white person looking to extract knowledge rather than building relationships and doing my own reflection. One of the things I learned from that experience is that there's no checklist for being anti-racist. In some spaces, I need to step back, while in others, I will be asked to step forward and be vulnerable. It's a journey that requires humility and accountability.

Prior to attending two intensive IGD facilitation trainings led by Anna Yeakley and Teresa Brett, I cobbled together bits and pieces of IGD from attending preconferences at the National Conference on Race and Ethnicity (NCORE) and the White Privilege Conference. If your institution has the resources, I highly recommend attending an intensive IGD facilitation training over several days. Due to the COVID-19 pandemic, many of the trainings are now offered online. In addition to the public trainings offered by Anna Yeakley, the University of Michigan, where IGD was developed, offers a summer institute. If your institution offers IGD for students, there may be an opportunity to participate. Even without a formal program, there may be colleagues in student life that you could partner with on campus.[34] There may also be opportunities to incorporate elements of IGD into library professional development as well as community conversations at your institution.[35]

There are many skills shared between IGD and community mediation. The community mediation trainings I've attended have increased my capacity for mindful listening, rephrasing, asking questions, and staying centered during conflict. These skills have supported me as both an academic librarian and a facilitator. Like IGD, mediation is a craft one needs to practice. If you are interested in learning and practicing community mediation, seek out a conflict resolution center in your area. Basic community mediation trainings are generally forty hours. The Social Mediation Institute also offers a forty-hour mediation training that focuses on multipartiality.

While the full IGD curriculum is not possible in a library one-shot, my facilitation and mediation experience has informed my instruction far more than my formal education. When classes moved online due to the COVID-19 pandemic, I learned so much from the community mediators and IGD facilitators who moved relational modalities to an online environment. Whether I'm teaching a library one-shot, facilitating, or mediating, there is a common thread of connection and holding space for folks as they continue their journey to transform relationships and systems.

Notes

1. Paulo Freire, *Pedagogy of the Oppressed*, 30th anniversary ed., trans. Myra Bergman Ramos (New York: Bloomsbury Academic, 2000).
2. Patricia Gurin, Biren (Ratnesh) A. Nagda, and Ximen Zúñiga, "Practice of Intergroup Dialogue," in *Dialogue across Difference: Practice, Theory, and Research on Intergroup Dialogue* (New York: Russell Sage Foundation, 2013), 44.
3. Ximena Zúñiga et al., "Intergroup Dialogue in Higher Education: Definition, Origins, and Practices," *ASHE Higher Education Report* 32, no. 4 (2007): 4–6, https://doi.org/10.1002/aehe.3204.
4. Gurin, Nagda, and Zúñiga, "Practice of Intergroup Dialogue," 43–44.
5. Sara Cobb and Janet Rifkin, "Practice and Paradox: Deconstructing Neutrality in Mediation," *Law and Social Inquiry* 16, no. 1 (Winter 1991): 35–62, https://doi.org/10.1111/j.1747-4469.1991.tb00283.x.
6. Leah Wing, "Mediation and Inequality Reconsidered: Bringing the Discussion to the Table," *Conflict Resolution Quarterly* 26, no. 4 (Summer 2009): 383–404, https://doi.org/10.1002/crq.240; Elli Nagai-Rothe, "Dialogue as a Tool for Racial Reconciliation: Examining Racialized Frameworks," *Journal of Dialogue Studies* 3, no. 1 (Spring 2015): 57–69.
7. Janet Rifkin, Jonathan Millen, and Sara Cobb, "Toward a New Discourse for Mediation: A Critique of Neutrality," *Mediation Quarterly* 9, no. 2 (Winter 1991): 151–64, https://doi.org/10.1002/crq.3900090206.
8. Cobb and Rifkin, "Practice and Paradox," 61.
9. Cobb and Rifkin, "Practice and Paradox," 41–44.
10. The term *master narrative* (also known as the dominant narrative) comes from critical theory. It describes the often invisible mythology that is used to legitimate and maintain oppression. I will be using the term *dominant narrative* to avoid the connotations of slavery. Maurianne Adams and Ximena Zúñiga, "Getting Started: Core Concepts for Social Justice Education," in *Teaching for Diversity and Social Justice*, 3rd ed., ed. Maurianne Adams and Lee Anne Bell (New York: Routledge, 2016), 113–48.
11. Leah Wing, "Whither Neutrality? Mediation in the Twenty-First Century," in *Re-centering Culture and Knowledge in Conflict Resolution Practice*, ed. Mary Adams Trujillo, S. Y. Bowland, Linda James Myers, and Phillip M. Richardset (Syracuse, NY: Syracuse University Press, 2008), 93–107.
12. Wing, "Whither Neutrality?" 100.
13. Leah Wing, "Mediation Training through a Social Justice Perspective," Social Justice Mediation Institute, accessed August 1, 2021, http://www.sjmediation.org.
14. Racial affinity groups are caucuses based on racial identity. They provide a space for BIPOC participants to explore solidarity with each other without getting derailed by white participants, as well as a space for white participants to learn about white racial identity and privilege without discharging their discomfort onto the BIPOC participants. In addition to both intergroup and racial affinity group

discussions, IGD participants may be invited to reflect on their experiences through journaling on their own.

15. Roger Fisher and Taryn Petryk, "Balancing Asymmetrical Social Power Dynamics," IGR Working Paper Series (Ann Arbor: University of Michigan, 2017), 4.

16. Chris Bourg, "The Library Is Never Neutral," in *Disrupting the Digital Humanities*, ed. Dorothy Kim and Jesse Stommel (Santa Barbara, CA: Punctum Books, 2018), 455–71.

17. Anastasia Chiu, Fobazi M. Ettarh, and Jennifer A. Ferretti, "Not the Shark, but the Water: How Neutrality and Vocational Awe Intertwine to Uphold White Supremacy," in *Knowledge Justice: Disrupting Library and Information Studies through Critical Race Theory*, ed. Sofia Y. Leung and Jorge R. López-McKnight (Cambridge, MA: MIT Press, 2021), 57.

18. Rise for Racial Justice offers racial literacy courses for teachers, parents, and youth. The courses are informed by critical race theory and IGD.

19. Teresa Brett and Anna Yeakley, "Stage 1: Introduction and Setting the Stage for Dialogue" (class lecture, Dialogue Facilitation Training, Anna Yeakley Consulting, online, May 1, 2021), https://annayeakley.com.

20. Maurianne Adams, "Pedagogical Foundations for Social Justice Education," in *Teaching for Diversity and Social Justice*, 3rd ed., ed. Maurianne Adams and Lee Anne Bell with Diane J. Goodman and Khyati Y. Joshi, (New York Routledge, 2016), 27–53.

21. D. Scott Tharp with Roger A. Moreano, *Doing Social Justice Education* (Sterling, VA: Stylus Publishing, 2020).

22. Eva Jo Meyers, "Boom Your Zoom: Avoid Burnout, Increase Engagement, Productivity, and Ease in Your Virtual Meetings" (workshop, Eva Jo Meyers Consulting, online, October 28, 2020), https://evajomeyers.com.

23. Eva Jo Meyers, "Virtual Facilitation Bootcamp: Creating Effective, Engaging Meetings and Events Online" (workshop, Eva Jo Meyers Consulting, online, February 20, 2021), https://evajomeyers.com.

24. Zúñiga et al., "Intergroup Dialogue in Higher Education," 93–94.

25. Tanya Williams and Elaine Brigham, "Developing and Sustaining Effective Co-facilitation across Identities," in *The Art of Effective Facilitation: Reflections from Social Justice Educators*, ed. Lisa M. Landreman (Herndon, VA: Stylus Publishing, 2013), 101–16.

26. Zúñiga et al., "Intergroup Dialogue in Higher Education," 100–101.

27. Micia Mosely and Kathy O'Bear, "Navigating Triggering Events: Critical Competencies for Facilitating Difficult Dialogues" (preconference institute, National Conference on Race and Ethnicity [NCORE], San Francisco, CA, May 31, 2016).

28. SEEDS Community Resolution Center, "Hooks and Activators" (workshop, online, April 2020), https://www.seedscrc.org.

29. Mosely and O'Bear, "Navigating Triggering Events."

30. Kathy O'Bear, "Navigating Triggering Events," in *The Art of Effective Facilitation: Reflections from Social Justice Educators*, ed. Lisa M. Landreman (Herndon, VA: Stylus Publishing, 2013), 151–72.

31. Paul Gorski and Marceline DuBose, "Learning to Be a Threat to Inequity: Intro to Equity Literacy" (online class, Equity Literacy Institute, January 28, 2021), https://www.equityliteracy.org/online-professional-learning.

32. Abigail Flanigan et al., "Confronting the Limits of Dialogue: Charlottesville, 2017," in *Libraries Promoting Reflective Dialogue in a Time of Political Polarization*, ed. Andrea Baer, Ellysa Stern Cahoy, and Robert Schroeder (Chicago: Association of College and Research Libraries, 2019), 49.

33. Flanigan et al., "Confronting the Limits of Dialogue," 50.

34. Lindsay Marlow and Kelly McElroy, "Reflective Dialogue across Difference in Libraries," in *Libraries Promoting Reflective Dialogue in a Time of Political Polarization*, ed. Andrea Baer, Ellysa Stern Cahoy, and Robert Schroeder (Chicago: Association of College and Research Libraries, 2019), 33–46.

35. Ione T. Damasco, "Creating Meaningful Engagement in Academic Libraries Using Principles of Intergroup Dialogue," in *Libraries Promoting Reflective Dialogue in a Time of Political Polarization*, ed. Andrea Baer, Ellysa Stern Cahoy, and Robert Schroeder (Chicago: Association of College and Research Libraries, 2019), 13–31.

Bibliography

Adams, Maurianne. "Pedagogical Foundations for Social Justice Education." In *Teaching for Diversity and Social Justice*, 3rd ed., edited by Maurianne Adams and Lee Anne Bell with Diane J. Goodman and Khyati Y. Joshi, 27–53. New York: Routledge, 2016.

Adams, Maurianne, and Ximena Zúñiga. "Getting Started: Core Concepts for Social Justice Education." In *Teaching for Diversity and Social Justice*, 3rd ed., edited by Maurianne Adams and Lee Anne Bell, 113–48. New York: Routledge, 2016.

Bourg, Chris. "The Library Is Never Neutral." In *Disrupting the Digital Humanities*, edited by Dorothy Kim and Jesse Stommel, 455–71. Santa Barbara, CA: Punctum Books, 2018.

Brett, Teresa, and Anna Yeakley. "Stage 1: Introduction and Setting the Stage for Dialogue." Class lecture, Dialogue Facilitation Training, Anna Yeakley Consulting, online, May 1, 2021, https://annayeakley.com.

Chiu, Anastasia, Fobazi M. Ettarh, and Jennifer A. Ferretti. "Not the Shark, but the Water: How Neutrality and Vocational Awe Intertwine to Uphold White Supremacy." In *Knowledge Justice: Disrupting Library and Information Studies through Critical Race Theory*, edited by Sofia Y. Leung and Jorge R. López-McKnight, 49–70. Cambridge, MA: MIT Press, 2021.

Cobb, Sara, and Janet Rifkin. "Practice and Paradox: Deconstructing Neutrality in Mediation." *Law and Social Inquiry* 16, no. 1 (Winter 1991): 35–62. https://doi.org/10.1111/j.1747-4469.1991.tb00283.x.

Damasco, Ione T. "Creating Meaningful Engagement in Academic Libraries Using Principles of Intergroup Dialogue." In *Libraries Promoting Reflective Dialogue in a Time of Political Polarization*, edited by Andrea Baer, Ellysa Stern Cahoy, and Robert Schroeder, 13–31. Chicago: Association of College and Research Libraries, 2019.

Fisher, Roger, and Taryn Petryk. "Balancing Asymmetrical Social Power Dynamics." IGR Working Paper Series. Ann Arbor: University of Michigan, 2017.

Flanigan, Abigail, Dave S. Ghamandi, Phylissa Mitchell, and Erin Pappas. "Confronting the Limits of Dialogue: Charlottesville, 2017." In *Libraries Promoting Reflective Dialogue in a Time of Political Polarization*, edited by Andrea Baer, Ellysa Stern Cahoy, and Robert Schroeder, 47–70. Chicago: Association of College and Research Libraries, 2019.

Freire, Paulo. *Pedagogy of the Oppressed*, 30th anniversary ed. Translated by Myra Bergman Ramos. New York: Bloomsbury Academic, 2000.

Gorski, Paul, and Marceline DuBose. "Learning to Be a Threat to Inequity: Intro to Equity Literacy." Online class, Equity Literacy Institute, January 28, 2021. https://www.equityliteracy.org/online-professional-learning.

Gurin, Patricia, Biren (Ratnesh) A. Nagda, and Ximena Zúñiga. "Practice of Intergroup Dialogue." In *Dialogue across Difference: Practice, Theory, and Research on Intergroup Dialogue*, 32–73. New York: Russell Sage Foundation, 2013.

Marlow, Lindsay, and Kelly McElroy. "Reflective Dialogue across Difference in Libraries." In *Libraries Promoting Reflective Dialogue in a Time of Political Polarization*, edited by Andrea Baer, Ellysa Stern Cahoy, and Robert Schroeder, 33–46. Chicago: Association of College and Research Libraries, 2019.

Meyers, Eva Jo. "Boom Your Zoom: Avoid Burnout, Increase Engagement, Productivity, and Ease in Your Virtual Meetings." Workshop, online, Eva Jo Meyers Consulting, October 28, 2020. https://evajomeyers.com.

———. "Virtual Facilitation Bootcamp: Creating Effective, Engaging Meetings and Events Online." Workshop, online, Eva Jo Meyers Consulting, February 20, 2021. https://evajomeyers.com.

Mosely, Micia, and Kathy O'Bear. "Navigating Triggering Events: Critical Competencies for Facilitating Difficult Dialogues." Preconference institute, National Conference on Race and Ethnicity (NCORE), San Francisco, CA, May 31, 2016.

Nagai-Rothe, Elli. "Dialogue as a Tool for Racial Reconciliation: Examining Racialized Frameworks." *Journal of Dialogue Studies* 3, no. 1 (Spring 2015): 57–69.

O'Bear, Kathy. "Navigating Triggering Events." In *The Art of Effective Facilitation: Reflections from Social Justice Educators*, edited by Lisa M. Landreman, 151–72. Herndon, VA: Stylus Publishing, 2013.

Rifkin, Janet, Jonathan Millen, and Sara Cobb. "Toward a New Discourse for Mediation: A Critique of Neutrality." *Mediation Quarterly* 9, no. 2 (Winter 1991): 151–64. https://doi.org/10.1002/crq.3900090206.

SEEDS Community Resolution Center. "Hooks and Activators." Workshop, online, April 2020, https://www.seedscrc.org.

Tharp, D. Scott, with Roger A. Moreano. *Doing Social Justice Education: A Practitioner's Guide for Workshops and Structured Conversations.* Sterling, VA: Stylus Publishing, 2020.

Williams, Tanya, and Elaine Brigham. "Developing and Sustaining Effective Co-facilitation across Identities." In *The Art of Effective Facilitation: Reflections from Social Justice Educators*, edited by Lisa M. Landreman, 101–16. Herndon, VA: Stylus Publishing, 2013.

Wing, Leah. "Mediation and Inequality Reconsidered: Bringing the Discussion to the Table." *Conflict Resolution Quarterly* 26, no. 4 (Summer 2009): 383–404. https://doi.org/10.1002/crq.240.

———. "Mediation Training from a Social Justice Perspective." Social Justice Mediation Institute. Accessed August 1, 2021. http://www.sjmediation.org.

———. "Whither Neutrality? Mediation in the Twenty-First Century." In *Re-centering Culture and Knowledge in Conflict Resolution Practice*, edited by Mary Adams Trujillo, S. Y. Bowland, Linda James Myers, and Phillip M. Richards, 93–107. Syracuse, NY: Syracuse University Press, 2008.

Zúñiga, Ximena, Biren (Ratnesh) A. Nagda, Mark Chesler, and Adena Cytron-Walker. "Intergroup Dialogue in Higher Education: Definition, Origins, and Practices." *ASHE Higher Education Report* 32, no. 4 (2007): 1–128. https://doi.org/10.1002/aehe.3204.

CHAPTER 2

Anti-ableism in Library Instruction

Considerations for Neurodivergent Students

Paige Crowl and Elizabeth C. Novosel

Introduction

This chapter is an expansion of the session "Optimizing the Learning Experience of Neurodivergent Students" from the 2020 Critical Librarianship and Pedagogy Symposium (CLAPS). The session provided conference attendees with an introduction to disability and neurodivergence, the medical and social models of disability, and how Universal Design for Learning (UDL) can be used as a guide to help librarians develop more inclusive instruction practices.

We will build upon the ideas originally presented in the CLAPS session by providing a brief overview of ableism in academic settings, discuss invisible disabilities and neurodivergence and their relevance for library instruction, and offer suggestions for ways instruction librarians can better support this subset of the student population by applying aspects of UDL. We are particularly interested in increasing

librarians' understanding of disability issues in the context of the one-shot session, a commonly requested format for library instruction. We recognize the one-shot, a single session covering a variety of information literacy and research skills, to be a fundamentally problematic instructional model.[1] However, because it is a frequently requested format and remains one of the most prevalent forms of library instruction, we believe that establishing more inclusive practices for the one-shot is a key step in making library instruction more accessible for neurodivergent students.

For librarians engaging in instruction sessions, we offer thoughts on how to make the one-shot more empowering for all students. Additionally, we hope to offer librarians who are not familiar with disability justice and invisible disabilities some insight into what students with these disabilities may struggle with in the higher education classroom. We invite our peers to reflect on their teaching methods and consider ways to make their instruction more inclusive.

Key Concepts
Invisible Disabilities

The words *disability* and *disabled* are often associated with physical disabilities or impairments that visibly impact the way a person engages with the world around them. These disabilities may require the use of a wheelchair, interpreter, guide dog, or other forms of physical assistance. This understanding of disability is incomplete as it fails to take into account the enormous range of disabilities that are not always, or never, visible to an observer.[2] Invisible disabilities span medical, psychological, and neurological conditions. These include learning disabilities (dyslexia, dysgraphia, dyscalculia), mental health issues (depression, anxiety, post-traumatic stress disorder), brain injuries (concussion, stroke), developmental disabilities (autism spectrum disorder, attention deficit hyperactivity disorder), autoimmune diseases (Crohn's disease, multiple sclerosis, lupus) and other conditions such as D/deafness*, blindness and low vision, sleep disorders, digestive/eating disorders and many more.

Neurodivergence

Neurodivergence is a term used to describe a subset of invisible disabilities that affect mood, thought, and behavior. Originally used to refer to autism

---

* The audiological condition of not hearing is referred to as deafness (lowercase). The term Deaf is used to refer to the group of deaf people who share the language American Sign Language and the cultural identity of Deafness. For more information on D/deafness, visit the website of the National Association of the Deaf at https://www.nad.org/.

spectrum disorder (ASD), it has expanded in meaning to include a range of conditions that involve an individual whose way of thinking, learning, or functioning in the world diverges from societal expectations of how someone with a "typical brain" thinks, acts, or functions. Examples of such conditions include dyslexia, attention deficit hyperactivity disorder (ADHD), Tourette's syndrome, and others.[3]

Some object to the emergence of the neurodiversity paradigm because they feel it implies that there are no downsides to some of these conditions.[4] Using this term, we do not intend to diminish the difficulty of adapting to a particular condition or living in a world that does not accommodate disability. We use the idea of neurodivergence to encourage librarians to consider their assumptions about normal thinking and behavior. All brains and ways of thinking have strengths and challenges.[5] It is important to understand that, while many neurodivergent people consider their disabilities to be a central part of their identity, others do not. Every disabled person's relationship to their disability or disabilities is unique.

Autistic librarian Zachary Tumlin argues that it is impossible to separate the experience of a person's life from their disability, and "curing" their impairment would likely strip away part of what makes them unique:

> Neurodivergence is not a gift or a curse, but a state of being. Everyone has strengths and weaknesses, period. Removing someone's impairment would give them a different set of attributes, not make them perfect or their lives hardship-free. However, their life would become easier, in many cases because they would fit into our ableist society better. That does not mean that we should be looking to cure all impairments as a racist society would seek to cure non-whiteness.[6]

Tumlin addresses the fact that in addition to typical strengths and weaknesses, neurodivergent people must contend with the reality that others often seek to change, or fix, a significant and basic aspect of their identity. Though neurodivergence can make life challenging in an ableist world, many neurodivergent people embrace their differences and do not desire to be cured. For these people, fully embracing neurodiversity can be liberating.[†]

---

† For more in-depth information on neurodiversity scholarship, we highly recommend Hanna Bertilsdotter Rosqvist, Nick Chown, and Anna Stenning, *Neurodiversity Studies: A New Critical Paradigm, Routledge Advances in Sociology 285* (London: Routledge, 2020), https://doi.org/10.4324/9780429322297.

Ableism

As defined by Bogart and Dunn, "Ableism is stereotyping, prejudice, discrimination, and social oppression toward people with disabilities."[7] An ableist society, therefore, is designed for and privileges those who are able-bodied and neurotypical. Many disabled people continually encounter discriminatory attitudes, situations, policies, physical environments, and other disabling barriers. They must also contend with societal messages that they are inferior due to their disabilities and that they would be better if they were "normal." Ableism and ableist attitudes place the blame for disabled people's disadvantages, lack of access, and challenges on the individual and their disability, ignoring that institutions and social structures create obstacles for disabled people. Much like racism, sexism, and many other isms, the institutionalized, pervasive nature of ableism both generates and perpetuates the oppressive disadvantages faced by disabled people.[8]

Ableism takes many forms, including assumptions, ideas and stereotypes, and physical barriers to facilities or information. It can also take the form of abusive or prejudicial treatment or actions toward disabled people. All these forms of ableism are oppressive[9] and are often perpetrated unintentionally, out of ignorance. Research has shown that disabled people face detrimental psychological impacts from experiences of being "patronized, avoided, ignored, or stared at."[10]

Disabled people may experience aggressive and overt forms of prejudice, such as violence, housing discrimination, and stigma.[11] They may also be subjected to derogatory or insulting language. There are also more subtle forms of ableism, which may present as the expression of sympathy, pity, or the need to give disabled people "charitable praise."[12] Disabled people are also cast in narratives of "inspiration porn," which frequently depict a disabled person overcoming their disadvantage in some way that inspires or captivates an able-bodied audience.[13] Some specific examples of common ableist microaggressions include asking a disabled stranger about their health history, providing a disabled person with help when they do not ask for it, assuming ability or disability in areas based on other disabilities (e.g., assuming a Deaf person cannot speak), patronizing disabled individuals by treating them as incapable or like children, and viewing disabled people as incapable of engaging in romantic or sexual relationships.[14]

These subtle manifestations of ableism are harmful. They serve to disempower disabled people and remind them of their "defects" as well as the stigma and oppression they regularly face.[15] Microaggressions also contribute to a negative higher education experience for disabled students. Lett, Tamaian, and Klest found that disabled students regularly facing ableist microaggressions reported distressing feelings of "embarrassment, anger, and frustration." Students frequently exposed to these microaggressions also reported "increased symptoms of anxiety and depression, as well as poorer academic self-concept."[16] These experiences of ableism significantly impact the ability of disabled students to succeed personally and academically.

Due to the less visible nature of their disability, neurodivergent people may not experience as much overt ableism as those with more visible differences. However, they do also encounter discrimination and stigma, especially when seeking accommodation for their disabilities. The stigma around psychological, neurological, and developmental disorders can lead neurodivergent people to hide their condition and not seek the help and accommodations they need.[17] Neurodivergent students may be challenged by institutional authorities who question whether they truly have a disability. Even if students do secure accommodations from their institution, professors may also imply that students with invisible disabilities are lazy or refuse to make voluntary accommodations because they do not look or act disabled.[18] In many contexts, it can be hard for people with these disabilities to find a supportive community and to have their experiences validated.

Librarians and other educators should consider that the students they interact with may have a neurodivergence-related disability they have not revealed. Since many students may not have officially identified themselves as disabled to their institution and formally requested accommodations, instructors will best serve their student populations by making efforts to include the needs of these students when designing instruction and teaching materials.

The Medical Model of Disability

Ableist attitudes are strongly influenced by the *medical model of disability*, which frames disability as an "individual pathology, abnormality, or difference from a standardized norm."[19] Most spaces and institutions were designed by and for nondisabled people. Accommodations make it possible for disabled people to navigate in these spaces, but they are disempowered and must ask for assistance or find ways to navigate systems not friendly to their needs.

The medical model employs experts and medical providers to diagnose, treat, and devise intervention strategies so that disabled people can get as close as possible to being "normal."[20] The solution, according to this view, is to fix the deficit rather than evaluate the greater world for ways it could be inclusive.[21] The medical model does not recognize the way environmental or social conditions contribute to the challenges disabled people face. To function in such a society, disabled people must devise ways to navigate the barriers of a world not designed for them. To get any sort of help, support, or accommodations, they must often prove that they are disabled enough by providing medical documentation and then negotiate for what they need. This process is exhausting, time-consuming, expensive, frustrating, and emotionally draining.

The Social Model of Disability

Unlike the medical model, the social model of disability recognizes that society is designed to privilege able-bodied individuals.[22] Kumbier and Starkey write in "Access Is Not Problem Solving: Disability Justice and Libraries" that the social model shifts away from medical diagnoses and accommodations to examine the limitations imposed on disabled people through "marginalization, stigmatization, disenfranchisement, stereotyping, and the perpetuation of inequitable living and working conditions."[23] The social model holds that a just society can—and should—be organized in a way that allows all people independence, opportunity, and access to resources. Disabled people should not have to adapt to society; society should be restructured to be inclusive and accessible to everyone. Importantly, the social model recognizes that in some cases, society cannot create access for all disabilities and that some disabled people need and benefit from medical interventions and a variety of accommodations. Disabilities can be painful and overwhelming, and medical technologies have made living with disabilities easier and more comfortable for many people. However, the social model acknowledges that the challenges of disability are currently compounded by the numerous barriers that disabled people must navigate, in addition to their existing impairments, and removing these barriers whenever possible is a matter of social justice. We believe that this way of viewing disability is vital for creating an anti-ableist and welcoming learning environment in the library classroom.

Challenges for Disabled Students in Higher Education

When disabled people enter academic spaces, they do not escape barriers and assumptions; discrimination toward disabled people thrives in academia. As disability studies scholar Jay Dolmage writes, "the ethic of higher education still encourages students and teachers alike to accentuate ability, valorize perfection, and stigmatize anything that hints at intellectual (or physical) weakness."[24] In addition to seeing those with disabilities as inferior, there is a long history in academia of viewing those with "non-elite and nonstandard bodies and minds"[25] as things or objects to study rather than as students, teachers, or valued members of the university community.

Margaret Price has comprehensively delineated the intersection of academic and medical rhetoric and how it results in the deliberate othering of mentally and neurologically disabled people in academia. She writes that "higher education clings to the notion that mental disability must be an aberration, something that emerges only rarely and, when it does emerge, should be stifled or expunged as quickly as possible."[26] Despite statements of inclusion and efforts to create a more inclusive culture on many campuses, many disabled students still encounter ableist stigma and institutional barriers. These experiences impress upon these students that they are not truly welcome in academia.

Self-Advocacy

All students, including those who are neurodivergent and disabled, must adapt to the intensive expectations of living and learning in an academic environment. Disabled students have the additional burden of securing accommodations and institutional support on their own. In primary and secondary education, parents, therapists, and administrators often decide on support structures for disabled students and how those accommodations are implemented. Because the role of primary advocate was previously assumed by others, students beginning higher education often have little preparation to take on the role of advocating for the services they need.[27] As a result, the shift to self-advocacy can be highly stressful and intimidating. In their research on why many college students delay disclosing their disabilities to their institutions, Lightener and colleagues found that many students avoid the process because it feels overwhelming. Of the forty-two disabled students they interviewed, many waited an entire academic year to pursue accommodations.[28] Students reported that they often waited to seek help until they faced academic distress, at which time they found they had inadequate time to secure accommodations to improve their immediate situation. Significantly, these students expressed that they had little knowledge of the supportive resources offered by their institutions and that they did not understand until it was "too late" that they could access services which could improve their experience and help them succeed. Lightener and colleagues argue that this lack of preparedness and understanding of disability services can be avoided by institutions providing stronger transition programming from high school to higher education.[29] In terms of the library classroom, it is important for instructors to be aware that disabled students may not be practiced self-advocates and in such cases may not ask for needed assistance.

Hesitation to Reveal Disabilities

In addition to the challenges of transitioning to college and the effort required to seek accommodations, disabled students also may not reveal their disabilities because they want to avoid stigma, assumptions, and lack of understanding from peers, institutional staff, and faculty. Many students with invisible disabilities are "routinely and systematically" dismissed, perceived as faking their conditions, or accused of asking for unfair advantages.[30] The fear of encountering these attitudes and accusations may discourage students from being open about their disabilities.[31] Instructors should also be aware that disabled students may be unwilling to complain if activities or aspects of their classes make them feel uncomfortable. Librarian J. J. Pionke surveyed functionally diverse patrons of the library at a large research university regarding their feelings toward the library in the context of their disabilities. Pionke found that many patrons said things like "I don't want to be a bother," or "I don't know how to ask [for help]," or "I'm intimidated by the (process, librarian, environment, etc.)." One patron indicated that this disempowerment deters students from asking for help in the library, stating: "I guess I'll just say that people with disabilities tend not to ask [for] what they need."[32] Such feelings can affect a student's experience in the classroom. For example, dyslexic students may not want to admit that they cannot read as quickly as other students or that they have short-term memory or information processing challenges.[33] This hesitancy to disclose their disability could make a student behave in such a way that they seem inattentive or as though they refuse to engage with class activities.

Internalized Ableism

Neurodivergent students and those with invisible disabilities may also struggle with their own feelings of inadequacy and shame. Research shows that disabled students may internalize external messages that tell them they are not as capable, smart, or able to succeed as other students.[34] If they are accused of trying to get unfair advantages, many students begin to doubt the reality or severity of their disability, which creates anxiety, shame, and a desire for secrecy.[35] It is important for instructors to affirm individual needs and proactively offer adjustments for all students. This could improve the classroom experience for those students who could benefit from accommodations but have not sought them. Later in this chapter, we will discuss some ways that library instructors can build these adjustments into their lesson planning.

Library Classrooms and Neurodivergence

Instruction librarians are at a disadvantage when working with students who have invisible disabilities or identify as neurodivergent, as they are often given no information on the accommodations required by students before a class visit. Some librarians mistakenly assume that all disabled students are assisted by the disability services office at their institution, leading them to devote little time or thought to the needs of disabled students in their classrooms. Yet even if librarians are told that there will be disabled students in a class, they may be unsure how to make their instruction more inclusive. Many librarians do not receive pedagogical training in MLIS programs,[36] and librarians may be uninformed about how neurodivergent students experience higher education classrooms,[37] but this information gap is difficult to overcome. Librarians researching the topic will find that there is a dearth of scholarly literature addressing ableism or advising librarians working with disabled students in instruction settings. These factors, when combined with the intense demands placed upon library instructors in the typical one-shot library session, can result in instructors not meeting the needs of disabled and neurodivergent students.

Despite growing evidence that a scaffolded, course-integrated approach leads to better student learning outcomes in library skills,[38] the expectation that librarians can cover all relevant information for students in a single one-shot session persists in many institutions.[39] Where this constraint exists, librarians must work to adapt their classrooms to provide the best instruction possible in the one-shot setting. Library instructors, highly conscious of these limitations, have worked as a profession to incorporate pedagogical best practices into their teaching. Unfortunately, some instructional practices commonly used by librarians create difficulties for neurodivergent students. To avoid this, librarians can work to integrate elements of UDL into their library instruction.

Universal Design for Learning

The field of universal design began with architecture in the 1980s, with the aim of making buildings, spaces, and products usable by everyone regardless of age, ability, or other characteristics. This philosophy aligns well with the social model of disability, which understands that external barriers compound the difficulties disabled people face. Following similar principles, UDL was developed in the 1980s by the Center for Applied Special Technology (CAST) with the goal of making learning more accessible to all students.[40] UDL is based on the premise that different brains function and learn differently. It recognizes variability among students and supports both the cognitive and emotional aspects of learning.

The three main principles of UDL are

1. Multiple means of engagement, which refers to the effort to tap into learners' interests, offer appropriate challenges, and increase motivation. An example of this is having students practice research skills by finding resources related to a topic of their choice, rather than creating a practice exercise with preselected research topics.

2. Multiple means of representation, which seeks to provide learners with various methods or platforms for acquiring information and knowledge. An example of this is offering students a choice to either read an article or watch a video covering the same content so they can access the information in the way that works best for them.

3. Multiple means of expression, which allows learners to demonstrate what they know in a variety of ways. An example of this is allowing students to either write a short-answer response or record themselves explaining a topic for an exam.

Instructors have utilized UDL to improve the classroom experiences of linguistically diverse learners and students with intellectual disabilities.[41] Integrating UDL into course design has been shown to reduce the need for intervention by campus disability services in undergraduate classrooms.[42]

We believe incorporating elements of UDL can greatly benefit library instruction sessions. UDL principles may feel overwhelming to library instructors who already must cover a great deal of material in a session, but it is not necessary to completely overhaul lesson plans to make use of UDL. These recommendations are not meant to be a list of rules or requirements, but rather a framework to help make instruction as accessible as possible. Dolmage recommends that instructors use these principles as a method of orienting their thoughts when designing instruction.[43] Some example questions to address include

- Is this activity simple and intuitive?

- Can a student make a mistake following these instructions that will make the activity difficult or impossible to complete?

- Does this require physical effort by students?

- Is there only one way for students to learn this content?

- Is there an accessible way for students to view this content if they are unable to attend the class session or miss a portion of the lesson?

Though UDL has been well studied in traditional classroom settings, specific articles including recommendations for librarians looking to use UDL in their instruction are limited. Samantha Peter and Kristina Clement of the University of Wyoming write in their 2020 article, "One Step at a Time: A Case Study of Incorporating Universal Design for Learning in Library Instruction," that there is little guidance or literature on integrating UDL into library instruction, especially since most of this instruction happens in one-shot sessions. Their article addresses two major barriers to implementing UDL: many librarians lack an understanding of how the principles of UDL relate to library instruction, and instructors often feel that they should implement everything in the framework at once. They advocate slowly incorporating these ideas into instruction because to do too much at once can be overwhelming and lead to burnout.[44]

We want to emphasize Peter and Clement's conviction that it is most successful to slowly integrate UDL into instructional practice. Ableism and barriers in instruction for students with invisible disabilities cannot be solved overnight. Undoing ableism is a long, slow process that involves self-education, experimenting with new strategies, reviewing student feedback, and self-reflection. This iterative process leads to improved methods over time with better outcomes for students and lower stress levels for instructors. Peter and Clement describe this process as circular, as there is a constant need to reevaluate teaching methods and tools as pedagogies evolve and changes occur within student needs and learning habits. They argue that ongoing reevaluation of the successes and limitations of lesson designs will gradually identify and break down environmental barriers to learning.

The goal of UDL is to move away from instruction that makes limiting assumptions regarding students' abilities to participate in instructional activities and reduces the barriers that hinder many kinds of learners, not just disabled ones. Beth Fornauf and Joy Erickson explain that approaching UDL as a framework rather than another sort of intervention

> allows us to acknowledge disabling environments and center the lived experiences of students with disabilities in our design. Furthermore, [institutions of higher education] can incorporate variation not only in perceived ability, but in language, race, gender, etc., without assuming the default position of a heteronormative, able-bodied individual as the standard toward which a UDL intervention could remediate students.[45]

Although developed with disabled people in mind, UDL can help instructors improve outcomes for many students with diverse needs.

Limitations of UDL

This is not to say that UDL is a perfect be-all and end-all solution to challenges in instruction. Some UDL resources found in pedagogical literature are certainly framed more as accommodating learning styles than accommodating disability. The theory of learning styles, an educational technique based on the theory that students have a preferred way to learn and will learn more effectively when taught using their preferred mode of delivery, has been tested repeatedly and shown to have little scientific evidence for its validity.[46] Despite this problematic lack of evidence, a great deal of higher education research literature still advocates its use.[47] Psychologist Guy Boysen has expressed concern that UDL shares "problematic parallels" with learning styles and cautions that educators should "examine it carefully, not accept it uncritically."[48] We agree that more research needs to be conducted on the effectiveness of UDL and more concrete recommendations are needed on the operationalization of UDL outcomes.

In our view, applications of UDL should be grounded in the understanding that the primary goal of this framework is to remove barriers for disabled students. As Anne-Marie Womack writes, teaching should create a space that "centers the experiences of disabled students within a universal design framework to create more inclusive pedagogy."[49] UDL, like other evidence-based pedagogical theory, is a tool to make instruction more accessible for students. Overall, like the social model of disability and the concept of neurodiversity itself, UDL invites us to reflect on what we consider good learning and teaching practice, how we share our knowledge with our students, and how they share their knowledge with us. It is up to instructors to do the work of observing students' learning, listening to their feedback, and making appropriate adjustments to their teaching.

Specific Library One-Shot Issues for Neurodivergent Students and Alternate Suggestions

In the CLAPS session that inspired this chapter, participants were asked the question "How does traditional library instruction disable students?" Many respondents expressed concern that one-shot library sessions are too short for students to learn complex research skills and that the efforts to teach these skills are hampered by jargon and a feeling of information overload. Attendees noted that instructors frequently make assumptions about the preexisting knowledge students have when they enter the library classroom and the ways students should participate in an instructional session. Instructors expect that students will behave normatively in a classroom, for example, appearing interested, making eye contact, and participating in classroom activities. Students are expected to have ready answers to questions when called on, to quickly read a page of text to answer questions, and to follow a fast-moving lesson plan without confusion. Neurodivergent students and students with other disabilities may be impeded by these and other classroom expectations and structures.

We will discuss examples of some common instructional practices found in library one-shots and highlight some of the ways they can be disabling to neurodivergent students. For each identified issue, we suggest more inclusive, UDL-informed alternatives.

Too Much Content

One-shots are notoriously crammed with instructional content. It is not unusual for librarians to cover library resources, database searching, and source evaluation in a single fifty-minute session. Either because librarians have been asked by faculty to cover everything the students may need to know or because they want to prove the usefulness of library instruction in a limited time frame, library instructors scramble to move quickly and cover as much ground as possible. When pressured to cover too much material, librarians often slip into using jargon that students do not know or understand, and the urgency of a hurried presentation can dissuade students from asking questions. All students are susceptible to information overload, but this experience can be especially overwhelming for those who struggle with processing information.

The most obvious recommendation for fixing this issue is to cover less content in one-shot sessions. With thoughtful use of UDL, less can be more in instructional settings. Maximizing the transfer and generalization of carefully selected skills and information for multiple settings can be more effective than presenting to learners scattershot information that they may or may not recall later.[50] Librarian Steven Hoover writes that when planning time-limited one-shots, it is important to "clarify priorities for what actually needs to be learned as opposed to what would be nice to learn."[51] We recommend that instructors be realistic about the number of topics that can be covered in a single sitting and focus on skills that are most transferable to other settings.

Next, think about instructional speed. Do students have enough time to understand and ask questions about each topic? Librarians may want to record themselves to get a sense of how fast they are speaking and take note if they are slipping into librarian jargon. It can also be helpful to have a colleague observe an instruction session and give feedback. Make a point of asking the course instructor for feedback later and check if they felt their students understood the key concepts of the session.

If it is necessary to include information on many disparate topics in a one-shot, make dedicated time for students to participate in personal formative assessment and conversation between sections. CAST's *UDL Guidelines* Checkpoint 6.4, "Enhance capacity for monitoring progress," suggests prompting learners to engage in self-reflection on their own progress and quality of understanding the class material.[52] A student may feel intimidated to bring a question up during a brief interlude of "Does anyone have questions? No?" A private assessment time allows participants to process what they have learned, check their own understanding, and prepare emotionally and mentally for the next segment of the lesson. This is an opportunity to consider student affect when designing a lesson—consider how students may be feeling throughout your session and how their emotional state may affect their ability to learn. A simple strategy for private formative assessment is to show and describe an example problem (in library instruction, this may be a source to evaluate, a research question that needs to be adapted or broken into keywords, a resource that a citation needs to be created for, etc.). Give the students time to work through the example on their own. The instructor can then solve it themselves, guiding the students through applying techniques taught in the lesson and explaining their thinking. Students will see a solution to the problem and can check their process against the librarian's. Then, crucially, check in after this exercise through an anonymous survey or similar tool (Poll Everywhere, Padlet, etc.), asking the students if they are comfortable using these techniques. This method of eliciting information anonymously also gives students a chance to ask questions they feel uncomfortable asking in front of peers.

Access to Materials

Many students are accustomed to a classroom experience mediated by a learning management system (LMS) where their instructor may post lesson plans, course materials and readings, and class recordings or slides. Because many librarians are considered a visitor to the class rather than a permanent resource for the course, materials they present may not be included in the LMS. Often it is difficult or impossible for students to access the materials and content before or after the session. Even students who have arranged to have class materials provided in advance as a disability accommodation may not have library session material provided for them if the faculty member does not give the library instructor advance notice. Not knowing how to access class materials later can cause considerable anxiety to students who may feel that this is their only opportunity to absorb and understand the library instructional content. Students who missed the session are also unable to make up the lesson without access to the lesson materials.

In general, it is good practice to provide students options in how they access content and resources, and we can extend this advice to one-shots as well. Create a packet of session contents that comprise the materials and skills covered in the session. Include in this packet an outline of the information covered in the session, a list of resources and links students can use, and any learning supplements or exercises given in class that could be done asynchronously. Explain each step in a clear and comprehensive way so any student, regardless of experience with library materials, can understand and employ the content. Ideally, this packet should be placed with other course resources—for example, in the course's LMS or online syllabus—but if this is not possible, put these instruction materials in another easily accessible online location, like a LibGuide or Google folder. A recording of the session could also be included with the permission of the participants or short instructional videos about the skills and information presented. Clearly state that these materials are available at the beginning of the session and demonstrate to the students how to find the content. When students know they can revisit the information and resources you are presenting, it relieves the pressure to get everything down during your session, a recommendation of UDL Checkpoint 6.3.[53] Access to materials allows the students to revisit the content on their own terms throughout their experience in the course and accommodates students who were not able to attend the session.

Unclear Goals

Instructors of short, fast-paced sessions may not take the time to give students an overview of the content of the session or provide a sense of structure. Without a brief overview of the session to come, students may not know what to expect or understand how the topics being covered interconnect. This may seem like an easy five minutes to cut when pressed for time in a one-shot. However, without clearly presented learning objectives and mastery goals, students are less capable of monitoring their personal progress and may not be able to determine from lesson activities what mastery of the content looks like.[54] Absent clearly laid out goals, students can get lost or overwhelmed. Highlighting the relevance of the library instruction to the course content up front also helps students who may otherwise have trouble connecting concepts or who may struggle to see the greater usefulness of library skills.

Clearly articulating the learning goals and outcomes to students at the beginning of a lesson helps students to focus their attention on what elements of the session will be most important. State these objectives, and the agenda for the session, clearly at the beginning of the lesson, and provide it in writing as well so students can follow along throughout the session. This supports continued understanding of the salience of goals and objectives, aligned with UDL Checkpoint 8.1, of which CAST writes, "it is important to build in periodic or persistent 'reminders' of both the goal and its value in order for them to sustain effort and concentration in the face of distracters."[55] For example, if a library instructor explains to student participants that the goal of the session is to become better at identifying appropriate articles in databases, this information helps students focus on the source evaluation portion of the lesson rather than getting overwhelmed and distracted by the many features in the library database.

Unclear Relevance

Highlighting how the research skills taught in the lesson will be useful going forward is also critical for increasing student motivation to learn. In studying student self-efficacy in library skills, librarian Wen-Hua Ren found that library instruction is most effective and useful for students when it "cultivate[s] in the students a positive attitude and a strong motivation to continue to learn and practice those skills on their own."[56] Library instructors cannot show students everything they will need in a single session, but by working to highlight the usefulness of library skills and demonstrate their utility with "authentic, meaningful activities," we can guide students to feel invested in their own learning and pursue it on their own time, as recommended by UDL Checkpoint 7.2.[57]

One way to prepare students for library instruction and show them in advance that the session will be useful is to create a pre-assignment or tutorial. This can be done via LibGuides or a shared slide deck. If the faculty instructor is willing to collaborate on the assignment, this can even be hosted or formally assigned on the course LMS page. A pre-assignment or tutorial focusing on the basics of the lesson will help students come to the lesson with similar background knowledge; a pre-lesson exercise is also a good opportunity to highlight how these skills can be used in context. If possible, design the assignment to be related to the subject area or assignment topic, and keep it brief—no more than ten or fifteen minutes for the student. This recommendation does require a time investment, but a template that can be edited and reused for courses is a simple way to significantly reduce the time requirement for creating multiple pre-assignments. As they work through a pre-assignment, students will be able to begin thinking about how they can utilize these skills going forward for this and other research projects. Creating a pre-assignment can also help to reduce the amount of content the library instructor needs to cover in the session, allowing students more time to absorb the material and ask questions in class.

Active Learning

A common recommendation to maximize the effectiveness of a short instructional session is incorporating active learning techniques, including in-class polling utilizing clickers or other online tools, small group work, or random calling.[58] Though there are pedagogical benefits to active learning techniques,[59] we want to call attention to the ways that they can also be disabling to many neurodivergent students. For example, Jennifer Cullen found in interviews with autistic students that "group work environments [may] simply accentuate their difficulties with social communication."[60] Discomfort with group work and cold calling in the classroom does not apply only to autistic learners; students who experience social anxiety also report discomfort in active learning classrooms.[61] Group assessment activities and clicker usage can also cause anxiety, primarily from the fear of negative evaluation by instructors and peers.[62] If a student is focusing on mediating their communication or controlling their social anxiety, they will not be in the optimal headspace to absorb the class material.

It is not necessary to stop using active learning techniques in the classroom to remedy these problems. Applying the UDL principle of multiple methods of engagement can make these activities more universally accessible to students. Group activities like think-pair-share are a useful way to get more students involved in discussion of instructional content, but some students will feel much more comfortable working alone. When designing sessions that include an active learning activity, consider preparing an alternative activity that does not require social interaction or group evaluation that also fulfills the learning objectives. It is also important to introduce these activities at the same time, rather than offering a non-active learning activity only if students request it. If students feel as if they are singled out or their disability is exposed, it can make them afraid of other students' reactions,[63] which they may have experienced as negative, critical, or shaming in the past. Making space for disabled students to choose their own engagement with the content reinforces that they have agency over their experience in the classroom and that they can interact with the material in a way that works for them.

Further Recommendations
Meeting Student Needs

Librarians need to empower students to make use of what we have and to feel comfortable telling us when they need help. Because neurodivergent students may fear judgment when asking for accommodations, it is also possible that disabled students have needs libraries have not yet considered. To address the issue of authentically making sure we are offering the right services to users, Pionke suggested that "observation and discussion with user experience and other ethnographic methods" can be part of a tool set to reach out and learn some of the needs of disabled patrons.[64] Observation and discussion may not be able to predict or infer every service and accommodation that may help disabled learners, but making preemptive efforts will show students that accessibility is a priority. If students perceive that their accommodation requests will be treated respectfully and the library will work to meet them, they may be more open to sharing their needs.

It is important to ask users with disabilities about how they experience library services and resources to understand their needs. This requires getting out there and talking with students, of course, but it can also mean asking other campus departments and resources—departments of residential life, departments of accessibility or disability services, or diversity, equity, and inclusion departments—to see what students are asking them about. Librarians Brannen, Milewski, and Mack suggest including disability services and disabled people in educational efforts so their voices and concerns are heard directly. Libraries rely on collaborative relationships to help students succeed, just as student affairs and disability services offices on campuses do.[65] These partnerships can highlight how to better serve students and will help other departments understand how to better direct students to library services. Learners should see the library as another support service that is there to help, especially for those with specialized needs.

Professional Development Resources

Though this process may seem intimidating, many step-by-step resources exist focusing on implementing UDL in instructional practice. As discussed earlier, implementing UDL is intended to be an iterative process that responds to and incorporates learner feedback over time. It can be helpful to consult and collaborate with colleagues, either at your institution or in online spaces, as you begin this journey. Several researchers suggest creating a community of practice to relieve stress while providing a forum to explore instructional ideas.[66] We also suggest forming a reading or discussion group with other interested library staff or faculty to share experiences and communicate about upcoming training opportunities across campus. Consistent, ongoing staff training is imperative to help support disabled students. Many webinars and free or low-cost trainings are available online—we recommend beginning with the learning resources on the CAST website. Disability services departments may also have recommendations for professional development resources for instructors hoping to make their work more accessible.

Disability Justice and Libraries

The ALA recognizes that "libraries should be fully inclusive of all members of their community and strive to break down barriers to access,"[67] but librarians still have a great deal of work to do to bring the practices of librarianship in line with the call to action of disability justice. The disability justice movement emerged in 2005 as a response to the single-issue, white-focused disability rights movement.[68] The movement has continued to grow due to the dedication and efforts of many disabled Black, brown, queer, and trans folks speaking up, rebelling, and doing the work in countless ways. Disability justice challenges us to approach ableism critically, as one of the many reflections of hegemonic oppression that we must call out and dismantle to make a more just world. Sins Invalid, a disability justice advocacy group, writes that ableism is deeply intertwined with heteropatriarchy, white supremacy, colonialism, and capitalism. Acknowledging this connection means acknowledging the ongoing "violence on bodies and minds deemed outside the norm and therefore 'dangerous.'"[69]

Librarians are dedicated to the success of students, and this extends beyond their academic endeavors to their experiences in university communities. Librarians actively engage with movements for social justice in academia and their local communities. Though the library profession has made great strides fighting for justice and bringing conversations about oppression into the library, disability justice remains an unfamiliar movement to many librarians. Some scholarship exists on the overlap between the ideals of librarianship and disability justice, but our field needs more thought and conversation in this area. Kumbier and Starkey write that "when we think of disability as a problem to be solved or limit our thinking to ADA compliance, we miss opportunities to understand disability in more nuanced ways and think more broadly about what creating accessible, inclusive libraries could mean."[70] Librarians need to take a critical look at our work and our values and strive to better integrate disability justice into our day-to-day work.

Conclusion

A review of the literature available on disabilities and libraries reveals that most research conducted on this topic is still approached with the medical model in mind. Most of this literature discusses making spaces and resources accessible to disabled patrons. Disabilities are identified, the difficulties they pose are discussed, and solutions are proposed without much comment on the "larger structural, systemic, or social transformations that could enable access for people with disabilities."[71] Autistic librarian Zachary Tumlin noted that there is also a distinct lack of neurodivergent authors producing LIS research.[72] We need to critically reexamine the narrative of disability in the library and approach our research with a non-paternalistic lens, including the voices of neurodivergent library professionals, students, and other library users. Their thoughts, opinions, and experiences should guide library services, policies, and instruction. We can and must work to dismantle ableism in libraries—for our students and for our profession.

A crucial element of this work is also how libraries function in relation to the educational institutions they serve. Rarely are disabled people mentioned as key members of the university community or as the focus of initiatives to change university policies, admissions, hiring, or programs.[73] Instead of making systemic changes toward increased accessibility, institutions leave disabled students to navigate bureaucratic systems to fight for individual accommodations, and librarians may believe they need to follow this pattern when approaching their instruction. The ALA Code of Ethics states,

> We affirm the inherent dignity and rights of every person. We work to recognize and dismantle systemic and individual biases; to confront inequity and oppression; to enhance diversity and inclusion; and to advance racial and social justice in our libraries, communities, profession, and associations through awareness, advocacy, education, collaboration, services, and allocation of resources and spaces.[74]

The code of ethics of our profession drives us to fight for better experiences for marginalized students in our spaces. We need to do more than grant excluded groups access to academic spaces. We need to transform the concepts of access and inclusion themselves.

We are asking librarians to be open to learning about instructing disabled students. Examine your own attitudes about disability and how you, personally, interact with neurodivergent students in the classroom. Take initiative beyond referring students to disability offices, and actively pursue changes in your teaching and attitudes toward disabled people. By embracing the principles of disability justice, working to make library instruction more accessible, and being open to disabled perspectives, librarians can create positive change and transform our educational environments.

Notes

1. Nicole Pagowsky, "The Contested One-Shot: Deconstructing Power Structures to Imagine New Futures," editorial, *College and Research Libraries* 82, no. 3 (2021), https://doi.org/10.5860/crl.82.3.300; Cinthya Ippoliti, "Re-imagining the One-Shot: The Case for Transformational Teaching," *Scholarship of Teaching and Learning, Innovative Pedagogy* 1, no. 1 (2018), https://digitalcommons.humboldt.edu/sotl_ip/vol1/iss1/3.
2. Shanna K. Kattari, Miranda Olzman, and Michele D. Hanna, "'You Look Fine!' Ableist Experiences by People with Invisible Disabilities," *Affilia* 33, no. 4 (November 2018): 478, https://doi.org/10.1177/0886109918778073.
3. Lynn Clouder et al., "Neurodiversity in Higher Education: A Narrative Synthesis," *Higher Education* 80, no. 4 (2020): 758, https://doi.org/10.1007/s10734-020-00513-6; Nick Walker, "Neurodiversity: Some Basic Terms and Definitions," *Neuroqueer* (blog), September 27, 2014, https://neuroqueer.com/neurodiversity-terms-and-definitions/.
4. Moheb Costandi, "Why the Neurodiversity Movement Has Become Harmful," Aeon, September 12, 2019, https://aeon.co/essays/why-the-neurodiversity-movement-has-become-harmful.
5. Clouder et al., "Neurodiversity in Higher Education," 758.
6. Zachary Tumlin, "'This Is a Quiet Library, Except When It's Not:' On the Lack of Neurodiversity Awareness in Librarianship," *Music Reference Services Quarterly* 22, no. 1–2 (2019): 6, https://doi.org/10.1080/10588167.2019.1575017.
7. Kathleen R. Bogart and Dana S. Dunn, "Ableism Special Issue Introduction," *Journal of Social Issues* 75, no. 3 (September 2019): 650, https://doi.org/10.1111/josi.12354.
8. Bogart and Dunn, "Ableism Special Issue Introduction," 651.
9. Bogart and Dunn, "Ableism Special Issue Introduction," 651.
10. Jenna A. Harder, Victor N. Keller, and William J. Chopik, "Demographic, Experiential, and Temporal Variation in Ableism," *Journal of Social Issues* 75, no. 3 (September 2019): 684, https://doi.org/10.1111/josi.12341.
11. Harder, Keller, and Chopik, "Demographic, Experiential, and Temporal Variation," 683–701.
12. Michelle R. Nario-Redmond, Alexia A. Kemerling, and Arielle Silverman, "Hostile, Benevolent, and Ambivalent Ableism: Contemporary Manifestations," *Journal of Social Issues* 75, no. 3 (2019): 727, https://doi.org/10.1111/josi.12337.
13. Jan Grue, "The Problem with Inspiration Porn: A Tentative Definition and a Provisional Critique," *Disability and Society* 31, no. 6 (2016): 840, https://doi.org/10.1080/09687599.2016.1205473.
14. Kayla Lett, Andreea Tamaian, and Bridget Klest, "Impact of Ableist Microaggressions on University Students with Self-Identified Disabilities," *Disability and Society* 35, no. 9 (2020): 1444–45, https://doi.org/10.1080/09687599.2019.1680344.

15. Rhoda Olkin et al., "The Experiences of Microaggressions against Women with Visible and Invisible Disabilities," *Journal of Social Issues* 75, no. 3 (September 2019): 781, https://doi.org/10.1111/josi.12342.

16. Lett, Tamaian, and Klest, "Impact of Ableist Microaggressions," 1445–51.

17. Jennifer Marie Martin, "Stigma and Student Mental Health in Higher Education," *Higher Education Research and Development* 29, no. 3 (2010): 259, https://doi.org/10.1080/07294360903470969.

18. Kattari, Olzman, and Hanna, "'You Look Fine!'" 481–83.

19. Bogart and Dunn, "Ableism Special Issue Introduction," 652.

20. Lydia Brown, "Disability in an Ableist World," *Autistic Hoya* (blog), August 12, 2012, https://www.autistichoya.com/2012/08/disability-in-ableist-world.html.

21. Louise M. Yoho, "Academic Discourse Surrounding College Students with Disabilities in the United States," *Disability and Society* 35, no. 8 (2020): 1267, https://doi.org/10.1080/09687599.2019.1680343.

22. Yoho, "Academic Discourse," 1269.

23. Alana Kumbier and Julia Starkey, "Access Is Not Problem Solving: Disability Justice and Libraries," *Library Trends* 64, no. 3 (Winter 2016): 473, https://doi.org/10.1353/lib.2016.0004.

24. Jay Dolmage, *Academic Ableism*, Corporealities: Discourses Of Disability (Ann Arbor: University of Michigan Press, 2017), 3.

25. Jay Dolmage, *Academic Ableism*, Corporealities: Discourses Of Disability (Ann Arbor: University of Michigan Press, 2017), 161.

26. Margaret Price, *Mad at School*, Corporealities: Discourses Of Disability (Ann Arbor: University of Michigan Press, 2011), 231.

27. Consuelo M. Kreider, Roxanna M. Bendixen, and Barbara J. Lutz, "Holistic Needs of University Students with Invisible Disabilities: A Qualitative Study," *Physical and Occupational Therapy in Pediatrics* 35, no. 4 (2015): 427, https://doi.org/10.3109/01942638.2015.1020407.

28. Kirsten L. Lightner et al., "Reasons University Students with a Learning Disability Wait to Seek Disability Services," *Journal of Postsecondary Education and Disability* 25, no. 2 (2012): 149.

29. Lightner et al., "Reasons University Students," 155.

30. Dolmage, *Academic Ableism*, 10.

31. Nario-Redmond, Kemerling, and Silverman, "Hostile, Benevolent, and Ambivalent Ableism," 737.

32. J. J. Pionke, "Toward Holistic Accessibility: Narratives from Functionally Diverse Patrons," *Reference and User Services Quarterly* 57, no. 1 (2017): 50–54.

33. Clouder et al., "Neurodiversity in Higher Education," 768–70.

34. Carla Branco, Miguel R. Ramos, and Miles Hewstone, "The Association of Group-Based Discrimination with Health and Well-Being: A Comparison of Ableism with Other 'Isms,'" *Journal of Social Issues* 75, no. 3 (September 2019): 840, https://doi.org/10.1111/josi.12340.

35. Nario-Redmond, Kemerling, and Silverman, "Hostile, Benevolent, and Ambivalent Ableism," 748.

36. Dani Brecher and Kevin Michael Klipfel, "Education Training for Instruction Librarians: A Shared Perspective," *Communications in Information Literacy* 8, no. 1 (2014): 44, https://doi.org/10.15760/comminfolit.2014.8.1.164.

37. Mary Beth Applin, "Instructional Services for Students with Disabilities," *Journal of Academic Librarianship* 25, no. 2 (March 1999): 139, https://doi.org/10.1016/S0099-1333(99)80015-9.

38. Karen Bordonaro and Gillian Richardson, "Scaffolding and Reflection in Course-Integrated Library Instruction," *Journal of Academic Librarianship* 30, no. 5 (September 2004): 391–401, https://doi.org/10.1016/j.acalib.2004.06.004; Alison Farrell, Janet Goosney, and Karen Hutchens, "Evaluation of the Effectiveness of Course Integrated Library Instruction in an Undergraduate Nursing Program," *Journal of the Canadian Health Libraries Association* 34, no. 3 (December 2013): 164–75.

39. Sarah Cisse, *The Fortuitous Teacher* (Cambridge, MA: Chandos, 2016), Safari Books Online.

40. CAST, "Timeline of Innovation," accessed July 28, 2021, https://www.cast.org/impact/timeline-innovation.

41. Patricia Rice Doran, "Language Accessibility in the Classroom: How UDL Can Promote Success for Linguistically Diverse Learners," *Exceptionality Education International* 25, no. 3 (2015): 1–12, https://doi.org/10.5206/eei.v25i3.7728; K. Alisa Lowrey et al., "More Than One Way: Stories of UDL and Inclusive Classrooms," *Research and Practice for Persons with Severe Disabilities* 42, no. 4 (December 2017): 225–42, https://doi.org/10.1177/1540796917711668.

42. Kari Lynne Kumar and Maureen Wideman, "Accessible by Design: Applying UDL Principles in a First Year Undergraduate Course," *Canadian Journal of Higher Education* 44, no. 1 (2014): 125.

43. Jay Dolmage, "Universal Design: Places to Start," *Disability Studies Quarterly* 35, no. 2 (2015), https://doi.org/10.18061/dsq.v35i2.4632.

44. Samantha Peter and Kristina Clement, "One Step at a Time: A Case Study of Incorporating Universal Design for Learning in Library Instruction," *Scholarship of Teaching and Learning, Innovative Pedagogy* 2, no. 1 (Fall 2020): article 3, https://digitalcommons.humboldt.edu/sotl_ip/vol2/iss1/3.

45. Beth S. Fornauf and Joy Dangora Erickson, "Toward an Inclusive Pedagogy through Universal Design for Learning in Higher Education: A Review of the Literature," *Journal of Postsecondary Education and Disability* 33, no. 2 (2020): 191.

46. Harold Pashler et al., "Learning Styles: Concepts and Evidence," *Psychological Science in the Public Interest* 9, no. 3 (December 2008): 105–19, https://doi.org/10.1111/j.1539-6053.2009.01038.x; Daniel T. Willingham, Elizabeth M. Hughes, and David G. Dobolyi, "The Scientific Status of Learning Styles Theories," *Teaching of Psychology* 42, no. 3 (July 2015): 266–71, https://doi.org/10.1177/0098628315589505.

47. Philip M. Newton, "The Learning Styles Myth Is Thriving in Higher Education," *Frontiers in Psychology* 6 (2015): 1908, https://doi.org/10.3389/fpsyg.2015.01908.

48. Guy A. Boysen, "Lessons (Not) Learned: The Troubling Similarities between Learning Styles and Universal Design for Learning," *Scholarship of Teaching and Learning in Psychology* (preprint, submitted in 2021), 5, https://doi.org/10.1037/stl0000280.

49. Anne-Marie Womack, "Teaching Is Accommodation: Universally Designing Composition Classrooms and Syllabi," *College Composition and Communication* 68, no. 3 (2017): 497.

50. CAST, *Universal Design for Learning Guidelines*, ver. 2.2 (Lynnfield, MA: CAST, 2018), https://udlguidelines.cast.org/representation/comprehension/transfer-generalization.

51. Megan Oakleaf et al., "Notes from the Field: 10 Short Lessons on One-Shot Instruction," *Communications in Information Literacy* 6, no. 1 (2012): 7, https://doi.org/10.15760/comminfolit.2012.6.1.114.

52. CAST, *Universal Design for Learning Guidelines*.

53. CAST, *Universal Design for Learning Guidelines*.

54. Helen S. Timperley and Judy M. Parr, "What Is This Lesson About? Instructional Processes and Student Understandings in Writing Classrooms," *Curriculum Journal* 20, no. 1 (March 2009): 57, https://doi.org/10.1080/09585170902763999.

55. CAST, *Universal Design for Learning Guidelines*.

56. Wen-Hua Ren, "Library Instruction and College Student Self-Efficacy in Electronic Information Searching," *Journal of Academic Librarianship* 26, no. 5 (September 2000): 323, https://doi.org/10.1016/S0099-1333(00)00138-5.

57. CAST, *Universal Design for Learning Guidelines*.

58. Kevin W. Walker and Michael Pearce, "Student Engagement in One-Shot Library Instruction," *Journal of Academic Librarianship* 40, no. 3–4 (May 2014): 281–90, https://doi.org/10.1016/j.acalib.2014.04.004; Katherine Strober Dabbour, "Applying Active Learning Methods to the Design of Library Instruction for a Freshman Seminar," *College and Research Libraries* 58, no. 4 (July 1997): 299–308, https://doi.org/10.5860/crl.58.4.299.

59. Scott Freeman et al., "Active Learning Increases Student Performance in Science, Engineering, and Mathematics," *Proceedings of the National Academy of Sciences* 111, no. 23 (May 12, 2014): 8410–15, https://doi.org/10.1073/pnas.1319030111.

60. Jennifer A. Cullen, "The Needs of College Students with Autism Spectrum Disorders and Asperger's Syndrome," *Journal of Postsecondary Education and Disability* 28, no. 1 (Spring 2015): 95, https://eric.ed.gov/?id=EJ1066322.

61. Matthew Cohen et al., "Think, Pair, Freeze: The Association between Social Anxiety and Student Discomfort in the Active Learning Environment," *Scholarship of Teaching and Learning in Psychology* 5, no. 4 (December 2019): 273, https://doi.org/10.1037/stl0000147.

62. Katelyn M. Cooper, Virginia R. Downing, and Sara E. Brownell, "The Influence of Active Learning Practices on Student Anxiety in Large-Enrollment College Science Classrooms," *International Journal of STEM Education* 5, no. 1 (2018): article 23, p. 10, https://doi.org/10.1186/s40594-018-0123-6.

63. Margaret M. Quinlan, Benjamin R. Bates, and Maureen E. Angell, "'What Can I Do to Help?' Postsecondary Students with Learning Disabilities' Perceptions of Instructors' Classroom Accommodations," *Journal of Research in Special Educational Needs* 12, no. 4 (2012): 229, https://doi.org/10.1111/j.1471-3802.2011.01225.x.
64. Pionke, "Toward Holistic Accessibility," 54.
65. Michelle H. Brannen, Steven Milewski, and Thura Mack, "Providing Staff Training and Programming to Support People with Disabilities: An Academic Library Case Study," *Public Services Quarterly* 13, no. 2 (2017): 65, https://doi.org/10.1080/15228959.2017.1298491.
66. Peter and Clement, "One Step at a Time," 32; Brannen, Milewski, and Mack, "Providing Staff Training and Programming," 71.
67. American Library Association, "Services to People with Disabilities: An Interpretation of the Library Bill of Rights," Issues and Advocacy, 2009, amended 2018, https://www.ala.org/advocacy/intfreedom/librarybill/interpretations/servicespeopledisabilities.
68. Leah Lakshmi Piepzna-Samarasinha, *Care Work* (Vancouver, BC: Arsenal Pulp Press, 2018).
69. Sins Invalid, "What Is Disability Justice?" *Sins Invalid* (blog), June 16, 2020, https://www.sinsinvalid.org/news-1/2020/6/16/what-is-disability-justice.
70. Kumbier and Starkey, "Access Is Not Problem Solving," 473.
71. Kumbier and Starkey, "Access Is Not Problem Solving," 478.
72. Tumlin, "This Is a Quiet Library, Except When It's Not," 15.
73. Yoho, "Academic Discourse Surrounding College Students," 1269–70.
74. American Library Association, "Code of Ethics," Professional Ethics, Tools, Publications and Resources, 1939, amended 1981, 1995, 2008, and 2021, https://www.ala.org/tools/ethics.

Bibliography

American Library Association. "Code of Ethics." Professional Ethics, Tools, Publications and Resources, 1939, amended 1981, 1995, 2008, and 2021. https://www.ala.org/tools/ethics.

———. "Services to People with Disabilities: An Interpretation of the Library Bill of Rights." Issues and Advocacy, 2009, amended 2018. https://www.ala.org/advocacy/intfreedom/librarybill/interpretations/servicespeopledisabilities.

Applin, Mary Beth. "Instructional Services for Students with Disabilities." *Journal of Academic Librarianship* 25, no. 2 (March 1999): 139–41. https://doi.org/10.1016/S0099-1333(99)80015-9.

Bogart, Kathleen R., and Dana S. Dunn. "Ableism Special Issue Introduction." *Journal of Social Issues* 75, no. 3 (September 2019): 650–64. https://doi.org/10.1111/josi.12354.

Bordonaro, Karen, and Gillian Richardson. "Scaffolding and Reflection in Course-Integrated Library Instruction." *Journal of Academic Librarianship* 30, no. 5 (September 2004): 391–401. https://doi.org/10.1016/j.acalib.2004.06.004.

Boysen, Guy A. "Lessons (Not) Learned: The Troubling Similarities between Learning Styles and Universal Design for Learning." *Scholarship of Teaching and Learning in Psychology*. Preprint, submitted in 2021. https://doi.org/10.1037/stl0000280.

Branco, Carla, Miguel R. Ramos, and Miles Hewstone. "The Association of Group-Based Discrimination with Health and Well-Being: A Comparison of Ableism with Other 'Isms.'" *Journal of Social Issues* 75, no. 3 (September 2019): 814–46. https://doi.org/10.1111/josi.12340.

Brannen, Michelle H., Steven Milewski, and Thura Mack. "Providing Staff Training and Programming to Support People with Disabilities: An Academic Library Case Study." *Public Services Quarterly* 13, no. 2 (2017): 61–77. https://doi.org/10.1080/15228959.2017.1298491.

Brecher, Dani, and Kevin Michael Klipfel. "Education Training for Instruction Librarians: A Shared Perspective." *Communications in Information Literacy* 8, no. 1 (2014): 43–49. https://doi.org/10.15760/comminfolit.2014.8.1.164.

Brown, Lydia. "Disability in an Ableist World." *Autistic Hoya* (blog), August 12, 2012. https://www.autistichoya.com/2012/08/disability-in-ableist-world.html.

CAST. "Timeline of Innovation." Accessed July 28, 2021. https://www.cast.org/impact/timeline-innovation.

———. *Universal Design for Learning Guidelines*, ver. 2.2. Lynnfield, MA: CAST, 2018. https://udlguidelines.cast.org.

Cisse, Sarah. *The Fortuitous Teacher: A Guide to Successful One-Shot Library Instruction*. Cambridge, MA: Chandos, 2016. Safari Books Online.

Clouder, Lynn, Mehmet Karakus, Alessia Cinotti, María Virginia Ferreyra, Genoveva Amador Fierros, and Patricia Rojo. "Neurodiversity in Higher Education: A Narrative Synthesis." *Higher Education* 80, no. 4 (2020): 757–78. https://doi.org/10.1007/s10734-020-00513-6.

Cohen, Matthew, Steven G. Buzinski, Emma Armstrong-Carter, Jenna Clark, Benjamin Buck, and Lillian Reuman. "Think, Pair, Freeze: The Association between Social Anxiety and Student Discomfort in the Active Learning Environment." *Scholarship of Teaching and Learning in Psychology* 5, no. 4 (December 2019): 265–77. https://doi.org/10.1037/stl0000147.

Cooper, Katelyn M., Virginia R. Downing, and Sara E. Brownell. "The Influence of Active Learning Practices on Student Anxiety in Large-Enrollment College Science Classrooms." *International Journal of STEM Education* 5, no. 1 (2018): article 23. https://doi.org/10.1186/s40594-018-0123-6.

Costandi, Moheb. "Why the Neurodiversity Movement Has Become Harmful," Aeon, September 12, 2019. https://aeon.co/essays/why-the-neurodiversity-movement-has-become-harmful.

Cullen, Jennifer A. "The Needs of College Students with Autism Spectrum Disorders and Asperger's Syndrome." *Journal of Postsecondary Education and Disability* 28, no. 1 (Spring 2015): 89–101. https://eric.ed.gov/?id=EJ1066322.

Dabbour, Katherine Strober. "Applying Active Learning Methods to the Design of Library Instruction for a Freshman Seminar." *College and Research Libraries* 58, no. 4 (July 1997): 299–308. https://doi.org/10.5860/crl.58.4.299.

Dolmage, Jay Timothy. *Academic Ableism: Disability and Higher Education*. Corporealities: Discourses of Disability. Ann Arbor: University of Michigan Press, 2017. https://www.jstor.org/stable/j.ctvr33d50.

———. "Universal Design: Places to Start." *Disability Studies Quarterly* 35, no. 2 (2015). https://doi.org/10.18061/dsq.v35i2.4632.

Doran, Patricia Rice. "Language Accessibility in the Classroom: How UDL Can Promote Success for Linguistically Diverse Learners." *Exceptionality Education International* 25, no. 3 (2015): 1–12. https://doi.org/10.5206/eei.v25i3.7728.

Farrell, Alison, Janet Goosney, and Karen Hutchens. "Evaluation of the Effectiveness of Course Integrated Library Instruction in an Undergraduate Nursing Program." *Journal of the Canadian Health Libraries Association* 34, no. 3 (December 2013): 164–75.

Fornauf, Beth S., and Joy Dangora Erickson. "Toward an Inclusive Pedagogy through Universal Design for Learning in Higher Education: A Review of the Literature." *Journal of Postsecondary Education and Disability* 33, no. 2 (2020): 183–99.

Freeman, Scott, Sarah L. Eddy, Miles McDonough, Michelle K. Smith, Nnadozie Okoroafor, Hannah Jordt, and Mary Pat Wenderoth. "Active Learning Increases Student Performance in Science, Engineering, and Mathematics." *Proceedings of the National Academy of Sciences* 111, no. 23 (May 12, 2014): 8410–15. https://doi.org/10.1073/pnas.1319030111.

Grue, Jan. "The Problem with Inspiration Porn: A Tentative Definition and a Provisional Critique." *Disability and Society* 31, no. 6 (2016): 838–49. https://doi.org/10.1080/09687599.2016.1205473.

Harder, Jenna A., Victor N. Keller, and William J. Chopik. "Demographic, Experiential, and Temporal Variation in Ableism." *Journal of Social Issues* 75, no. 3 (September 2019): 683–706. https://doi.org/10.1111/josi.12341.

Ippoliti, Cinthya. "Re-imagining the One-Shot: The Case for Transformational Teaching." *Scholarship of Teaching and Learning, Innovative Pedagogy* 1, no. 1 (2018). https://digitalcommons.humboldt.edu/sotl_ip/vol1/iss1/3.

Kattari, Shanna K., Miranda Olzman, and Michele D. Hanna. "'You Look Fine!' Ableist Experiences by People with Invisible Disabilities." *Affilia* 33, no. 4 (November 2018): 477–92. https://doi.org/10.1177/0886109918778073.

Kreider, Consuelo M., Roxanna M. Bendixen, and Barbara J. Lutz. "Holistic Needs of University Students with Invisible Disabilities: A Qualitative Study." *Physical and Occupational Therapy in Pediatrics* 35, no. 4 (2015): 426–41. https://doi.org/10.3109/01942638.2015.1020407.

Kumar, Kari Lynne, and Maureen Wideman. "Accessible by Design: Applying UDL Principles in a First Year Undergraduate Course." *Canadian Journal of Higher Education* 44, no. 1 (2014): 125–47.

Kumbier, Alana, and Julia Starkey. "Access Is Not Problem Solving: Disability Justice and Libraries." *Library Trends* 64, no. 3 (Winter 2016): 468–91. https://doi.org/10.1353/lib.2016.0004.

Lett, Kayla, Andreea Tamaian, and Bridget Klest. "Impact of Ableist Microaggressions on University Students with Self-Identified Disabilities." *Disability and Society* 35, no. 9 (2020): 1441–56. https://doi.org/10.1080/09687599.2019.1680344.

Lightner, Kirsten L., Deborah Kipps-Vaughan, Timothy Schulte, and Ashton D. Trice. "Reasons University Students with a Learning Disability Wait to Seek Disability Services." *Journal of Postsecondary Education and Disability* 25, no. 2 (2012): 145–59.

Lowrey, K. Alisa, Aleksandra Hollingshead, Kathy Howery, and John B. Bishop. "More Than One Way: Stories of UDL and Inclusive Classrooms." *Research and Practice for Persons with Severe Disabilities* 42, no. 4 (December 2017): 225–42. https://doi.org/10.1177/1540796917711668.

Martin, Jennifer Marie. "Stigma and Student Mental Health in Higher Education." *Higher Education Research and Development* 29, no. 3 (2010): 259–74. https://doi.org/10.1080/07294360903470969.

Nario-Redmond, Michelle R., Alexia A. Kemerling, and Arielle Silverman. "Hostile, Benevolent, and Ambivalent Ableism: Contemporary Manifestations." *Journal of Social Issues* 75, no. 3 (2019): 726–56. https://doi.org/10.1111/josi.12337.

Newton, Philip M. "The Learning Styles Myth Is Thriving in Higher Education." *Frontiers in Psychology* 6 (2015): 1908. https://doi.org/10.3389/fpsyg.2015.01908.

Oakleaf, Megan, Steven Hoover, Beth Woodard, Jennifer Corbin, Randy Hensley, Diana Wakimoto, Christopher Hollister, Debra Gilchrist, Michelle Millet, and Patty Iannuzzi. "Notes from the Field: 10 Short Lessons on One-Shot Instruction." *Communications in Information Literacy* 6, no. 1 (2012): 5–23. https://doi.org/10.15760/comminfolit.2012.6.1.114.

Olkin, Rhoda, H'Sien Hayward, Melody Schaff Abbene, and Goldie VanHeel. "The Experiences of Microaggressions against Women with Visible and Invisible Disabilities." *Journal of Social Issues* 75, no. 3 (September 2019): 757–85. https://doi.org/10.1111/josi.12342.

Pagowsky, Nicole. "The Contested One-Shot: Deconstructing Power Structures to Imagine New Futures." Editorial. *College and Research Libraries* 82, no. 3 (2021): 300–309. https://doi.org/10.5860/crl.82.3.300.

Pashler, Harold, Mark McDaniel, Doug Rohrer, and Robert Bjork. "Learning Styles: Concepts and Evidence." *Psychological Science in the Public Interest* 9, no. 3 (December 2008): 105–19. https://doi.org/10.1111/j.1539-6053.2009.01038.x.

Peter, Samantha, and Kristina Clement. "One Step at a Time: A Case Study of Incorporating Universal Design for Learning in Library Instruction." *Scholarship of Teaching and Learning, Innovative Pedagogy* 2, no. 1 (Fall 2020): article 3. https://digitalcommons.humboldt.edu/sotl_ip/vol2/iss1/3.

Piepzna-Samarasinha and Leah Lakshmi. *Care Work: Dreaming Disability Justice*. Vancouver, BC: Arsenal Pulp Press, 2018.

Pionke, J. J. "Toward Holistic Accessibility: Narratives from Functionally Diverse Patrons." *Reference and User Services Quarterly* 57, no. 1 (2017): 48–56.

Price, Margaret. *Mad at School: Rhetorics of Mental Disability and Academic Life*. Corporealities: Discourses of Disability. Ann Arbor: University of Michigan Press, 2011.

Quinlan, Margaret M., Benjamin R. Bates, and Maureen E. Angell. "'What Can I Do to Help?' Postsecondary Students with Learning Disabilities' Perceptions of Instructors' Classroom Accommodations." *Journal of Research in Special Educational Needs* 12, no. 4 (2012): 224–33. https://doi.org/10.1111/j.1471-3802.2011.01225.x.

Ren, Wen-Hua. "Library Instruction and College Student Self-Efficacy in Electronic Information Searching." *Journal of Academic Librarianship* 26, no. 5 (September 2000): 323–28. https://doi.org/10.1016/S0099-1333(00)00138-5.

Sins Invalid. "What Is Disability Justice?" *Sins Invalid* (blog), June 16, 2020. https://www.sinsinvalid.org/news-1/2020/6/16/what-is-disability-justice.

Timperley, Helen S., and Judy M. Parr. "What Is This Lesson About? Instructional Processes and Student Understandings in Writing Classrooms." *Curriculum Journal* 20, no. 1 (March 2009): 43–60. https://doi.org/10.1080/09585170902763999.

Tumlin, Zachary. "'This Is a Quiet Library, Except When It's Not': On the Lack of Neurodiversity Awareness in Librarianship." *Music Reference Services Quarterly* 22, no. 1–2 (2019): 3–17. https://doi.org/10.1080/10588167.2019.1575017.

Walker, Kevin W., and Michael Pearce. "Student Engagement in One-Shot Library Instruction." *Journal of Academic Librarianship* 40, no. 3–4 (May 2014): 281–90. https://doi.org/10.1016/j.acalib.2014.04.004.

Walker, Nick. "Neurodiversity: Some Basic Terms and Definitions." *Neuroqueer* (blog), September 27, 2014. https://neuroqueer.com/neurodiversity-terms-and-definitions/.

Willingham, Daniel T., Elizabeth M. Hughes, and David G. Dobolyi. "The Scientific Status of Learning Styles Theories." *Teaching of Psychology* 42, no. 3 (July 2015): 266–71. https://doi.org/10.1177/0098628315589505.

Womack, Anne-Marie. "Teaching Is Accommodation: Universally Designing Composition Classrooms and Syllabi." *College Composition and Communication* 68, no. 3 (2017): 494–525.

Yoho, Louise M. "Academic Discourse Surrounding College Students with Disabilities in the United States." *Disability and Society* 35, no. 8 (2020): 1248–73. https://doi.org/10.1080/09687599.2019.1680343.

Information Studies for Social Justice

Praxis in an Undergraduate Course

Lua Gregory and Shana Higgins

This chapter shares our experiences developing a credit-bearing course that integrates critical information literacy (CIL) practices with the exploration of social justice movement rhetorical strategies. Librarians will find this chapter useful if they are interested in teaching courses that integrate theory, CIL, and analyzing and practicing media production and writing with the aim of advocacy. For us, the journey to teaching this course was a long one, taking place after years of incremental transformation of our library instruction program to include critically informed perspectives and outcomes.[1] We taught the first iteration of LIB 201: Information Studies for Social Justice, a four-credit semester-length course, listed under our library department in spring 2020. Although our department does not offer a library and information science (LIS) degree, this class is essentially an LIS course for undergraduates and responds to the important work of Nicole A. Cooke, Miriam E. Sweeney, and Safiya Umoja Noble and of Amelia N.

Gibson and Sandra Hughes-Hassell, in which they call for LIS faculty to embed social justice in their work, including the classroom.[2]

The following questions informed the creation of this course: How might we explore the intersections of CIL and social justice? In what ways might we, as social justice advocates, best support the development of student agency? How do we connect critical theories to social justice movement practice in order to embody praxis? With these questions guiding course design, we integrated theory, skill practice, and community and cultural knowledge to engage with advocacy.

This course was also an opportunity to participate in the first-year implementation of a recently adopted general education (GE) curriculum. One core requirement in the new curriculum is an introductory experience of information and media literacy. This experience can be integrated with a second GE requirement for writing and research. We decided to combine these two GE requirements so that writing, research, and information and media literacy skills necessarily became entwined with our efforts to support student agency and explore praxis.

In bringing these skills together, we also asked, How are writing and media production leveraged to effect change, specifically by social justice movements? We explored with students the ways in which practicing information literacy, writing, and producing media are forms of action that can transform reality. Furthermore, by connecting theory to practice, and by encouraging students to actively engage with movements and organizations that seek to redress social inequities, we realized *praxis** in more meaningful ways than we've felt possible in one-shot sessions with students.[3]

Classroom Community Context

The private liberal arts university where we work is located in the Inland Empire region of Southern California, an area where African American, Black, Hispanic, Latinx, and Native American communities combined make up more than half the population. It is an historically White institution that recently sought and received recognition as an Hispanic-serving institution (HSI). The undergraduate core of the university, roughly 2,600 students, remains predominantly

---

* At the heart of critical pedagogy is praxis, the joining of theory and practice. It is communal, inclusive, and empowering. As critical librarians, we aim for a theoretically informed practice, one that contributes to social justice work.

White[†] and middle-class. Entering undergraduates are primarily from Southern California counties, with first-generation students and Cal Grant recipients making up about half of our first-year student population, and Pell Grant recipients one-third. Demographically our class in spring 2020 was a mix of first-, second-, and third-year students. Through in-class activities, group discussions, and formal assignments, students disclosed a range of socioeconomic statuses, some as first-generation college-going, a majority woman-identifying, as well as self-identification as Asian American, African American, Black, Latinx, and White.

Knowing that some of the students enrolled in our class to fulfill a GE requirement and others because of their interest in social justice, with some straddling both, we opened the first week of classes by recognizing these different motives. We asked students, despite their reasons for being in the class, to be open to reflecting on the meanings of social justice and the ways in which writing and research are tools for effecting change. We explicitly described the learning outcomes for the course and decisions we made regarding assignments, reading material, and subject matter. In our syllabus and in our introduction to the course, we used the words of bell hooks to set expectations for classroom engagement: "As a classroom community, our capacity to generate excitement is deeply affected by our interest in one another, in hearing one another's voices, in recognizing one another's presence."[4] In this way, we took care to set the tone and climate for the class in an effort to create an environment in which meaningful discussions could take place. We acknowledged that there would be assigned reading and viewing and conversations that would be uncomfortable for them and for us. We asked students "to become comfortable with being uncomfortable."[5] Cooke, Sweeney, and Noble note that "conversations about sensitive and possibly inflammatory topics are not easy and require sincere effort to be productive; as such, a conducive and safe learning environment must be established early in the course."[6]

We do our students a great disservice, and perpetuate the status quo, if we shrink "from discussions about institutionalized racism, sexism, ableism,

---

[†] Recent years have seen revisions to citation styles to recognize Black and Brown as racial categories, with compelling arguments for and against the capitalization of White. We have decided to follow the recommendation from Nell Irvin Painter, author of *The History of White People*, who wrote in an op-ed in the *Washington Post* that "in terms of racial identity, white Americans have had the choice of being something vague, something unraced and separate from race" and that "Capital-W 'Whiteness' is less saliently linked to white nationalism than to racial neutrality or absence. We should capitalize 'White' to situate 'Whiteness' within the American ideology of race, within which 'Black,' but not 'White,' has been hypervisible as a group identity." Making the decision to capitalize White challenges the racial invisibility of White people.

classism, and other forms of structural oppression" to assuage our "fear of being perceived as partisan or politically biased by students or administrators."[7] Additionally, teaching during a time in which the movements for Black lives and immigrant rights were met with White rage, blatant acts of racism, and state-sponsored violence meant we were intensely aware of the injustices taking place around us and of the trauma our students and colleagues were experiencing. Although we didn't address the Trump administration directly in this class, some of our discussions involved issues that intersected with the administration's policies, including institutionalized racism and xenophobia. Michelle Gohr and Vitalina A. Nova explore the challenges of teaching under the forty-fifth administration without causing harm, stating that librarians must "be affective, critically self-reflective and rooted in critical pedagogy."[8] Thus we reflected on our own positionalities and critiqued the cultures of our institutions with our class so that our students felt comfortable reflecting and sharing their own experiences. With this mental and emotional preparation, and with students knowing they would take control of class content and discussion during the second part of the semester, we established a sense of community and reciprocity in the classroom.

Theory for Social Justice

To provide frameworks for discussions on social justice, we front-loaded the class with theory by assigning readings from Brian Barry, Iris Marion Young, Patricia Hill Collins, and Paulo Freire. Although each of these authors approaches social justice with a different lens, deconstructing power relations and systems of oppression is a shared goal. By assigning these readings, we hoped to inspire students to deconstruct these systems present in their day-to-day lives, to inspect them and question them, inside and out. Excerpts from Barry's *Why Social Justice Matters* provided a traditional liberal conception of social justice.[9] Specifically, Barry discusses a distributive, or redistributive, model of social justice that does not challenge capitalist systems or the ways in which gendered and raced identities intersect with the free market and egalitarian notions of redistribution. Young's "Five Faces of Oppression" encouraged thinking beyond only economic disadvantage to consider multiple forms of oppression that impact the material conditions and lived experiences of individuals and groups.[10] Popular discourse in the United States tends to decontextualize the concept of privilege from oppression such that one can recognize membership in a privileged group without accepting the concomitant responsibilities of dismantling complicity as a passive oppressor. Young helps restore the relationship between privilege and oppressor. Grappling with the various forms of oppression experienced by those who belong to and are associated with particular social groups, in the sociological sense, facilitated our understanding of systemic oppression.

In "Toward a New Vision," Collins connects systemic oppression with individual lived experience: our positionality. For example, the "basic relationship of domination and subordination"[11] shapes "our personal biographies" and Collins argues it's our individual and collective responsibility to build "new theories of how race, class and gender have shaped the experiences …of all groups."[12] Collins clearly articulates how differences in our experiences with oppression, and in our relationships with power, obstruct our willingness or ability to build coalition across differences. Nevertheless, Collins describes a path toward collective action around common cause, a path that requires self-reflection, empathy, and accountability. Drawing from Audre Lorde's work, Collins calls for each of us to consciously attempt to "root out the piece of the oppressor planted within."[13] To actualize Collins's work, we asked students to reflect on their personal biographies, their dimensions of privilege, and to explore these in depth throughout the semester in relation to course content. This critical social theory provided a framework for future discussions, in which students were prepared to consider the connections between systemic and individual, political and personal, as we examined specific social justice issues and movements.

We introduced students to Freire's life and work in graphic form, drawing from *Portraits of Violence: An Illustrated History of Radical Thinking*,[14] which focused on the importance of critical consciousness raising and the possibilities of action and transformation—we *can* make change. We also discussed how Freire's pedagogical methods of dialogue and problem posing, as opposed to traditional ways of learning (the "banking model" of education), were going to be utilized in our class throughout the semester. One useful method involving critical questioning is described in *Reading Paulo Freire: His Life and Work* by Moacir Gadotti.[15] Gadotti explains how cultural circles* would come together to approach words or phrases with generative questions that encompassed life from a philosophical perspective, as well as questions that considered social and political contexts.[16] Gadotti provides an excellent example of this exercise on the topic of wages.[17] We used this in our class, writing the word *wages* on the board for everyone to visualize and contemplate. We then began generating questions, pausing after each for discussion, and encouraging the group to generate their

---

* Gadotti defines cultural circles, in a note on page 165 of *Reading Paulo Freire*, as a "teaching unit that replaces the traditional school. It is formed by a group of people who get together to discuss their work, local and national realities, their family life, etc. There is no place for the traditional (banking) teacher—the one who knows everything—nor is there for the pupil who knows nothing."

own questions, such as: What is the value of work? What are wages? How do we use wages? What is a minimum wage? What is a fair and just wage? What if everyone were paid the same wage? While Gadotti highlights the salaries of rural farm workers, we focused on salaries of immigrant farm workers, fast-food workers, and the Fight for $15 movement to generate more questions and to make transparent and deconstruct the political, social, and economic systems that affect *wages* in a context closer to our students' lives. This questioning and dialogue engaged students in the critical process Freire described as the *unveiling of reality*, a process that awakens our critical consciousness and subsequent interventions.[18]

Social Justice Movements in Practice

Information and media produced by social justice movements and activist organizations were prioritized in course content to support the learning goals for the course. We assigned materials, such as AIDS Coalition to Unleash Power (ACT UP) graphics, documents and radio from Indians of All Tribes, Black Lives Matter reports and tweets, and Riot Grrrl zines. Class sessions often first focused on a discussion of core concepts, theories, and historical contexts to frame analysis and understanding of primary source documents. A practice of CIL was enabled through the integration of critical theory, rhetorical strategies of social justice movements, and information literacy skills: recognizing how particular systems construct authority; how the creation, distribution, and uses of information can effect change; and how systematically marginalized groups find and develop alternative forms of knowledge production and sharing.[19]

Here is one example of practicing critical reading and CIL skills: students discussed readings on the concept of settler colonialism, watched Richard Oakes's delivery of the "Alcatraz Proclamation"[20] and listened to an episode of Radio Free Alcatraz.[21] Both are examples of media created by activists associated with Indians of All Tribes during the occupation of Alcatraz in 1969. This material offered students concrete examples of production practices aimed at social justice work. Students also read press releases from the Standing Rock Sioux Tribal Chairman, Dave Archambault II, issued during the Dakota Access Pipeline protests (2016–2017)[22] and explored the Standing Rock website[23] to investigate ongoing Indigenous resistance to settler colonialism across decades. Dialogue centered on an understanding of settler colonialism by exploring the following questions: What are some of the privileges settlers enjoy today? What methods are used to make Indigenous peoples invisible? In what ways is colonialism ongoing? To draw on our collective experiences, we asked students,

"How does learning about settler colonialism alter your understanding of living in Southern California? How do you benefit from settler colonialism?"

To practice writing strategies employed by social justice movements, we asked students to respond to weekly writing prompts. One especially successful writing exercise focused on letter writing. Before the assignment, we traced the history of some powerful letters, including James Baldwin's "My Dungeon Shook: Letter to My Nephew on the One Hundredth Anniversary of the Emancipation," Martin Luther King Jr.'s "Letter from a Birmingham Jail," Ta-Nehisi Coates's *Between the World and Me,* and Alicia Garza's "A Love Letter to Black People."[24] The history also included activist letter writing in recent anthologies, such as Jesmyn Ward's *The Fire This Time* and Carolina De Robertis's *Radical Hope: Letters of Love and Dissent in Dangerous Times,* both of which respond to Baldwin's work.[25] De Robertis explains the uniqueness of letter writing in that "Baldwin showed us that letter-essays, as a form, are perfectly situated to blend incisive political thought with intimate reflections, to fold them into a single embrace"[26] such that love is the essential ingredient that brings the political and personal together. Further, De Robertis writes, "In a letter, the thoughts at hand are undergirded by the need to connect with the intended recipient—and this spirit of extension beyond oneself can link social themes to our personal spheres, to what cuts the closest and matters most."[27] With this background, and in this spirit, students penned letters to their ancestors, to their younger selves, to family members, and to the children of immigrant parents.

Exploring Praxis: Student Agency and Voice

Praxis is the joining of reflection and action, theory and practice, in order to transform the world. Throughout our class, we sought to reflect through dialogue with students as well as to encourage reflection and action through writing. Specifically, we explored how student engagement with writing and production strategies used by social movements could foster student action and agency. Definitions of student agency are numerous, though we are concerned primarily with student agency as it relates to praxis. Lauren Smith discusses the importance of *political agency*, when one possesses a "heightened awareness of social injustices" as well as the skills or tools needed to challenge them.[28] Thus, an individual's capacity to take informed, reflexive action, to transform the world by redressing inequities, is the definition of agency that most aligns with the goals for the LIB 201 course. Further, as Jennifer Simpson writes, "Agency and implicatedness are inseparable. Implicatedness involves the understanding that all of us are situated within a web of relationships and power. Understanding one's implicatedness requires an ongoing regard for the various 'we's' in which one is situated. Students live in a 'we' at home, at school, and at work; and with family and friends."[29] Then agency, the ability to act, to effect change, is embedded in the relationships, systems, and structures of everyday life. Agency is contextual and multidimensional,[30] and its development is a social (or collective) and individual process, one that "demands a personal commitment from individuals to identify the forces influencing their lives."[31]

To support student agency in a college classroom, one must recognize these relationships by drawing from students' community knowledge, identities, and lived experiences.[32] We must also consider student voice.[33] Gr Keer describes the process of *giving voice* in a classroom setting as one that requires the instructor not to "silence the student and that the course material, teaching methods, and classroom atmosphere allow each student to retain her voice,"[34] and further writes that "giving voice means not only giving students the opportunity to speak, but also being aware, as an instructor, of one's own speech patterns, word choice, and attitude toward non-standard English in the classroom."[35] bell hooks, in *Teaching to Transgress*, points out the importance of redirecting focus and attention from the teacher's voice and centering the voices of students, because "the more students recognize their own uniqueness and particularity, the more they listen."[36] Nevertheless, as Julie Mcleod asserts:

> Voice is not simply speech; it can mean identity or agency, or even power, and perhaps capacity or aspiration; it can be the site of authentic reflection and insight or a radical source for counter narratives. Voice can be a code word for representing difference, or connote a democratic politics of participation and inclusion, or be the expression of an essentialized group identity. It can evoke practices attuned to the power of inter-subjectivity and the politics of the personal; it can have a therapeutic resonance; it can be a latent yet need-to-be-released attribute attached to some groups and not others. It can suggest an ideal, a political agenda and a basis for policy reform and action; it can declare difference and it can homogenize it; it has methodological and pedagogical dimensions and is rarely—if ever—simply a matter of creating opportunities for unfettered expression.[37]

Opportunities for developing student voice must move beyond simple expression.[38] Rather, through the process of dialogue, speaking, and listening as co-teachers and co-learners; through problematizing the world around us and unveiling structures of power; and through the reflective process of writing, student voice evolves.

Sarbani Sen Vengadasalam contends that developing one's voice is a way of becoming, of actively taking part in the social production of meaning.[39] Practicing writing is one method of developing voice. Growing into one's voice is to become empowered. In order to cultivate student voice, those teaching writing should encourage risk-taking, enable choice, share authority, support students' unique voices rather than enforcing social norms (in this case, academic writing norms), and promote a shared understanding that writing is meaning making.[40]

The course focused on the ways in which distinct voices were expressed in social justice movements, through writing, visual, and aural genres to advocate and empower, to urge toward agency and action. Students both practiced analysis of these methods of giving and taking voice and established their own voices through writing, discussion, and visual production. Considering these complexities for developing student agency and voice, we asked students, on the first day of class, to respond to an in-class writing prompt: What is social justice? Snippets from student responses include:

- That is a big question to ask on the first day lol.

- The first thing that comes to my mind is equality.... It means everyone is treated fairly.

- Social justice is a political movement that pursues equity for marginalized groups.

- Social justice insinuates that there are current social issues that need resolving.

- I believe it is the act of righting a wrong.

- It is an ongoing movement, maybe one that will never end.

The student responses were shared in the next class session so that we could arrive at a collective understanding, drawing from existing student knowledge, of what we mean by social justice. This activity at the beginning of the course illustrates a move away from the traditional lecture provided by the teaching authority toward an embrace of co-investigation with students.

In addition to in-class writing exercises and weekly writing prompts, student-led discussions were also successful in developing student voice and agency. Students chose two to three readings or examples of media for their peers to read or watch and crafted several discussion questions that were shared before class. We asked students, when selecting course materials for their peers, to consider the academic and lived experiences of the authors, as well as their classmates' prior knowledge and positionality. We found these recommendations to be helpful for students in selecting course materials that would provoke thoughtful discussion. Most importantly, student-facilitated class sessions flipped the power dynamic of the classroom in a positive way, providing a space for students to share and discuss with their peers social justice issues they were passionate about. Students developed voice and practiced their agency through defining course content, by choosing to explore incarceration, juvenile justice, gendered and raced wage gaps, child poverty, diversity in schools and segregation, migrant worker rights, and violence against women.

Conclusion

We structured work to build up to the creation of a zine, the final assignment, something that students would be able to share beyond the classroom. An annotated bibliography assignment provided background research for their zines and practice in searching and evaluating multiple forms of information on an issue, movement, or organization. This was followed by a zine proposal, which outlined zine content, described how evidence identified in annotated bibliographies would be used, explored action or solutions for the issue under consideration, and outlined a distribution plan to reach the audience of their zine. The scaffolded zine proposal fulfilled writing and research and information and media literacy learning outcomes for a multi-draft, sourced composition that attended to audience and purpose.

In mid-March 2020, due to the COVID-19 pandemic, we held our last in-person class. Students living in dorms had to quickly vacate and return home. They struggled with working in environments not conducive to learning, experiencing inequities in access to technology, and shifting to online classes. We reduced some of the workload to take these issues into account by canceling the final (the creation of the zine) and focused on writing and revising the zine proposal as the final assignment. Although these changes to the course worked well given the circumstances, we hope to teach the class again to see the media production practices of our students come to fruition.

Regardless of the challenges a pandemic presented, we engaged in a variety of dialogic and writing exercises throughout the semester, in which students came "to recognize that their voices and participation are politically powerful resources that can be collectively generated in the interest of social justice, human rights, and economic democracy."[41] We found this course to be an opportunity to enact a critical pedagogy that "link[s] the political with the personal in order to understand how power is mediated, resisted, and reproduced in daily life,"[42] where students were empowered to "recognize [their] own agency, [their] capacity to be active participants in the pedagogical process,"[43] and to attempt to create a classroom community that critically interrogated difference to build solidarity and empathy needed for social change.[44] Ultimately, the course was an exploration of how to realize praxis within a college classroom by practicing theoretically informed information literacy, writing, and media production, mediums through which we can develop voice and agency, through which we can reflect and act.

Notes

1. Lua Gregory and Shana Higgins, *Information Literacy and Social Justice* (Sacramento, CA: Library Juice Press, 2013); Lua Gregory and Shana Higgins, "Reorienting an Information Literacy Program toward Social Justice: Mapping the Core Values of Librarianship to the ACRL Framework," *Communications in Information Literacy* 11, no. 1 (2017): 42–54, https://doi.org/10.15760/comminfolit.2017.11.1.46.
2. Nicole. A. Cooke, Miriam E. Sweeney, and Safiya Umoja Noble, "Social Justice as Topic and Tool: An Attempt to Transform an LIS Curriculum and Culture," *Library Quarterly: Information, Community, Policy* 86, no. 1 (2017): 107–24; Amelia N. Gibson and Sandra Hughes-Hassell, "We Will Not Be Silent: Amplifying Marginalized Voices in LIS Education and Research," *Library Quarterly: Information, Community, Policy* 87, no. 4 (2017): 317–29.
3. Kenny Garcia, "Finding and Analyzing Information for Action and Reflection: Possibilities and Limitations of Popular Education in One-Shot Library Instruction," in *Critical Library Pedagogy Handbook*, vol. 1, ed. Kelly McElroy and Nicole Pagowsky (Chicago: Association of College and Research Libraries, 2016), 97–98; Karen P. Nicholson, "'Taking Back' Information Literacy: Time and the One-Shot in the Neoliberal University," in *Critical Library Pedagogy Handbook*, vol. 1, ed. Kelly McElroy and Nicole Pagowsky (Chicago: Association of College and Research Libraries, 2016), 25–39.
4. bell hooks, *Teaching to Transgress* (New York: Routledge, 1994), 8.
5. Cooke, Sweeney, and Noble, "Social Justice as Topic and Tool," 117.
6. Cooke, Sweeney, and Noble, "Social Justice as Topic and Tool," 117.
7. Gibson and Hughes-Hassell, "We Will Not Be Silent," 322.
8. Michelle Gohr and Vitalina A. Nova, "Student Trauma Experiences, Library Instruction and Existence under the 45th," *Reference Services Review* 48, no. 1 (2020): 189.
9. Brian Barry, *Why Social Justice Matters* (Malden, MA: Polity Press, 2005).
10. Iris Marion Young, "Five Faces of Oppression," in *Justice and the Politics of Difference* (Princeton, NJ: Princeton University Press, 1990), 39–65.
11. Patricia Hill Collins, "Toward a New Vision: Race, Class, and Gender as Categories of Analysis and Connection," *Race, Sex, and Class* 1, no. 1 (1993): 29.
12. Collins, "Toward a New Vision," 27.
13. Collins, "Toward a New Vision," 43.
14. Bradley Evans and Sean Michael Wilson, *Portraits of Violence,* illus. Inko, Carl Thompson, Robert Brown, Chris Mackenzie, Michiru Morikawa and Yen Quach (Oxford, UK: New Internationalist, 2016), 49–56.
15. Moacir Gadotti, *Reading Paulo Freire*, trans. John Milton (Albany, NY: SUNY Press, 1994).
16. Gadotti, *Reading Paulo Freire*, 20.
17. Gadotti, *Reading Paulo Freire*, 20.
18. Paulo Freire, *Pedagogy of the Oppressed*, 30th anniversary ed., trans. Myra Bergman Ramos (New York: Continuum, 2000), 81.

19. Lua Gregory and Shana Higgins, "Mapping Our Values across the Curriculum: A Social Justice Oriented Program at a Liberal Arts University" (poster presentation, European Conference on Information Literacy, Prague, Czech Republic, October 2016), https://library.redlands.edu/ecil2016.

20. Intelligent Channel, "Richard Oakes Delivering the Alcatraz Proclamation during the Occupation of Alcatraz (1969)—from THE EDUCATION ARCHIVE," recorded November 1969, posted March 21, 2013, YouTube video, 7:00, https://youtu.be/7QNfUE7hBUc.

21. Radio Free Alcatraz, "Radio Free Alcatraz 1969-12-28 and 1969-12-29," American Archive of Public Broadcasting, accessed May 28, 2021, https://americanarchive.org/catalog/cpb-aacip-28-pz51g0jc7r.

22. Dave Archambault II, "Aug 16, 2016—Statement from Standing Rock Sioux Tribal Chairman on the Dakota Access Pipeline," August 16, 2016, https://lastrealindians.com/news/2016/8/16/aug-16-2016-statement-from-standing-rock-sioux-tribal-chairman-on-the-dakota-access-pipeline.

23. Standing Rock Sioux Tribe, Stand with Standing Rock home page, accessed January 2, 2022, https://standwithstandingrock.net/.

24. James Baldwin, "My Dungeon Shook: Letter to My Nephew on the One Hundredth Anniversary of the Emancipation," in *The Fire Next Time* (New York: Dial Press, 1963), 17-24; Martin Luther King Jr., "Letter from a Birmingham Jail [King, Jr.]," April 16, 1963, African Studies Center, University of Pennsylvania, accessed June 18, 2021. https://www.africa.upenn.edu/Articles_Gen/Letter_Birmingham.html; Ta-Nehisi Coates, *Between the World and Me* (New York: Spiegel & Grau, 2015); Wesley Lowery, "Black Lives Matter: Birth of a Movement," *Guardian*, January 17, 2017, https://www.theguardian.com/us-news/2017/jan/17/black-lives-matter-birth-of-a-movement.

25. Jesmyn Ward, ed., *The Fire This Time* (New York: Scribner, 2016); Carolina De Robertis, ed., *Radical Hope* (New York: Vintage Books, 2017).

26. Carolina De Robertis, "A Symphony of Voices," in *Radical Hope: Letters of Love and Dissent in Dangerous Times*, ed. Carolina De Robertis (New York: Vintage Books, 2017), 6.

27. De Robertis, "Symphony of Voices," 6.

28. Lauren Smith, "Towards a Model of Critical Information Literacy Instruction for the Development of Political Agency," *Journal of Information Literacy* 7, no. 2 (2013): 15.

29. Jennifer Simpson, *Longing for Justice* (Toronto: University of Toronto Press, 2014), 211.

30. Margaret Vaughn, "Where to from Here: Fostering Agency across Landscapes," *Theory into Practice* 59, no. 2 (2020): 234–43, https://doi.org/10.1080/00405841.2019.1702391.

31. Bill Johnston, Sheila MacNeill and Keith Smyth, "Information Literacy, Digital Capability, and Individual Agency," in *Conceptualising the Digital University: The Intersection of Policy, Pedagogy and Practice* (Cham, Switzerland: Palgrave Macmillan, 2018), 118.

32. Margaret Vaughn, "What Is Student Agency and Why Is It Needed Now More Than Ever?" *Theory into Practice* 59, no. 2 (2020): 115, https://doi.org/10.1080/00405841.2019.1702393.

33. Louie F. Rodríguez and Tara M. Brown, "From Voice to Agency: Guiding Principles for Participatory Action Research with Youth," *New Directions for Youth Development* 2009, no. 123 (Fall 2009): 19–34, https://doi.org/10.1002/yd.312.

34. Gr Keer, "Critical Pedagogy and Information Literacy in Community Colleges," in *Critical Library Instruction: Theories and Methods*, ed. Maria Accardi, Emily Drabinski, and Alana Kumbier (Duluth, MN: Library Juice Press, 2010), 154.

35. Keer, "Critical Pedagogy and Information Literacy," 154.

36. hooks, *Teaching to Transgress*, 151.

37. Julie McLeod, "Student Voice and the Politics of Listening in Higher Education," *Critical Studies in Education* 52, no. 2 (2011): 181, https://doi.org/10.1080/17508487.2011.572830.

38. Antonia Darder, *Reinventing Paulo Freire* (Boulder, CO: Westview Press, 2002), 106.

39. Sarbani Sen Vengadasalam, "Transformative Pedagogy and Student Voice: Using S.E.A. Principles in Teaching Academic Writing," *Journal of Effective Teaching in Higher Education* 3, no. 2 (Fall 2020): 13, https://doi.org/10.36021/jethe.v3i2.95.

40. Vengadasalam, "Transformative Pedagogy and Student Voice," 14.

41. Darder, *Reinventing Paulo Freire*, 106.

42. Henry A. Giroux, "Theories of Reproduction and Resistance in the New Sociology of Education: A Critical Analysis," *Harvard Educational Review* 53, no.3 (1983): 293.

43. hooks, *Teaching to Transgress*, 183.

44. Collins, "Toward a New Vision."

Bibliography

Archambault, Dave, II. "Aug 16, 2016—Statement from Standing Rock Sioux Tribal Chairman on the Dakota Access Pipeline." Last Real Indians, August 16, 2016. https://lastrealindians.com/news/2016/8/16/aug-16-2016-statement-from-standing-rock-sioux-tribal-chairman-on-the-dakota-access-pipeline.

Baldwin, James. *The Fire Next Time*. New York: Dial Press, 1963.

Barry, Brian. *Why Social Justice Matters*. Malden, MA: Polity Press, 2005.

Coates, Ta-Nehisi. *Between the World and Me*. New York: Spiegel & Grau, 2015.

Collins, Patricia Hill. "Toward a New Vision: Race, Class, and Gender as Categories of Analysis and Connection." *Race, Sex, and Class* 1, no. 1 (1993): 25–45.

Cooke, Nicole A., Miriam E. Sweeney, and Safiya Umoja Noble. "Social Justice as Topic and Tool: An Attempt to Transform an LIS Curriculum and Culture." *Library Quarterly: Information, Community, Policy* 86, no. 1 (2017): 107–24.

Darder, Antonia. *Reinventing Paulo Freire: A Pedagogy of Love*. Boulder, CO: Westview Press, 2002.

De Robertis, Carolina, ed. *Radical Hope: Letters of Love and Dissent in Dangerous Times*. New York: Vintage Books, 2017.

Evans, Bradley, and Sean Michael Wilson. *Portraits of Violence: An Illustrated History of Radical Thinking*. Illustrated by Inko, Carl Thompson, Robert Brown, Chris Mackenzie, Michiru Morikawa and Yen Quach. Oxford, UK: New Internationalist, 2016.

Freire, Paulo. *Pedagogy of the Oppressed*, 30th anniversary ed. Translated by Myra Bergman Ramos. New York: Continuum, 2000.

Gadotti, Moacir. *Reading Paulo Freire: His Life and Work*. Translated by John Milton. Albany, NY: SUNY Press, 1994.

Garcia, Kenny. "Finding and Analyzing Information for Action and Reflection: Possibilities and Limitations of Popular Education in One-Shot Library Instruction." In *Critical Library Pedagogy Handbook*, vol. 1, edited by Kelly McElroy and Nicole Pagowsky, 93–99. Chicago: Association of College and Research Libraries, 2016.

Gibson, Amelia N., and Sandra Hughes-Hassell. "We Will Not Be Silent: Amplifying Marginalized Voices in LIS Education and Research." *Library Quarterly: Information, Community, Policy* 87, no. 4 (2017): 317–29.

Giroux, Henry A. "Theories of Reproduction and Resistance in the New Sociology of Education: A Critical Analysis." *Harvard Educational Review* 53, no. 3 (1983): 257–93.

Gohr, Michelle, and Vitalina A. Nova. "Student Trauma Experiences, Library Instruction and Existence under the 45th." *Reference Services Review* 48, no.1 (2020): 183–99.

Gregory, Lua, and Shana Higgins. *Information Literacy and Social Justice: Radical Professional Praxis*. Sacramento, CA: Library Juice Press, 2013.

———. "Mapping Our Values across the Curriculum: A Social Justice Oriented Program at a Liberal Arts University." Poster presentation, European Conference on Information Literacy, Prague, Czech Republic, October 2016. https://library.redlands.edu/ecil2016.

———. "Reorienting an Information Literacy Program toward Social Justice: Mapping the Core Values of Librarianship to the ACRL Framework." *Communications in Information Literacy* 11, no. 1 (2017) 42–54. https://doi.org/10.15760/comminfolit.2017.11.1.46.

hooks, bell. *Teaching to Transgress: Education as the Practice of Freedom*. New York: Routledge, 1994.

Intelligent Channel. "Richard Oakes Delivering the Alcatraz Proclamation during the Occupation of Alcatraz (1969)—from THE EDUCATION ARCHIVE." Recorded November 1969. Posted March 21, 2013. YouTube video, 7:00. https://youtu.be/7QNfUE7hBUc.

Johnston, Bill, Sheila MacNeill, and Keith Smyth. "Information Literacy, Digital Capability, and Individual Agency." In *Conceptualising the Digital University: The Intersection of Policy, Pedagogy and Practice*, 105–25. Cham, Switzerland: Palgrave Macmillan, 2018.

Keer, Gr. "Critical Pedagogy and Information Literacy in Community Colleges." In *Critical Library Instruction: Theories and Methods*, edited by Maria Accardi, Emily Drabinski, and Alana Kumbier, 149–59. Duluth, MN: Library Juice Press, 2010.

King, Martin Luther, Jr. "Letter from a Birmingham Jail [King, Jr.]." April 16, 1963. African Studies Center, University of Pennsylvania. Accessed June 18, 2021. https://www.africa.upenn.edu/Articles_Gen/Letter_Birmingham.html.

Lowery, Wesley. "Black Lives Matter: Birth of a Movement." *Guardian,* January 17, 2017. https://www.theguardian.com/us-news/2017/jan/17/black-lives-matter-birth-of-a-movement.

McLeod, Julie. "Student Voice and the Politics of Listening in Higher Education." *Critical Studies in Education* 52, no. 2 (2011): 179–89. https://doi.org/10.1080/17508487.2011.572830.

Nicholson, Karen, P. "'Taking Back' Information Literacy: Time and the One-Shot in the Neoliberal University." In *Critical Library Pedagogy Handbook*, vol. 1, edited by Kelly McElroy and Nicole Pagowsky, 25–39. Chicago: Association of College and Research Libraries, 2016.

Painter, Nell Irvin. "Why 'White' Should Be Capitalized, Too." *Washington Post*, July 22, 2020. https://www.washingtonpost.com/opinions/2020/07/22/why-white-should-be-capitalized/.

Radio Free Alcatraz. "Radio Free Alcatraz 1969-12-28 and 1969-12-29." American Archive of Public Broadcasting. Accessed May 28, 2021. https://americanarchive.org/catalog/cpb-aacip-28-pz51g0jc7r.

Rodríguez, Louie F., and Tara M. Brown. "From Voice to Agency: Guiding Principles for Participatory Action Research with Youth." *New Directions for Youth Development* 2009, no. 123 (Fall 2009): 19–34. https://doi.org/10.1002/yd.312.

Simpson, Jennifer. *Longing for Justice: Higher Education and Democracy's Agenda*. Toronto: University of Toronto Press, 2014.

Smith, Lauren. "Towards a Model of Critical Information Literacy Instruction for the Development of Political Agency." *Journal of Information Literacy* 7, no. 2 (2013): 15–32.

Standing Rock Sioux Tribe. Stand with Standing Rock home page. Accessed January 2, 2022. https://standwithstandingrock.net/.

Vaughn, Margaret. "What Is Student Agency and Why Is It Needed Now More Than Ever?" *Theory into Practice* 59, no. 2 (2020): 109–18. https://doi.org/10.1080/00405841.2019.1702393.

———. "Where to from Here: Fostering Agency across Landscapes." *Theory into Practice* 59, no. 2 (2020): 234–43. https://doi.org/10.1080/00405841.2019.1702391.

Vengadasalam, Sarbani Sen. "Transformative Pedagogy and Student Voice: Using S.E.A. Principles in Teaching Academic Writing." *Journal of Effective Teaching in Higher Education* 3, no. 2 (Fall 2020): 12–27. https://doi.org/10.36021/jethe.v3i2.95.

Ward, Jesmyn, ed. *The Fire This Time: A New Generation Speaks about Race*. New York: Scribner, 2016.

Young, Iris Marion. "Five Faces of Oppression." In *Justice and the Politics of Difference*, 39–65. Princeton, NJ: Princeton University Press, 1990.

PART II
Feminist Library Practices

What Is Authority?

A Feminist Investigation of Personal Experience as Knowledge in Student Research and Writing

Martinique Hallerduff and Hannah Carlton

Introduction

Feminist pedagogy, both in librarianship and more generally, and the ACRL *Framework for Information Literacy for Higher Education* (hereafter referred to as the Framework) are both concerned with the idea of authority, although each deals with authority in a different way. At its core, feminist pedagogy envisions the classroom as a liberatory environment and emphasizes reflective engagement with oneself and others to dismantle oppressive structures and collectively create knowledge.[1] It provides us with tools to interrogate and challenge traditional structures of authority—in information literacy instruction between instructor

and students, in the larger structures of higher education institutions, and in scholarly publishing and knowledge creation systems. Among these structures that must be interrogated is the exclusion of student personal experience as a legitimate form of knowledge in academic environments.

In this chapter, we conduct a deeper dive into the literature of feminist pedagogy, the Authority Is Constructed and Contextual (ACC) frame, and what the frame refers to as "unlikely voices." In concert with our review of the literature, we investigate how students understand personal experience as a form of authority through an analysis of student writing, in the form of students' written reflections on their "best source." Students submitted this reflection paper for a required information literacy corequisite course paired with a 100-level English composition course. We're interested in both how undergraduate students connect personal experience with knowledge or expertise and how personal experience is addressed in feminist pedagogy, critical information literacy, and the Framework.

Literature Review

Our interest in feminist pedagogy, the Framework—specifically how it upholds a novice/expert binary—and personal experience as knowledge drive our investigation of our students' use of personal experience in their research. We focus on literature that looks at all of these: foundational thinkers in feminist pedagogy such as bell hooks and Patricia Hill Collins, as well as librarians engaging with feminist pedagogy. We also draw on the work of writer and activist Sonya Renee Taylor to explore the idea of hierarchies of knowledge and apply these to higher education.

Feminist Pedagogy and Personal Experience

In "What is Feminist Pedagogy?" Carolyn Shrewsbury defines the feminist classroom as one in which the "teacher-student and student-teacher act as subjects, not objects."[2] This definition introduces several key elements of feminist pedagogy. The first is the decentering of authority in the classroom and the role of the instructor, moving teachers from a role of absolute authority to a more collaborative model in which teacher and students learn and grow together. The second is a change in the centering of student experience in the classroom and construction of knowledge. Foundational feminist pedagogues Patricia Hill Collins and bell hooks critique "the social institutions that legitimate knowledge,"[3] such as scholarly journals, presses, colleges, and universities. Collins reminds us that "the system of knowledge 'devalues and excludes' the knowledge of many subjugated groups and yet we ask these groups to participate in their own devaluing and exclusion when we tell them that only this system of knowledge is to be trusted."[4] In *Teaching to Transgress*, bell hooks advocates using and valuing personal experience in the classroom is "a way of knowing that exists in a nonhierarchical way with other ways of knowing, and she explains that these nonhierarchical ways of knowing "[lessen] the possibility that it [personal experience] can be used to silence."[5] Feminist pedagogy welcomes the personal experience of students and instructors into the classroom in an effort to collaboratively develop new understanding and knowledge.

Feminist Pedagogy and Library Instruction

In the last decade, librarians have begun to integrate feminist pedagogy into information literacy instruction. In the influential text *Feminist Pedagogy for Library Instruction*, Maria Accardi argues that feminist pedagogy and library instruction already share foundational tenets, favoring "active learning, a nurturing environment, and learner-centered pedagogy."[6] Accardi writes that "feminist approaches to teaching …primarily seek to destabilize traditional, hierarchical, and sexist models of teaching and learning,"[7] with the potential to create transformative learning experiences for both learners and instructors and have effects beyond the classroom and students' time in academia. Other published works and conference presentations by librarians share a centering of social justice in information literacy instruction and an emphasis on designing lessons that encourage students to work collaboratively, engage in self-reflection, and question oppressive systems.[8]

While librarianship has begun to enter the conversation about feminist pedagogy in higher education, there has been relatively little published on the subject of feminist analyses of information literacy dealing directly with authority, and instruction librarians have yet to grapple with the inclusion of personal experience in our treatment and consideration of authority in information literacy instruction. Accardi also explores the changes in the relationship between instruction librarian and student in a feminist classroom, suggesting that "feminist pedagogy is also concerned with the validity of experiential knowledge… and privileging students' voices over the teacher's voice, which is no longer viewed as the ultimate authority."[9] However, Accardi's text predates the Framework and does not directly address authority as it is presented in the ACC frame.

The Framework and ACC Frame

Many librarians within our field have reflected on and critiqued the Framework and the ACC frame. Many of these critiques engage with the ACC frame in relation to conceptions of truth and definitions of expertise. Rinne questions the absence of discussion of nonsubjective truth in relation to authority, while Baer scrutinizes the relationship between contextual authority and relativism.[10] Meszaros and Agnell and Tewell deal with students' conceptions of authority and scholarly expertise within academia.[11] Notably, Dudley shares strategies to encourage Indigenous studies students to critically view academic knowledge structures:

> For purposes of information literacy instruction in Indigenous Stud-
> ies, which is fundamentally concerned with the interface between
> starkly contrasting worldviews, as well as for topics related to gender
> and sexuality that explore different expressions of human identity,
> the frame Authority is Constructed and Contextual [ACC] assists
> students in recognizing the power inherent in naming both "worlds"
> and the structural power and ideologies underlying social categories.[12]

Dudley notes that Western knowledge systems have actively oppressed Indigenous knowledge. Critiquing these systems allows students to situate their own experience and knowledge within those structures for the purposes of research.

Within the Framework, the ACC frame shapes our professional conversation about authority with a focus on recognition, but not necessarily action. The ACC frame sets up a novice/expert binary as it relates specifically to undergraduates' abilities to value unlikely voices:

> Experts know how to seek authoritative voices but also recognize
> that unlikely voices can be authoritative, depending on need. Novice
> learners may need to rely on basic indicators of authority, such as type
> of publication or author credentials, where experts recognize schools
> of thought or discipline-specific paradigms.[13]

The frame positively acknowledges the difference in how authority may be shaped in various communities: "Authority is constructed in that various communities may recognize different types of authority,"[14] but it also creates the binary separating novices and experts into separate poles or categories. Other scholars have also noted that the Framework does attempt to acknowledge different types of authority, including Saunders and Budd, who point out that the ACC frame exhorts students to "question traditional notions of granting authority and recognize the value of diverse ideas and worldviews."[15] This suggests that diverse ideas and worldviews may not be readily available in academic environments.

The Framework indicates that experts know how to "seek authoritative voices," but it also suggests that *only experts* "recognize that unlikely voices can be authoritative, depending on needs."[16] The Framework doesn't question the system that creates exclusionary knowledge and information systems and instead charges librarians (experts) with teaching students (novices) to navigate this system as they move closer to expert. The Framework suggests that experts or scholars should know how to work around academia's knowledge-legitimating system to bring unlikely voices into their work instead of questioning which voices are designated likely or unlikely.

Given the complexity of approaching the evaluation of expertise through the ACC frame and limited by the well-known constraints on library instruction (time, assignment requirements, etc.), it is easy for library instruction to fall into patterns that emphasize "surrogates and heuristics for authority"[17] (e.g., the CRAAP test*), rather than exploring more complicated constructions of authority and expertise. This type of work is complex and time-consuming, and it is often outside the scope of the opportunities librarians have to interact with students. However, relying on surrogates and heuristics often recreates traditional hierarchies of knowledge within academia—and beyond—and has, arguably, led to an erosion of trust of traditional academic authority both inside and outside of higher education. In "Lizard People in the Library," Barbara Fister traces the emerging distrust of conventional forms and sources of authority to the pervasive feeling of a lack of information agency, or the "ability to define what constitutes knowledge,"[18] and a distrust not only of conventional authority, but also of the "social systems that create expertise."[19] This erosion of trust in traditional constructions of authority and epistemologies is both a challenge and an opportunity for feminist practitioners in information literacy instruction and highlights the need to address students' complicated and personal constructions of authority and expertise.

Hierarchies and Information Literacy

To further our examination of hierarchies in higher education, we wanted to look outside of our field and incorporate unlikely voices into our exploration of personal experience and feminist pedagogy in library instruction. Sonya Renee Taylor, activist and author of *The Body is Not an Apology*, discusses the danger in devaluing particular bodies. Taylor explains "we have all been situated on a

---

* The C.R.A.A.P test is a popular mnemonic device for source evaluation. Students evaluate a source's currency, relevance, authority, accuracy, and perspective and eventually make a binary determination of the source's value: good or "crap."

ladder of hierarchy"[20] and discusses the US Constitution as one of the foundational documents that encodes the value difference in bodies. She provides as examples the exclusion of suffrage for all but able-bodied, white, land-owning men, and the lack of marriage equality.[21] Taylor contends that our foundational documents matter, that they shape our embodied experiences of violence or freedom and remind us that "changing the systemic and structural oppressions that regard us in perfunctory and myopic ways requires sweeping changes in our laws, policies, and social norms."[22]

If we look then at our guiding document for teaching information literacy—the Framework—it also delineates a hierarchy of expert and novice and an associated value difference. In the ACC frame, we read that "Experts understand," "experts view," "experts know how to," "experts recognize" and that "novice learners come to respect expertise."[23] Of course, the positions of novice and expert are different from the embodied existence to which Taylor refers, but they are similar in that they are rigidly assigned. The ACC frame provides a narrow path to the position of expert, which comes with the power to be believed.[24] In *Radical Information Literacy,* Andrew Whitworth deconstructs the relationship between knowledge and power, connecting Taylor's reference to the colonial period to Collins's ideas and hierarchies and to the context of information literacy in academic libraries:

> Colonialism also works by devaluing communicatively-rational processes in particular contexts. Is the intersubjective permitted to override the objective (or, in a monarchy, the subjective) authority? Who is *permitted* to address a problem? Whose learning will be attended to, and how? Whose purposes are served by the learning process? Hierarchism promotes "scientific" decisions, taken by designated experts and consultants, over the deliberative process of organisational members.[25]

Taylor, hooks, Collins, and Whitworth converge on the idea of existing hierarchies, which value some and devalue others.

Methodology

At a small, private, Catholic, Hispanic-serving institution, we, two members of the library faculty, taught an established information literacy corequisite (Library Information Literacy, LIB 102), which was a series of four class sessions for students co-enrolled in a required composition course, English 102. (The authors are no longer associated with the university where the research took place.) Librarians individually developed their syllabi using common assignments, learning outcomes, and learning activities. We collected copies of the final LIB 102 assignment from all eight sections of the course. This assignment, a Best Source Reflection Paper, asked students to do the following:

> Choose the scholarly or popular source that has been the most helpful or informative in leading you to answer your research question. Most commonly this will be a scholarly source you're actively using (quoting from, paraphrasing, analyzing) in your research paper, but in some cases it may be a popular source that helped shape your understanding of your topic or question. This reflection asks you to carefully analyze multiple aspects of the source beyond its content. [see appendix A for full assignment.]

Several areas were suggested for analysis, including these:

1. Type of source and why it matters to your research
2. Audience for the source
3. Date that the source was published
4. Author of your source
5. Author's research question
6. Source's main argument and/or any sub-arguments
7. Evidence used within the source and how it contributes to the argument and/or your own understanding

The Best Source Reflection Paper assignment was the final assignment in the information literacy course. In an earlier assignment, Research Proposal and Topic (see appendix B), students were asked to list two different types of people who might be affected by their research topic and to consider those with personal experience. Including personal experience in this early assignment likely established for students that personal experience is worthy of consideration when conducting research. However, personal experience is not mentioned in the assignment description for the Best Source Reflection Paper.

There were 155 students enrolled in the course. According to institutional research, approximately 63 percent identified as Hispanic of any race, 24 percent as White, 6 percent as Black or African American, and a very small number of students from other racial or ethnic categories. We received papers from 139 students; 16 students did not submit the assignment. We downloaded all 139 papers, removed student names, and assigned papers a two-digit number to protect student privacy and mitigate potential bias based on student names, such as gender/sex, ethnicity, or race.

We divided the papers in half, and each of us read 69 or 70 papers. All papers that mention personal experience in any capacity were moved into a new folder for closer analysis. We then reviewed one another's initial reading and moved any additional papers that mention personal experience to the folder for analysis. Of the 139 papers, 28 mentioned personal experience at least once. There were 32 unique quotes across the 28 papers that mention personal experience. Several quotes were assigned to multiple categories. For example, the following quote demonstrates how personal experience functioned both as evidence and as adding meaning to the students' research:

> I personally find it completely logical for the stereotype to have so many detrimental effects, especially with how Asian Americans feel burdened with the societal expectations of fulfilling the label or meeting the expectations of their families. I am also Asian American, so I relate to many of the topics stated in this article since I felt the need to be viewed as an intelligent student in my earlier years.

We counted this quote in the category "personal experience as evidence" because of how the student validates the research by indicating that they share the same experience, and in the category "personal experience adds meaning" because of how they discuss relating to "many of the topics," indicating that the research has been a potentially affirming experience in general.

We extracted these quotes into a new document and coded the quotations based on four categories related to how personal experience functions in the paper and three categories for whose personal experience is discussed. What follows is an analysis of how undergraduate students understand and value personal experience as a way of validating information and creating meaningful connections to their research.

Results

We identified three categories for types of personal experience: the student's personal experience, the author's personal experience, or the personal experience of others (see table 9.1). Because some papers included more than one distinct mention of personal experiences, these numbers equal more than our total sample of 28.

Table 9.1

Types of personal experience

Types of personal experience	No.
Student's personal experience	24
Author's personal experience	10
Others' personal experience	6

We also categorized how personal experience functions in students' papers. Our approach found that it functions in four ways (see table 9.2)—as evidence, adding meaning or significance, revealing research gaps, and to persuade—noting that some papers belonged in more than one of these categories and were counted accordingly.

Table 9.2

How personal experience functions in student's paper

Function of Personal Experience	No.
Personal experience as evidence	24
Personal experience adds meaning or significance	12
Personal experience reveals research gaps	3
Personal experience used to persuade	1

"Personal experience as evidence" was assigned to student responses that express an affirmation of published literature based on what the student has observed, witnessed, or experienced. We assigned the category "personal experience adds meaning or significance" to student responses where students' inclusion of personal experience introduced a new perspective on their research topic, deepened students' understandings, or added meaning to their research. Finally, we assigned the category "personal experience reveals research gaps" to papers where students used personal experience (or the lack of it) to reveal research gaps in published literature. Separately, we noted that six students who discussed personal experience connect it to their own increase in empathy for a group of people, typically groups with historically marginalized identities.

Discussion and Interpretation of Results
Personal Experience as Evidence

In terms of how personal experience functions in the students' papers, our largest category was students using personal experience (theirs or others') as evidence (see table 9.2). Students often describe personal experience as a way to verify or validate what they found in published research. The following example demonstrates this: "My sources tend to agree about bike sharing programs being beneficial to the environment. *I agree with this position because I experienced the benefits myself*" (emphasis added). From the student perspective, the alignment of their personal experience and published research adds credibility and authority to the source. In several cases, students explicitly describe personal experience as evidence, for example: "(the author) uses her personal experience and the statistics of linguists as her evidence." The students' discussion of personal experience provides a bridge between what students know to be true from their own experience and what their professors will accept as truth. More typically, students are expected to distance themselves from their research and use scholarly or statistical evidence to make an argument and to rely on the credibility of experts. However, it becomes clear in our study that students rely heavily on their own personal experience when evaluating information. Another student was researching the topic "Why one should consider being multilingual, for it benefits the individual in a way that develops their personality" and generalizes the information from their scholarly source: "I agree with this position that speaking a different language can have an effect on your personality and emotions." The student shares what other sources say, but their argument eventually comes together when they use the specifics of their own experience: "I agree …because when I speak English, I am very calm but shy; however, when I speak Spanish, I feel very confident and powerful because of how the language is, so it raises my self-esteem."

In lesser numbers students also use their personal experience to disagree with or identify a gap in the published research, creating a nuanced conversation with the research. One student writes, "However, I disagree with Allen's argument…. I believe that slang can be used within one group of people, as I personally experience on a daily basis." Another student uses personal experience to go deeper into a conversation with their source, both agreeing and disagreeing with the author:

> I agree that the assumptions and stereotypes placed upon poor students are hindering their abilities to be successful in life. I know

firsthand what it is like to be told that I am just not capable of succeeding because of where I am from, and my social class. Yes, because of where we come from and the lack of resources, we have available make it harder to succeed compared to those of a higher class, but it definitely does not make it impossible.

The student seems to be saying that, on the one hand, the source partially matches their experience, but on the other hand, there are limits to the research and the student knows this because of their own personal experience. This is a sophisticated research move that dissects an argument, notices the limits of published research, and compares it with existing knowledge. As practitioners of feminist pedagogy, we can observe how personal experience among novice researchers *is* in fact knowledge and that unlikely voices can answer back to published voices.

Personal Experience Reveals Research Gaps

While in much fewer numbers, students used personal experience (or the lack of it) to reveal research gaps and, in at least one instance, to persuade. One student is able to identify a gap in the source because of their personal experience:

> I agree with this source. I am speaking from a Latin-American perspective, so I am biased on the side of Latino perception. The way the women within the focus group talk is accurate in terms of the way I was raised as a child. I however wish that she would have asked where the line is drawn or along with familismo and respecto, had the women go into depth on what the repercussions are for not following the values.

This example suggests that the author lacks a complete picture of the research and the student knows this *because of their experience*. This student's personal experience—upbringing, understanding of their own culture—allows them to ask different questions than someone with an external perspective. The student here is engaging with the frame Scholarship as Conversation in that they are talking back to the source, asking questions of it, and bringing in another perspective— their own. Furthermore, the student tells us that they speak "from a Latin-American perspective" and, as mentioned earlier, academic research is steeped in whiteness. This student reminds the academy that systemic racism, which shapes scholarly publishing and published research, is incomplete precisely because it has left out unlikely voices. If they were not allowed to talk about themself but wanted to represent this idea, they would need to find a more "credible" source that said what they intrinsically knew, devaluing their voice and perspective. Perhaps more likely, they would leave out this perspective entirely and let the expert speak uninterrupted.

Another student expresses a desire for more personal experience to validate the research, in particular the experience and voices of marginalized people. This student is exploring first-wave feminism and writes:

> Her main argument was the [sic] black women were erased from the history of feminism despite playing such a key role in all women gaining rights. Ginzberg uses evidence from peer-reviewed, published work that also happen [sic] to be written by black women authors. This creates a strong sense of credibility because she backed up her argument with facts and quotes that were just as strong in credibility. The books were factually correct and the authors had lengthy background knowledge to the issue at hand…. I think that it would be a good idea to cite from a source where the author has personal experience in the topic that they are writing about. Moving forward, I want to try to find more sources where the people who write them have personal experience in that topic so they can give a more personal and thoughtful insight.

The student here makes a distinction between what credible sources provide: "factually correct," "lengthy background knowledge to the issue" (which presumably means expertise status due to previous publication or education and credentials), and "quotes," which she contrasts with personal experience which provides a "personal and thoughtful insight." She is saying that she wants to read about personal experiences of nineteenth-century racial marginalization within feminism. This student wants to engage deeply with her research by approximating personal experience by way of primary sources. In the following section we will further explore the ways in which students similarly express how the inclusion of personal experience enriches their research.

Personal Experience Adds Meaning or Significance

Student responses in this category express a change, expansion, or affirmation of their understanding of their research in relation to personal experience, their own or the experience of others, and the information presented in the source. The correlation between the appearance of personal experience in students' evaluation of their best sources and transformative interpretations of their sources mirrors one of the key tenants of critical and feminist pedagogy; issues that affect the personal or the local are the sites of true learning and growth for students. In this category, students demonstrate that they choose research topics that they clearly care deeply about and to which they are personally connected. Many students mention their families and draw on their own emotional understanding of their source and research topic.

In one example, a student has read about the personal experience of others in their source and explains how this has expanded their understanding of a marginalized group:

> This article contributed to my research by giving me personal experiences of non-English speakers in New York that were impacted by a language barrier when dealing with law enforcement.... The article has made me understand [emphasis in original] that not sharing the same language bring [*sic*] lack of communication, safety issues and the likelihood of being ignored.

The student's emphasis on and empathy for the stories of people experiencing language barriers hints at a transformation of their understanding of their topic. Another student, whose research focuses on "the emotional distress of divorce" writes, "My sources tend to agree about the impacts that divorce has on child development. It leaves a child in personal, emotional and mental distress. I agree with these classifications because since my parents are happily married, it kills me to see them ever get into an argument or a fight." While the student has not experienced the situation described in the source personally, the research prompts the student to imagine and empathize with others' experiences, and the student utilizes their own experience to understand the information in the source within the context of their own life. Another student demonstrates the significance of their own personal experience to their research: "In my understanding of the article what stuck out to me were the statistics of the suicide rate of veterans.... To me this stuck out not only because I have family members that are veterans." The connection to the student's family and personal experience with veterans guides the student's reading of the source and the direction of the student's research. Throughout their analysis of the source, the student draws on their personal experience to make a passionate argument for specific policies in conversation with the original source, demonstrating reflective and critical engagement with the source. For these students, the personal connection between their own lived experiences, their research topics, and the evaluation of their sources inspires empathic responses and an understanding of their topics that extends beyond the scope of the assignment or the classroom.

Implications

Our students used personal experience to interact with and converse with their sources, an approach not traditionally encouraged in academia. This use of personal experience in their research demonstrates the depth of their engagement with their sources. Students utilized what many would consider novice perspectives to integrate their understanding of their research topics and acquired academic knowledge. The fifth knowledge practice of the ACC frame calls for students to "acknowledge they are developing their own authoritative voices and recognize the responsibilities this entails, including seeking accuracy and reliability ...and participating in communities of practice."[26] This invites students to participate in the knowledge production in the academy but uses language that again requires that students position themselves within the novice/expert binary, without acknowledging the value of experience and expertise students bring with them into the classroom and into their time in higher education. Deliberately excluding that perspective silences and devalues the ways in which students integrate sources into new epistemologies and removes a rich opportunity for transformative learning, critical growth, learning with the potential for real impact on students' experiences—and their impact on others—outside of the classroom.

The knowledge hierarchies we identified in the Framework, higher education, and the larger information ecosystem are reinforced when we exclude student experience. This also has deeper implications for the way expertise and scholarship are integrated into popular knowledge structures and viewed by the public. Barbara Fister reminds us that "too often what passes as information literacy continues to be instruction on how to satisfy the requirements of assignments that may explicitly forbid students from using information that doesn't pass through traditional gatekeeping channels."[27] In an information environment in which both experts and novices must contend with misinformation, disinformation, conspiracy theories, and a growing distrust of institutions and traditional forms of authority, integrating students' personal experiences into library instruction is critical. By including and legitimizing the ways in which students choose to create meaning in their research, information literacy instruction has the potential to serve as a bridge between academia and those it has historically and systemically excluded.

Limitations

We recognize that in analyzing students' work, submitted for grading, we are analyzing students' performance of academic writing, thought, and research. Students' performance reflects the values of a dominant culture controlled by "Western structures of knowledge validation," which reflect the "interests of powerful white men."[28] Inevitably, students are writing for a faculty audience, which shapes what they share about their own thoughts.[29] Furthermore, other limitations include the small sample size of students at one university. We acknowledge that our research did not include qualitative interviews or other methods of acquiring students' self-described processes of validating information or their first-person accounts of how they value personal experience as a form of knowledge.

Conclusion

Students bring their lived experience into the classroom, and this affects the way they process and interact with information—and ultimately their interaction with the process of scholarly knowledge production. The 28 students who identified personal experience in their paper took risks in doing so, as it wasn't asked for and is often discouraged in academia, but we must ask: What if they were told it belonged? A feminist approach to teaching students about expertise in the context of information literacy requires balancing an understanding of the systems and processes used to create and regulate academic knowledge and an understanding of the harm these systems have caused in silencing voices and knowledge. If we want to facilitate critical engagement with information, we cannot dismiss the unique perspective that students bring to their own research, and we need to create a spectrum rather than a binary when we think of novices and experts.

We must include our students in discussions of authority, the scholarly publishing machine, and how expertise is narrowly understood, or we are participating in perpetuating these inequities. There are small ways we can participate in empowering students—many of them suggested by other feminist and critical pedagogues. These might include educating our colleagues about assignment design and advocating for the inclusion of personal experience in assignments. We can also create learning activities that validate personal experience as a way of making meaning and dissecting scholarly sources for missing voices. More concretely, in a one-shot class, strategies might include these:

- asking students what information they trust the most (not to dissuade them, but out of curiosity) and facilitating a discussion around this

- asking students to reflect emotionally on the sources they find via a free-write or anonymous posts to a Google Doc, Padlet, or Jamboard

- conducting in-class activities where we invite different perspectives into the classroom—for example, taking a topic like eating disorders and asking students to generate what questions different people might ask (e.g., doctors, psychologists, someone with an eating disorder, parent or friend of someone with an eating disorder)

- acknowledging and discussing how information is organized and labeled (e.g., subject headings that are disempowering) and how it might feel to encounter these as you research

We recommend that further research would similarly ask students to reflect on their source, but only after explicitly inviting personal experience as knowledge into the information literacy pedagogy. The conversation around student experience in research, or as a way of validating or understanding information, is just beginning. We are curious to see how students might engage differently with information after this invitation. Further research might also investigate questions such as these: What if we *expected* research to be meaningful to students and determined to facilitate meaning making for our students? What if there were a place for the emotional impact of research? What if students could dwell in the grief that emerges when they are left out of the research, when no one speaks for them? What if they could speak to the joy of affirmation? These questions could be investigated with qualitative studies that engage students in reflective conversations about personal experience and research.

APPENDIX A

Best Source Reflection Paper

Instructions

Choose the scholarly or popular source that has been the most helpful or informative in leading you to answer your research question. Most commonly this will be a scholarly source you're actively using (quoting from, paraphrasing, analyzing) in your research paper, but in some cases it may be a popular source that helped shape your understanding of your topic or question. This reflection asks you to carefully analyze multiple aspects of the source beyond its content. Reflecting in this way should help you when you choose sources in the future. For ideas about what or how to evaluate, refer back to earlier assignments.

Details

- There are two sections: Evaluate the Details and Evaluate the Research Conversation.
- One to one-and-a-half pages TOTAL single-spaced *or* no more than three double-spaced pages TOTAL.
- 12 point font and 1" margins.
- Written as a narrative in paragraph form, not as bullet-pointed sections.
- Include a **citation in proper MLA format** at the end of the paper and use parenthetical citations throughout.

Evaluate the Details

Consider the evaluation methods you have used in previous assignments, and thoroughly evaluate this source using the criteria below. For some criteria you will write only 1 or 2 sentences, other criteria you will write multiple sentences; you are not simply supplying simple answers to these questions but explaining how each criterion contributes to the quality or usefulness of your source. For example, you are *evaluating the author as you've done previously*, not simply providing their name.

1. Type of source and why it matters to your research.

2. Audience for the source.

3. Date that the source was published.

4. Author of your source.

5. Author's research question—Like you, the author of this article began their work on this source with a question, and this article or book is their answer or explanation. This will be stated in the form of a question. This won't be explicitly stated; you need to determine what it is by examining the article.

6. Source's main argument and/or any sub-arguments.

7. Evidence used within the source and how it contributes to the argument and/or your own understanding.

Evaluate the Research Conversation and Your Place in It

Describe how this source fits in to the larger conversation about your topic:

- On what points do your *other sources* agree with the arguments or conclusions in this source? (Include the source and a *short* paraphrase or summary to illustrate.)

- On what points do your other sources disagree? (Include a *short* paraphrase or summary to illustrate.)

- On what points do <u>you</u> agree or disagree with this source or another source?

APPENDIX B

Research Proposal and Topic

1. A research topic is

   The answer to your research question

   The broad subject area you will research

   A specific, focused aspect of research you will investigate

2. Which of the following are aspects of a good research question?

   Of interest to you

   Can be answered with a yes or no

   Leads to new insights

   Is in the news

   Provides research direction

   Is a current issue

   Can be analyzed

3. Using the Who, What, Where, When, Why, How model from the "Developing a Research or Guiding Question" video you just completed, select the *best* research question for the following pair:

   When did the Olympic Committee outlaw performance-enhancing drugs?

   When do children begin experimenting with drugs?

4. Using the Who, What, Where, When, Why, How model from the "Developing a Research or Guiding Question" video you just completed, select the *best* research question for the following pair:

   What is Alcoholics Anonymous?

What kinds of treatment options tend to be the most effective for seniors?

5. Using the Who, What, Where, When, Why, How model from the "Developing a Research or Guiding Question" video you just completed, select the *best* research question for the following pair:

    Why do doctors prescribe opioid painkillers?

    Why is the opioid epidemic discussed in more sympathetic terms in the media than the crack epidemic?

6. What topic do you want to research? Describe it in the broadest sense in just a few words.

    For example, racial/ethnic stereotypes

7. The next step after selecting a research topic is exploring the possible subtopics. Subtopics are more specific, narrowed-down ideas that exist within your larger topic. What are three different subtopics of your larger topic that interest you? These will likely be multiple-word phrases.

    For example, for "racial ethnic stereotypes" you might list representation of race in movies and TV, psychological impact of racism, police stereotypes of criminals.

8. Choose one subtopic from Question 7 and list at least two different types of people who might study that issue. Consider professionals who work in a field related to your topic, researchers, and experts on your topic.

    For example, for "racial/ethnic stereotypes," you might list psychologists, an expert on racism, people who study police or criminal justice.

9. Using the same subtopic as above, list two different types of people who might be affected by this issue. Consider those with personal experience and people by identity factors.

For example, for "racial/ethnic stereotypes," you might list Latinx actors, a cousin who has been harassed by police, a self-identified white supremacist.

10. Imagine you could ask one person from each category (someone who studies this and someone impacted by it) a question about your topic. Who and what would you ask? Be sure you are asking a specific question and that the question matches the person's experience or expertise.

For example, I would ask someone who studies racism how watching movies with a lot of white characters affects children of color, and I would ask my cousin how it felt when he was stopped by police and if it's affected the decisions he makes now.

Notes

1. Carolyn M. Shrewsbury, "What Is Feminist Pedagogy?" *Women's Studies Quarterly* 25, no. 1 (1997): 166–67.
2. Shrewsbury, "What Is Feminist Pedagogy?" 166.
3. Patricia Hill Collins, *Black Feminist Thought* (New York: Routledge, 2009), 271.
4. Collins, *Black Feminist Thought*, 272.
5. bell hooks, *Teaching to Transgress* (New York: Routledge, 1994), 84.
6. Maria Accardi, *Feminist Pedagogy for Library Instruction* (Sacramento, CA: Library Juice Press, 2013), 57.
7. Accardi, *Feminist Pedagogy*, 61.
8. Dory Cochran, "Using Pop Culture, Feminist Pedagogy, and Current Events to Help Students Explore Multiple Sides of an Argument," in *Critical Library Pedagogy Handbook*, vol. 2, ed. Nicole Pagowsky and Kelly McElroy (Chicago: Association of College and Research Libraries, 2016), 109–15, https://digitalcommons.usu.edu/cgi/viewcontent.cgi?article=1269&context=lib_pubs; Gina Schlesselman-Tarango, "Cyborgs in the Academic Library," *Behavioral and Social Sciences Librarian* 33, no. 1 (2014): 29–46, https://doi.org/10.1080/01639269.2014.872529; Courtney Baron et al., "From Theory to Practice: Using Feminist Pedagogy to Teach Information Literacy" (presentation, Georgia International Conference on Information Literacy (cancelled due to Hurricane Irma), Savannah, GA, September 15–16, 2017, presentation 29, https://digitalcommons.georgiasouthern.edu/gaintlit/2017/2017/29.
9. Accardi, *Feminist Pedagogy*, 37.
10. Andrea Baer, "It's All Relative? Post-truth Rhetoric, Relativism, and Teaching on 'Authority as Constructed and Contextual,'" *College and Research Libraries News* 79, no. 2 (2018) 72–97, https://doi.org/10.5860/crln.79.2.72; Nathan Aaron Rinne, "The New Framework: A Truth-less Construction Just Waiting to Be Scrapped?" *Reference Services Review* 45, no. 1 (2017): 54–66, https://doi.org/10.1108/RSR-06-2016-0039; Laura Saunders and John Budd, "Examining Authority and Reclaiming Expertise," *Journal of Academic Librarianship* 46, no. 1 (January 2020): 102077, https://doi.org/10.1016/j.acalib.2019.102077.
11. MaryBeth Meszaros, "Who's in Charge Here? Authority, Authoritativeness, and the Undergraduate Researcher," *Communications in Information Literacy* 4, no. 1 (2010): 5–11, https://doi.org/10.15760/comminfolit.2010.4.1.84; Katelyn Angell and Eamon Tewell, "Teaching and Un-teaching Source Evaluation: Questioning Authority in Information Literacy Instruction," *Communications in Information Literacy* 11, no. 1 (2017): 95–121, https://doi.org/10.15760/comminfolit.2017.11.1.37.

12. Michael Dudley, "Exploring Worldviews and Authorities: Library Instruction in Indigenous Studies Using Authority Is Constructed and Contextual," *College and Research Libraries News* 81, no. 2 (2020): 69, https://doi.org/10.5860/crln.81.1.66.

13. Association of College and Research Libraries, *Framework for Information Literacy for Higher Education* (Chicago: Association of College and Research Libraries, 2016), https://www.ala.org/acrl/standards/ilframework.

14. Association of College and Research Libraries, *Framework*.

15. Saunders and Budd, "Examining Authority," 3.

16. Association of College and Research Libraries, *Framework*.

17. Saunders and Budd, "Examining Authority," 2.

18. Barbara Fister, "Lizard People in the Library," Project InfoLit, February 3, 2021, https://projectinfolit.org/pubs/provocation-series/essays/lizard-people-in-the-library.html.

19. Fister, "Lizard People."

20. Sonya Renee Taylor, interview by Brené Brown, "Brené with Sonya Renee Taylor on 'The Body Is Not an Apology,'" September 16, 2020, in *Unlocking Us with Brené Brown*, podcast audio, 1:17:19, https://brenebrown.com/podcast/brene-with-sonya-renee-taylor-on-the-body-is-not-an-apology/.

21. Sonya Renee Taylor, *The Body Is Not an Apology* (Oakland, CA: Barrett-Koehler, 2018), 7.

22. Taylor, *Body Is Not an Apology*, 8.

23. Association of College and Research Libraries, *Framework*.

24. Collins, *Black Feminist Thought*, 270.

25. Andrew Whitworth, *Radical Information Literacy* (Oxford, UK: Chandros, 2014), 108.

26. Association of College and Research Libraries, *Framework*.

27. Fister, "Lizard People."

28. Collins, *Black Feminist Thought*, 268, 271.

29. David Bartholomae, "Inventing the University." *Journal of Basic Writing* 5, no. 1 (1986): 6.

Bibliography

Accardi, Maria. *Feminist Pedagogy for Library Instruction*. Sacramento, CA: Library Juice Press, 2013

Angell, Katelyn, and Eamon Tewell. "Teaching and Un-teaching Source Evaluation: Questioning Authority in Information Literacy Instruction." *Communications in Information Literacy* 11, no. 1 (2017): 95–121. https://doi.org/10.15760/comminfolit.2017.11.1.37.

Association of College and Research Libraries. *Framework for Information Literacy for Higher Education* (Chicago: Association of College and Research Libraries, 2016). https://www.ala.org/acrl/standards/ilframework.

Baer, Andrea. "It's All Relative? Post-truth Rhetoric, Relativism, and Teaching on 'Authority as Constructed and Contextual.'" *College and Research Libraries News* 79, no. 2 (2018): 72–97. https://doi.org/10.5860/crln.79.2.72.

Baron, Courtney, Elliott Kuecker, Gabrielle Dudley, and Felicia Fulks. "From Theory to Practice: Using Feminist Pedagogy to Teach Information Literacy." Presentation, Georgia International Conference on Information Literacy (cancelled due to Hurricane Irma), Savannah, GA, September 15–16, 2017, presentation 29. https://digitalcommons.georgiasouthern.edu/gaintlit/2017/2017/29.

Bartholomae, David. "Inventing the University." *Journal of Basic Writing* 5, no. 1 (1986): 4–23.

Brown, Brené. "Brené with Sonya Renee Taylor on 'The Body Is Not an Apology.'" September 16, 2020, in *Unlocking Us with Brené Brown*. Podcast audio, 1:17:19. https://brenebrown.com/podcast/brene-with-sonya-renee-taylor-on-the-body-is-not-an-apology/.

Cochran, Dory. "Using Pop Culture, Feminist Pedagogy, and Current Events to Help Students Explore Multiple Sides of an Argument." In *Critical Library Pedagogy Handbook*, vol. 2, edited by Nicole Pagowsky and Kelly McElroy, 109–15. Chicago: Association of College and Research Libraries, 2016. https://digitalcommons.usu.edu/cgi/viewcontent.cgi?article=1269&context=lib_pubs.

Collins, Patricia Hill. *Black Feminist Thought: Knowledge, Consciousness, and the Politics of Empowerment*. New York: Routledge, 2009.

Dudley, Michael. "Exploring Worldviews and Authorities: Library Instruction in Indigenous Studies Using Authority Is Constructed and Contextual." *College and Research Libraries News* 81, no. 2 (2020): 66–69. https://doi.org/10.5860/crln.81.1.66.

Fister, Barbara. "Lizard People in the Library." Project InfoLit, February 3, 2021. https://projectinfolit.org/pubs/provocation-series/essays/lizard-people-in-the-library.html.

Hofer, Amy R., Lori Townsend, and Korey Brunetti. "Troublesome Concepts and Information Literacy: Investigating Threshold Concepts for IL Instruction." *portal: Libraries and the Academy* 12, no. 4 (October 2012): 387–405. https://doi.org/10.1353/pla.2012.0039.

hooks, bell. *Teaching to Transgress: Education as the Practice of Freedom.* New York: Routledge, 1994.

Meszaros, MaryBeth. "Who's in Charge Here? Authority, Authoritativeness, and the Undergraduate Researcher." *Communications in Information Literacy* 4, no. 1 (2010): 5–11. https://doi.org/10.15760/comminfolit.2010.4.1.84.

Rinne, Nathan Aaron. "The New Framework: A Truth-less Construction Just Waiting to Be Scrapped?" *Reference Services Review* 45, no. 1 (2017): 54–66. https://doi.org/10.1108/RSR-06-2016-0039.

Saunders, Laura, and John Budd. "Examining Authority and Reclaiming Expertise." *Journal of Academic Librarianship* 46, no. 1 (January 2020): 102077. https://doi.org/10.1016/j.acalib.2019.102077.

Schlesselman-Tarango, Gina. "Cyborgs in the Academic Library: A Cyberfeminist Approach to Information Literacy Instruction." *Behavioral and Social Sciences Librarian* 33, no. 1 (2014): 29–46. https://doi.org/10.1080/01639269.2014.872529.

Shrewsbury, Carolyn M. "What Is Feminist Pedagogy." *Women's Studies Quarterly* 25, no. 1 (1997): 166–73.

Taylor, Sonya Renee. *The Body Is Not an Apology.* Oakland, CA: Barrett-Koehler, 2018.

Whitworth, Andrew. *Radical Information Literacy.* Oxford, UK: Chandros, 2014.

CHAPTER 5

Situated Data
Feminist Epistemology and Data Curation

Scout Calvert

Introduction

In the last decade or more, academic libraries have taken up the challenge of providing data curation and research data support, bringing expertise in metadata and digital preservation to key aspects of the research data life cycle. This activity has hastened since 2013, when the White House Office of Science and Technology Policy (OSTP) issued a memo directing federal funding agencies to require data, among other products of research, to be shared as a condition of funding.[1] The OSTP memo did not come out of the blue, but recognized changes in data practice in some disciplines as the costs of sharing data digitally declined and the open science movement gained steam. The practice of open science seeks to improve the reliability and efficiency of science by making it possible to share digital tools and products of research, including data, more readily. Data sharing is said to promote scientific transparency, maximize the value of federal research support, create opportunities for reanalysis and reuse, discourage fraud, and perhaps most idealistically, provide a means for reproducibility and replication, indicators of objectivity in high-stakes science.

During this same time, a body of thought within librarianship has coalesced under the phrase "critical librarianship" or "critical library practice" as

practitioners apply critical theories available in other disciplines to their work. Critical approaches to library practices have called neutrality, along with the profession's traditional commitment to it, into permanent question, enlarging the conversation about objectivity within library and information sciences. Conceptions of objectivity and neutrality are also central concerns in the study of scientific practice, a transdisciplinary domain of inquiry that is well developed within some strains of information science. Critical library practice is inflected by this scholarship, and together they can extend rigorous interrogation of practice to data curation, the specialty subdiscipline that cares for the stuff of scientific claims, research data.

In this chapter, I bring these conversations together through a feminist theory of knowledge production, or epistemology, and propose "situated data" as a framework for critical data practice. By connecting feminist epistemology to data curation, I provide a frame for understanding data sharing as a critical library practice with the potential for engaging a wider range of knowers in scientific knowledge production and producing better, more objective, and more just accounts of the world.

The feminist standpoint theory framework I develop for data curation also has crucial ramifications for librarianship more generally. First, this account of objectivity and neutrality is one that library practitioners can act on, not merely contemplate. Second, the framework developed here is useful not only for data curation, but also for concrete library practices such as collection development, cataloging, and classification, and I point to others articulating feminist epistemology for these purposes. Third, these challenges to objectivity and neutrality as conventionally understood are forceful correctives that can aid practitioners in their struggles for genuinely better, more inclusive, and more responsible collections, catalogs, and library spaces, and this discussion should make better versions of objectivity available through the literature.

Finally, while feminist standpoint theory is useful in application to specific library functions, it also pertains to the knowledge produced through library practice, that is, by library workers. Library science diversity, equity, and inclusion (DEI) discourse still largely assumes a white, gender and heteronormative, settler colonialist, bourgeois, patriarchal, and nondisabled library profession in the process of generously making itself more inclusive out of beneficence to members of underrepresented groups who, in exchange, can be expected to adopt the professional norms and standards for objectivity and neutrality established through the history of librarianship, which are inheritances from unreconstructed positivism. By marking the dominant culture from which librarianship springs as an overlapping set of specific, nonuniversal, nonobjective subject positions, I foreground the transformative potential for more robust, reliable, objective, and responsible knowledge about library practices and technologies that comes from genuine inclusion of marginalized knowers in library practice and knowledge making.

In what follows, I will first share definitions of data and metadata that pertain to data curation and connect data to the empiricist research tradition. I then turn to philosophy of science to trace the co-emerging histories of feminist standpoint epistemology and positivist reconsiderations of objectivity and neutrality. I briefly trace the roots of feminist epistemologies in theories of ideology and class consciousness and show their interconnections with other standpoint epistemologies, including Black and postcolonial standpoint theory. I elaborate on crucial feminist contestations of objectivity and neutrality that form the basis of "strong objectivity" and "situated knowledges," which offer more robust standards for objectivity that can inform data curation and, crucially, the wider set of all library practices. Finally, I offer some specific approaches for data curators and data literacy instructors to situate data and contribute to responsible, objective knowledge production.

Data Sharing, Data Curation, and the Practice of Science

Scholarly conversations about what data is (or are) are wide ranging. However, for the purposes of this essay, I define data as observations of some phenomenon and thus evidence for some claim or description of that phenomenon. This pragmatic definition of data accords with the definition used by the National Science Foundation and other granting agencies, based on the definition of research data from the Code of Federal Regulations (§200.315(e)): "the recorded factual material commonly accepted in the scientific community as necessary to validate research findings."*

However, as librarians and data curators know, data cannot speak for itself. Data requires documentation of some sort to explain what it is, that is, how recorded information counts as evidence or a description of a phenomenon. This is what data stewards call *metadata*. The National Science Foundation addresses

---

* In this chapter, I am mostly talking about "stuff" we call data. In this context, I typically treat *data* as a noncount noun, like *water*. However, when the topic is the phenomenon referenced by specific data, or data as evidence, that is, observations or measurements, then I treat *data* in the strict sense, as a plural noun. I think this makes sense, but have no stake in correcting people who say "data is" or chiding people who say "data are." The reader may also detect inconsistencies in my application.

the need for metadata to accompany recorded material in data packages: "This definition includes not only original data but also metadata (e.g., experimental protocols, software code written for statistical or experimental analyses or for proofs-of-concept, etc.)."[2] For the purposes of this chapter, I will use this expansive definition of *metadata* as the documentation necessary for data to be intelligible as observations *of* something, in addition to more familiar metadata schemata.

Data curation is a set of processes for managing and caring for data, in infrastructures that allow it to be found, understood, used, and preserved, and is often understood through the model of a research data life cycle that tracks the care of data through the research process. Metadata is fundamental to data curation, as well as to emerging frameworks for maximizing the sharing and reuse of research data, such as the FAIR data principles for making data findable, accessible, interoperable, and reusable.[3]

The requirement for metadata in a data package embeds a tacit acceptance that data are observer dependent in a fundamental way, speaking to tenets of standpoint epistemology, in addition to a host of other fields that study how science works. Without documentation, or metadata, it cannot be known what the data are supposed to describe or how they might count as evidence. Nor can the circumstances under which data were observed, or generated and captured, be reproduced. Without metadata, there are no data. Without data, there is no scientific knowledge. The necessity for metadata, for documentation, demonstrates that science is a social process that must justify its grounds for objectivity in the context in which it was conducted. Thus, data curation can be a site for critical interventions in scientific knowledge production.

Feminist Epistemology and Philosophy of Science

Science is a set of practices for producing knowledge, and the core concern of epistemology, as with library science, is how people know and create knowledge about the world and universe we live in. *Epistemology*, at its simplest, means theory of knowledge.* How are human powers of perception and capacities for

---

* Sometimes it may seem easier to say *knowledge system* or *theory of knowledge*, but one aim of this essay is to bring readers into the centuries-long stream of conversation about what counts as knowledge, and that means familiarizing them with the jargon of the domain. Every community of practice is defined in part by what it can take for granted (Geoffrey C. Bowker and Susan Leigh Star, *Sorting Things Out* [Cambridge, MA: MIT Press, 1999], 35). I hope that this essay will welcome more practitioners of library science into critical conversations about data curation, knowledge production, and epistemology.

reasoning and thought related to what we know? How do we revise or update our explanations for the world around us in light of new experiences? What parts of the world exist outside of our experience of it? What is the role of our social milieu in allowing some things to seem true or even thinkable? That is, what processes, discipline, or cognitive activity does it take for a person to be said to know or to discover something knowable? Questions like these became urgent with the expansion of Western science, as natural philosophers, or scientists, as they would be known, struggled to understand the explanatory power of science.

Epistemologies may be formal theories of what counts as knowledge (versus opinion or belief, for example), or they may be implicit or embedded in practices for interpreting the world and sharing experiences of it, as, for example, metadata practice. Epistemologies may also imply or stipulate certain knowers, or people who may be qualified within the theory to know something or produce valid knowledge. I also refer to knowers as "subjects" to point to the social and psychological processes through which people come to be knowing and agential selves, or as Katie King says, "acting-thinking ones."[4]

Crucially, some philosophers struggled to explain the relationship between human reasoning and accounts of reality as though such accounts could be human-independent. In the Western tradition, Kant and Hegel were among many involved in this inquiry, influencing, on the one hand, Karl Marx's efforts to explain the relationship between labor, profit, and commodities under capitalism, and on the other hand, empiricist philosophers who informed the positivist tradition, among others.[†] Feminist epistemologies, like other theories of knowledge, are shaped and influenced by both philosophical traditions.

Antecedents: Objectivity and Epistemology in Library Practice

Failures of objectivity in library practice, particularly classification and subject access, have been remarked for decades, as exemplified by the landmark *Revolting Librarians* (1972), containing Joan Marshall's "LC Labeling: An Indictment" and other relevant and passionately expressed criticisms, and Sanford Berman's *Prejudices and Antipathies*.[5] Neither volume, written from the politically engaged

---

[†] I do not hold that a reader must read backward in an infinite chain of citation to "really understand" the philosophy of science. I trace direct influences on standpoint theory, and not the wider body of empiricist and natural philosophers whose ideas also shape received beliefs about objectivity. Readers whose appetite has been whetted may benefit from starting with Harding (2004) and Bottomore's (1991) edited volumes, Sandoval (2000), Zammito (2004), or Lukács (1971) and work backward through Marx (1976), Hegel (1977) and Kant (2003).

margins of librarianship, has been made obsolete by changes in library practice, but both laid groundwork for further challenges to unexamined conceptions of objectivity and neutrality in the scholarly literature of LIS. Hope Olson's "Power to Name" shows how library catalogs adopt "mainstream culture's positioning of men as knowing subjects ...and women as objects to be known."[6] Olson and Schlegl draw on Marshall's insights and others to show the limitations of traditional objectivity in subject access.[7] This prior work allows Angela Kublik and colleagues to propose interventions across Dewey Decimal Classification schedules to improve the representation of topics relevant or pertaining to women.[8]

Explicitly feminist epistemology has gained traction in analysis of library science practices. Melodie Fox and Olson review key concepts in feminist epistemology for application to the organization of knowledge, including standpoint theory in their analysis.[9] Melanie Feinberg draws on situated knowledge to explore a more robust approach to analysis of bias in information systems.[10] Michelle Caswell develops the concept of "feminist standpoint appraisal" to interrogate the "view from nowhere" in archival practice and provide an intellectual trajectory for archival collections to address power-differentiated gaps and silences.[11] These examples show that politically engaged, avowedly "biased," not neutral, approaches generate vital knowledge for responsible and objective library practice.

Positivism to Post-positivism

Justifications for data sharing and data curation, as well as for traditional research library functions, are heavily dependent on conceptions of science and objectivity inherited from the positivist tradition. Positivism is a theory of knowledge (in other words, an epistemology) that says that objective knowledge is based on sensory input, that is information from the senses (or instruments that extend our senses), which is in turn processed with reason and logic. Since genuine knowledge, in the positivist view, can be acquired only this way, positivism gives rise to scientism and a privileging of knowledge produced through recognized scientific practices. Positivism is also associated with the view of science as the incremental, progressive, inevitable accretion of more correct facts and beliefs.[12] Indeed, we could say that typical rationales for data sharing are largely positivist in nature, demonstrating faith that scientific processes are objective, neutral and self-correcting, lead inevitably to new and more true knowledge, and thus that the accumulation of more data will lead inexorably to more objective knowledge. One strongly contested tenet of positivism is the position that to conduct objective science, it is necessary to separate science from social influence.

However, positivist philosophy gave rise to post-positivism as thinkers within that tradition, the logical positivist philosophers of the Vienna Circle, contested their own account of objectivity in the first half of the twentieth century. Powerful challenges came in three related assertions: first, that any theory of a phenomenon predetermines what will count as evidence (all observations are theory-laden); second, that there's no external measure of how much evidence is enough to prove or disprove a theory (theory is underdetermined by evidence); and finally, since all language is social, not even scientific or logical language can be extracted from social context (the inscrutability of reference).[13] These challenges imply the impossibility of drawing a boundary between the practice of science and the social circumstances in which it is practiced, the boundary that positivists said is necessary to the objectivity and functioning of science, and which enforced the belief that socially marked knowers, in distinction to unmarked and hence neutral white, bourgeois men, could not conduct objective, unbiased science.

Although positivist explanations for scientific knowledge persist, conversations within the Vienna Circle gave way to another influential body of thought for understanding scientific practice: post-positivism, with Karl Popper and Thomas Kuhn among the best-known thinkers. Kuhn may be familiar to readers as the originator of the concept of scientific paradigms,[14] while Popper is known for his work on falsifiability.[15] For those invested in positivist conceptions of objectivity, including many library practitioners, in which social concerns can have only a corrupting influence on science, the inseparability of science from society condemns the possibility of reliable explanations of the universe. However, for standpoint epistemologists and post-positivists, the entanglement of science and society is not a barrier to but a condition for objectivity, as I will describe below.

Objectivity and Class Consciousness

If science is inextricable from the social context in which it is practiced, what is the basis for objective knowledge? Feminist standpoint theory explores gender as a resource for reliable knowledge of the world, not as a barrier to it, as it had been conceived and enacted for most of the history of Western science. The seed of standpoint theory was developed through conversation with and critique of Marx's description of how the working classes come to know the reality of production under capitalism.

In Marx's analysis, objective knowledge of class arises through the subjective experience of people who must work for wages in order to live, in the development of class consciousness. The gap between how the social order is naturalized (it is the natural order of things for profit to go to the employer) and objective reality (it is a historically contingent social arrangement to privilege the capitalist over the worker) is *ideology* in the Marxist sense. To simplify Marx's account, when laborers stop identifying with the interests of the capitalist class, they can begin to stop taking the social order as a given and see the role of power (specifically, the ownership of capital) in establishing that order and making it seem natural and inevitable.

Marx's accounts of ideology and class consciousness in turn informed generations of philosophers and social theorists, notably György Lukács and scholars of the Frankfurt School, who elaborated the mechanisms of both concepts in the twentieth century. They also indirectly influenced many others in the nascent social sciences. One consequence of the elaboration of Marx's ideas—themselves developed from within the Enlightenment tradition with all the baggage that entails—was a philosophical explanation for how socially embedded knowers can nevertheless engage in objective reasoning.

From Class Consciousness to Standpoint Epistemology

Standpoint theory was born from the recognition that we make knowledge in social contexts from the subject positions we occupy, not just as class subjects, but racialized, gendered, colonized—indeed, intersectional—subjects as well. Subject positions from which we know and conduct science are socially produced and historically contingent, not voluntaristic or adopted identities. Lukács, working in the early twentieth century, developed Marx's analysis of class consciousness, calling it the "standpoint of the proletariat."[16] *Standpoint* in turn became a resource for understanding the development not just of class consciousness but of consciousness from other subject positions that produce knowledge that is contrary to normative understandings of social processes, including science. As Nancy Hartsock explains, the concept allows the development of "an important epistemological tool for understanding and opposing *all forms of domination* [my emphasis]—a feminist standpoint."[17] *Standpoint* thus informs theories of knowledge across many conversations, including many that do not explicitly name Marx or standpoint epistemology.

As a theory of knowledge, standpoint epistemology asserts that our social circumstances can make it harder or easier to know some things than others, as in Marx's observation that workers can develop objective awareness of their own circumstances through class struggle and thus become able to refute dominant accounts of economic activity. Additionally, standpoint epistemology offers a critique of mainstream knowledge production:

> The ruling group's vision may be *both* perverse *and* made real by means of that group's power to define the terms for the community as a whole. In Marxian analysis, this power is exercised in both control of ideological production, and in the real participation of the worker in exchange.[18]

Under standpoint theory, knowers from subjugated social positions have the potential for insights that challenge accounts that maintain the power of dominant groups. Patricia Hill Collins argues that "outsiders within occupy a special place—they become different people, and their difference sensitizes them to patterns that may be more difficult for established sociological insiders to see."[19] Collins notes that "to become sociological insiders, Black women must assimilate a standpoint that is quite different than their own" with "white male subjectivity at the center of analysis [which thus] assigns Afro-American womanhood a position on the margins."[20] Librarians from marginalized groups may also find they must decenter their own knowledge of the world in order to engage the collection, description, and classification practices of the profession which are positioned as neutral and objective.

Outsider perspectives can be a potent resource for better accounts of the world, as Collins articulates in this classic example:

> Afro-American women have long been privy to some of the most intimate secrets of white society. Countless numbers of Black women have ridden busses to their white "families," where they not only cooked, cleaned, and executed other domestic duties, but where they also nurtured their "other" children, shrewdly offered guidance to their employers, and frequently became honorary members of their white "families." These women have seen white elites, both actual and aspiring, from perspectives largely obscured from both their Black [male] spouses and from the white families themselves.[21]

Standpoint theory has been invigorated by feminist and decolonial thinkers who contribute to scholarship about the formation of subjectivities and knowledge from the perspective of the "Other" even when this does not travel under the name *standpoint theory*. Chela Sandoval names theorists including Franz

Fanon, Aimé Césaire, Gloria Anzaldúa, Audre Lorde, and others as "thinkers who rose from myriad populations but who similarly survived conquest, colonization, and slavery in order to develop insurgent theories and methods for outlasting domination" and thus contributing to her "methodology of the oppressed," which she identifies as "situated knowledges" in conversation with Donna Haraway's essay by that name.[22] Scholars insisting on lived truth have articulated how interlocking systems of oppression construct knowing subjects not just along the axis of class, but through racism, sexism, colonialism, and imperialism as well, giving rise to standpoint concepts including "the outsider within," "mestiza consciousness," "differential consciousness," and "oppositional consciousness," challenging knowledge constituted through power.

Standpoint Is Achieved

Because standpoint theories name social groups whose perspectives may provide unique insights, some critics mistakenly dismiss them as identity politics or imply they are exclusionary. Sandra Harding explains, "Standpoint theories argue that what we do in our social relations both enables and limits (it does not determine) what we can know."[23] Nor does standpoint theory claim that access to a more complete, less partial perspective is guaranteed by virtue of occupying an oppressed category, or by a knower's *identity* as a member of a social group. Sandoval's emphasis on standpoint theory as a *methodology* for decolonizing the imagination speaks to this tenet: consciousness is an achievement and does not come automatically from occupying a subjugated social category.

Rather, knowers occupy social locations, or subject positions, which are power-differentiated categories that produce different experiences of the world; through the development of attention to this difference, subjects become capable of perceiving the contingent historical and social relations that produce our objective conditions. As with class consciousness, feminist standpoint

> is achieved rather than obvious, a mediated rather than immediate understanding. Because the ruling group controls the means of mental as well as physical production, the production of ideals as well as goods, *the standpoint of the oppressed represents an achievement both of science (analysis) and of political struggle* [my emphasis] on the basis of which this analysis can be conducted.[24]

Moreover, as feminist and other scholars have noted, subject positions are not singularly *class* or *gender* or *racial* subject positions, but these and more, simultaneously: Collins notes that the "interlocking nature of race, gender, and class oppression" has been part of Black feminist analysis since at least the 1970s,[25] and Crenshaw's articulation of intersectionality remains salient to this discussion.[26]

Strong Objectivity, Situated Knowledges, and Agential Realism

How can valid, transferable knowledge be possible, given the challenges to conventional versions of neutrality and objectivity issuing from positivism, post-positivism, and standpoint theory, among others? Standpoint epistemology demands recognition that all knowledge comes from standpoints; because knowledge is an embodied and social process, there is no neutral position from which to get better knowledge. Critics of feminist epistemology may suggest that there are no alternatives to the "view from nowhere" that implies a knower who can transcend embodiment. But feminist epistemologies "can direct the production of less partial and less distorted beliefs"[27] that are thus more objective because they understand social location as a potential resource for detecting problematic bias, generating new research questions, and producing better, more accountable knowledge. Here, I briefly explain three conditions for robust objectivity that can be readily understood in library practice: strong objectivity, situated knowledges, and agential realism.

As Sandra Harding observes, traditional conceptions of objectivity have not been able to prevent distortions in science. Because we typically look for bias only in known cases of scientific failure, we rarely look at what social factors promote successful science. Harding calls the identification of social factors that enable the generation of less distorted science "strong objectivity" because traditional accounts of objectivity are too weak to ensure robust knowledge claims.[28] In Harding's words:

> A feminist standpoint epistemology requires strengthened standards of objectivity.... They call for the acknowledgement that all human beliefs—including our best scientific beliefs—are socially situated, but they also require a critical evaluation to determine which social situations tend to generate the most objective knowledge claims.[29]

From this insight, Harding and other feminist epistemologists argue that socially engaged science can produce better knowledge, as for example when the women's health movements of the 1970s demanded an end to the exclusive use of young, white men as universal, neutral subjects for health research. The Black Panthers similarly worked to counter medical inattention to sickle cell anemia as they provided health education and genetic screening for community members, framing "sickle cell anemia within a matrix of mediating factors that included not only biology but racism and poverty."[30] Today we know that not reckoning with discrimination under the pretense of neutrality has led to bad research design and poor conceptualization of health across marginalized populations.

However, while feminist, decolonial standpoints offer the potential for better knowledge of the lives and experiences of marginalized people, standpoint epistemology does not limit the domain in which Black, feminist, decolonial, and other perspectives can contribute to more objective knowledge to only the social sciences. Rather, feminist epistemologies, such as the situated knowledges framed by Sandoval as the methodology of the oppressed, or "a set of processes, procedures, and technologies for decolonizing the imagination,"[31] offer conditions of objectivity for all scientific knowledge production.

Objectivity posed as "the view from nowhere," which suggests the possibility of science conducted from outside any subject position, is both impossible and irresponsible, in Donna Haraway's account. She argues for "situated knowledges" that are accountable for knowledge production, including our conditions of possibility and our responsibility to other knowers. She argues that better knowledge comes from coming together with other knowers with admittedly partial perspectives, since all knowledge is situated, that is, comes from a set of social, historical, and material locations. For this reason, Haraway calls for "politics and epistemologies of location, positioning, and situating, where partiality and not universality is the condition of being heard to make rational knowledge claims."[32] The gathering together of partial perspectives is not mere accretion of knowledge in the progressivist sense, but rather, engaging together in creating, contesting, and revising knowledge claims with responsibility to how those claims could come to be made and how they might be used.

Situating and locating as conditions for objectivity are also expressed in theoretical physicist Karen Barad's conception of agential realism. Barad coined *agential realism* to describe how objective accounts of knowledge are possible in light of challenges to our fundamental understanding of the universe provoked by quantum theory in the early twentieth century. Barad elaborates the implications of the complementarity principle developed by Niels Bohr to account for wave-particle duality. As Bohr showed, we are ultimately unable to say whether elementary particles like photons are a wave or a particle without also referencing the instrument we used to detect them, and thus both the particle and the instrument are inseparable attributes of the phenomenon.

Barad's feminist elaboration of Bohr's insight explains that we can't draw clear boundaries between our objects of study and the experimental apparatuses we need to measure and record information about those objects. In her account, objects always exist as part of phenomena that include the experimental setup. Determining the boundaries of the experimental setup is what Barad calls "agential realism." To achieve realism, or objectivity, in our knowledge, we have to understand that our experimental setups also exert influence (or agency) over how things appear in the world, as does the object of study. To conceptually separate them is what Barad describes as an epistemological "cut" between the object and agencies of observation (the observer together with the observational apparatus). She says, "Object and subject emerge through and as part of the specific nature of the material practices that are enacted" in order to observe things in the world.[33]

According to Barad, the "condition for objective knowledge is that the referent is a phenomenon (and not an observation-independent object)."[34] In her account, science doesn't merely describe, but also produces its objects of study; that is, through iterative processes, science identifies and thus cocreates phenomena in the world as objects for study. Strong knowledge claims must include the contexts in which we have come to know about the phenomena we say our data describe, how we come to make a "cut" between the object of study and the apparatus we use to understand the object, including the knowing subject. Together, strong objectivity, situated knowledges, and agential realism demonstrate feminist commitments to reliable, socially engaged, and responsible knowledge production that can guide critical approaches to library practice, including data curation.

Feminist Epistemology, Critical Library Practice, and Data Curation: Situated Data

Returning now to critical library practice, we can relate key insights from feminist epistemology to data curation. As we learn from several strains of philosophy, science is an inseparably social process. Our contexts, or social locations, can allow some knowledge claims (from the "view from nowhere") to escape scrutiny that is otherwise reserved for marginalized knowers. As Harding notes, "When a scientific community shares assumptions, there is little chance that more careful application of existing scientific methods will detect them."[35] Location, or standpoint, is a resource for what Harding calls "strong objectivity" and what Haraway calls "situated knowledges"—knowledge that does not efface the social conditions for its production. Barad's "cut" is another articulation of what it takes to be accountable—and hence objective—to our research objects. Situated knowledges can also be a resource for decolonizing our mental capacities for understanding our social and natural worlds.[36]

Thus, curating research data for meaningful sharing can throw into sharp relief the social processes that constitute scientific knowledge production and provide opportunities for researchers, curators, producers, and users of research data to observe the constructedness of all knowledge claims, not just those that emanate from oppressed subject positions, and not just those about the social world.

The common baseline for sharing research data is that the data package should include necessary documentation for the data to be intelligible to other researchers with the same disciplinary training without further communication between researchers. That standard is relatively challenging, as we learn from case studies of scientific practice, such as H. M. Collins's account of the sharing of tacit knowledge in laser development.[37] Providing that kind of context requires encoding a fair amount of information about the experiment or the study, the measurements, the instruments, and the analysis, which is so challenging that data managers are developing ways to automate metadata collection as much as possible.

Sharing data packaged with metadata and documentation, or context, partially situates the data and the knowledge claims that are grounded on the data. This context can help make visible at least some of the theories with which the data is laden, allowing scrutiny of the theories and background beliefs that situate the data as evidence. FAIR standards articulate metadata requirements so that data can be made findable, accessible, interoperable, and reusable (i.e., FAIR) when ingested into a FAIR data repository. This requires not only human-readable documentation but also machine-readable metadata, including persistent identifiers, which can be used to collate information related to the researcher, the funding agency, the researcher's organizational affiliation, the methods or kinds of analysis used in the study, study protocols, experimental materials, and sometimes the specific scientific instrument used in the study—all elements of Barad's agential realism.

Different benchmarks for data curation could involve preparing data for use by more knowers or to make it findable and accessible to a wider range of knowers than the narrow disciplinary audience. There is no absolute demarcation for metadata sufficiency. Sufficient metadata for whom, and for what purpose? With a higher bar than meaningful reuse by another person from the same disciplinary background, criteria likely to reproduce the same perspective without detecting distortion, data curation can strive to situate data so that the documentation can provide thick descriptions of the data's conditions of possibility and the theories with which the data are laden as a resource to new knowers. Situated data challenges data curators to reflect on the Baradian "cut" in the determination that the provided context is sufficient and for which knowers, and to embed new norms in curatorial practice, including demands made on researchers to provide generous documentation along with data files.

Addressing Limitations

Sharing documented data is a starting point for responsibility to knowledge production—and hence objectivity—not a fulfillment of the obligation. While curating situated data is a step in the direction of responsibility for the enabling conditions of the research, it is limited. It does not guarantee that knowers from oppressed groups will have the disciplinary, methodological, or computational resources to contest, validate, aggregate, analyze, or reuse the data. Most research data are outputs from science conducted from the center, not the margins. Data sharing and curation is no substitute for situated science conducted from marginalized subject positions. Starting from the lives of women and Indigenous and people of color, as Collins, Harding, and their interlocutors encourage, means that members of these overlapping groups set research agendas, compose the questions, and design research, with enhanced potential to generate knowledge that does not reify existing social hierarchies. As Haraway puts it, "We are also bound to seek perspective from those points of view, which can never be known in advance, which promise something quite extraordinary, that is, knowledge potent for constructing worlds less organized by axes of domination."[38]

Additionally, some impulses toward data sharing are at odds with situated knowledges. While legal context is vital for research materials and data (e.g., human subjects protection programs, NAGPRA [North American Graves Protection and Repatriation Act], intellectual property, open licensing), these frameworks do not exhaust the responsibility of researchers to other knowers or research subjects. Indigenous data sovereignty and respect for other knowledge regimes will require data curators to challenge our received beliefs about ownership and openness of knowledge.[39] It may be especially difficult for those of us from dominant research paradigms to detect breaches of consent and trust or instrumental and appropriative uses of data. Joanna Radin's discussion of how Akimel O'odham health data became fodder for machine learning research is a good starting point for data curators to think about how open data practices may contribute to knowledge colonialism.[40]

Critical data curation documentation could include references to power-differentiated relationships between researchers and research subjects, be they human (including human remains) or nonhuman (as in the case of animals, historic human habitations, and ecologies). Situated data would demand of data curators continuous effort toward enriching and revising curatorial practice and standards through attention to subjugated knowledges, including intellectual property regimes that appropriate and allow the abuse of data and traditional knowledges. Here, responsibility to knowledge production will involve acknowledging the need of Indigenous communities for data with which to make knowledge claims and the right to govern data generated by and about them. The growing global Indigenous data sovereignty movement can inform data curators working from the center in taking up Sandoval's invitation to decolonize our imaginations to generate data curation practices made more objective and less appropriative through Indigenous standpoints.[41]

Situating Data

The following queries can be addressed to the contents of a data package as a starting point for testing and redressing the situatedness of its data. Such queries can guide data literacy activities or initiate new studies in the history and practice of science.

- What is the object of study, how is it being defined, and how did it become so?

- What are the agencies of observation? What are some implications of making this particular Baradian "cut" between the object and agencies of observation?

- What beliefs about the world, the universe, or society are embedded in the study, research questions, and prior research the study references?

- What context—theory, methods, instruments—frames how the phenomenon will be understood?

- How are the variables defined, and what histories might be relevant? (For example, see Duana Fullwiley's discussion of the definition of race categories used in genomic data sets.[42])

- For which group of knowers will this be sufficient documentation for reanalysis and reuse of the data? What would it take for this data to be made useful for a different or broader audience?

- What is the history of the method, instrument, analysis, theory, or object described in this data set?

- How was the study funded, and what other conditions of possibility were required?

- What historical conditions of possibility brought the research organization or team into existence? (See, for example, "Land-Grab Universities."[43])

- Is all the labor of the study accounted for, or are there people (grad students, lab assistants, participants, community members) who may not have been acknowledged for their role in knowledge production?

- Does the data set include observations of communities that prefer or are entitled to group consent processes or who are involved in struggles for sovereignty over data, samples, or resources? (See, for example, OCAP Principles.[44])

- Does this study acknowledge impacts on the environment, community, and participants?

Conclusion

Norms for the practice of science are changing, in part because of declining costs of computation and data storage and the development of robust and reliable data repositories and standards for documenting data and making it shareable. Data curation shows that many practices are required to produce objectivity while simultaneously showing that scientific practice is embedded within particular social conditions. Because data curation requires the inclusion of crucial context for the research data life cycle, it could provide means for new knowers to intervene and participate in science. This suggests the potential for critical approaches for data curation that I have named "situated data."

Data curation informed by feminist epistemology can create the conditions for "strong objectivity," more robust standards of objectivity than promised by traditional scientific norms. This involves situating ourselves, being responsible for the conditions of possibility for our knowledge production, being accountable to other knowers, and putting our experimental assumptions on the table for inspection. We understand that the quantity of metadata that we include in a data package is arbitrary and could include much more and that data sets don't stand on their own, but as partial accounts of the world that can be inspected, augmented, contextualized, contested, and joined with other accounts.

Because all observations (i.e., data) are theory laden, situating data means including and expanding context to make data accessible to a wider range of knowers who can reanalyze, reinterpret, contest, augment, or aggregate data for new projects, enabling conditions for objectivity. Curation for situated data can power social justice movements and citizen science projects on a host of concerns, including social determinants of health, police violence, environmental racism, and genomics. But more than this: situating data can bring more knowers into important scientific conversations across every discipline, banish the view from nowhere, and enable conditions for accountability and objectivity in scientific and curatorial practice.

Feminist epistemologies are a resource for challenging definitions of objectivity and neutrality that have been a barrier to reliable, responsible knowledge and the inclusion of marginalized knowers in scientific practice, including the practice of library and information science. Librarians can draw on their own standpoints as workers and as members of power-differentiated groups to interrogate the ways LIS engages in ideological production, allowing us not just to situate data and collections but to create and contest knowledge claims from within library discourse.

Acknowledgments

I would like to thank Eli Landaverde, Sara Miller, and Autumn Faulkner of the Critical Practice Reading Group at Michigan State University Libraries for sustaining conversations, and Kelly Barrick, Paul Roth, Donna Haraway, and Karen Barad for planting the seed of this chapter long ago.

Notes

1. John P. Holdren, "Increasing Access to the Results of Federally Funded Scientific Research" memorandum, Office of Science and Technology Policy, Executive Office of the President, February 22, 2013, https://obamawhitehouse.archives.gov/sites/default/files/microsites/ostp/ostp_public_access_memo_2013.pdf.
2. National Science Foundation, "Data Management Guidelines for CISE Proposals and Awards," accessed August 30, 2021, https://www.nsf.gov/cise/cise_dmp.jsp.
3. Mark D. Wilkinson et al., "The FAIR Guiding Principles for Scientific Data Management and Stewardship," *Scientific Data* 3, no. 1 (2016): article 160018, https://doi.org/10.1038/sdata.2016.18.
4. Katie King, "Acting-Thinking One," January 11, 2022.
5. Joan Marshall, "LC Labeling: An Indictment," in *Revolting Librarians*, ed. Celeste West (San Francisco: Booklegger Press, 1972), 45–49; Sanford Berman, *Prejudices and Antipathies* (Metuchen, NJ: Scarecrow Press, 1971).
6. Hope A. Olson, "The Power to Name: Representation in Library Catalogs," *Signs* 26, no. 3 (2001): 647.
7. Hope A. Olson and Rose Schlegl, "Standardization, Objectivity, and User Focus: A Meta-analysis of Subject Access Critiques," *Cataloging and Classification Quarterly* 32, no. 2 (2001): 61–80.
8. Angela Kublik et al., "Adapting Dominant Classifications to Particular Contexts," *Cataloging and Classification Quarterly* 37, no. 1 (2003): 13–31.
9. Melodie J. Fox and Hope A. Olson, "Feminist Epistemologies and Knowledge Organization," in *Cultural Frames of Knowledge*, ed. Richard P Smiraglia and Hur-Li Lee (Würzburg, Germany: Ergon Verlag, 2012), 79–97.
10. Melanie Feinberg, "Hidden Bias to Responsible Bias: An Approach to Information Systems Based on Haraway's Situated Knowledges," *Information Research* 12, no. 4 (October 2007), https://d-scholarship.pitt.edu/25116/1/colis/colis07.html.

11. Michelle Caswell, "Dusting for Fingerprints: Introducing Feminist Standpoint Appraisal," *Journal of Critical Library and Information Studies* 3, no. 2 (2021), https://doi.org/10.24242/jclis.v3i2.113.

12. John H. Zammito, *A Nice Derangement of Epistemes* (Chicago: University of Chicago Press, 2004), 6.

13. Zammito, *Nice Derangement of Epistemes*, 16.

14. Thomas S. Kuhn, *The Structure of Scientific Revolutions*, 3rd. ed. (Chicago: University of Chicago Press, 1996).

15. Karl Popper, *The Logic of Scientific Discovery* (1935), (London: Hutchinson, 1980).

16. György Lukács, *History and Class Consciousness* (Cambridge, MA: MIT Press, 1971).

17. Nancy Hartsock, *The Feminist Standpoint Revisited and Other Essays* (Boulder, CO: Westview Press, 1998). 106.

18. Hartsock, *Feminist Standpoint Revisited*, 110.

19. Patricia Hill Collins, "Learning from the Outsider Within: The Sociological Significance of Black Feminist Thought," in *The Feminist Standpoint Reader*, ed. Sandra Harding (New York: Routledge, 2004), 122.

20. Collins, "Learning from the Outsider Within," 118.

21. Collins, "Learning from the Outsider Within," 103.

22. Chela Sandoval, *Methodology of the Oppressed* (Minneapolis: University of Minnesota Press, 2000), 7.

23. Sandra Harding, "'Strong Objectivity': A Response to the New Objectivity Question," *Synthese* 104, no. 3 (1995): 341.

24. Hartsock, *Feminist Standpoint Revisited*, 110.

25. Collins, "Learning from the Outsider Within," 109.

26. Kimberlé Crenshaw, "Demarginalizing the Intersection of Race and Sex: A Black Feminist Critique of Antidiscrimination Doctrine, Feminist Theory and Antiracist Politics," *University of Chicago Legal Forum* 1989, no. 1 (1989): 139–67.

27. Sandra G. Harding, *Whose Science? Whose Knowledge?* (Ithaca, NY: Cornell University Press, 1991), 138.

28. Harding, "Strong Objectivity."

29. Harding, Whose Science? 142.

30. Alondra Nelson, *Body and Soul* (Minneapolis: University of Minnesota Press, 2011), 116.

31. Sandoval, *Methodology of the Oppressed*, 69.

32. Donna J. Haraway, "Situated Knowledges: The Science Question in Feminism and the Privilege of Partial Perspective," in *Simians, Cyborgs, and Women: The Reinvention of Nature* (New York: Routledge, 1991), 195.

33. Karen Barad, *Meeting the Universe Halfway* (Durham, NC: Duke University Press, 2007), 359.

34. Karen Barad, "Agential Realism: Feminist Interventions in Understanding Scientific Practices," in *The Science Studies Reader*, ed. Mario Biagioli (New York: Routledge, 1999), 5.

35. Harding, "Strong Objectivity," 340.

36. For a compelling application of feminist theory to data science and data ethics more generally, see Catherine D'Ignazio and Lauren F. Klein, *Data Feminism* (Cambridge, MA: MIT Press, 2020).

37. H. M. Collins, "The TEA Set: Tacit Knowledge and Scientific Networks," in *The Science Studies Reader*, ed. Mario Biagioli (New York: Routledge, 1999), 95–109; Paul N. Edwards et al., "Science Friction: Data, Metadata, and Collaboration," *Social Studies of Science* 41, no. 5 (2011): 667–90.

38. Haraway, "Situated Knowledges," 192.

39. International Working Group for Indigenous Affairs, *The Indigenous World 2021: Indigenous Data Sovereignty*, accessed January 14, 2022, https://iwgia.org/en/ip-i-iw/4268-iw-2021-indigenous-data-sovereignty.html; Global Investigative Journalism Network, "Indigenous Data Sovereignty," GIJN/NAJA Guide for Indigenous Investigative Journalists, accessed January 14, 2022, https://gijn.org/indigenous-data-sovereignty/.

40. Joanna Radin, "'Digital Natives': How Medical and Indigenous Histories Matter for Big Data," *Osiris* 32, no. 1 (2017): 43–64, https://doi.org/10.1086/693853.

41. Jacqueline M. Quinless, *Decolonizing Data* (Toronto: University of Toronto Press, 2022).

42. Duana Fullwiley, "The Molecularization of Race: Institutionalizing Human Difference in Pharmacogenetics Practice," *Science as Culture* 16, no. 1 (2007): 1–30.

43. Robert Lee and Tristan Ahtone. "Land-Grab Universities: Expropriated Indigenous Land Is the Foundation of the Land-Grant University System," *High Country News*, March 30, 2020. https://www.hcn.org/issues/52.4/indigenous-affairs-education-land-grab-universities.
44. First Nations Information Governance Centre, "The First Nations Principles of OCAP," accessed March 12, 2022, https://fnigc.ca/ocap-training/.

Bibliography

Barad, Karen. "Agential Realism: Feminist Interventions in Understanding Scientific Practices." In *The Science Studies Reader*, edited by Mario Biagioli, 1–11. New York: Routledge, 1999.

———. *Meeting the Universe Halfway: Quantum Physics and the Entanglement of Matter and Meaning*. Durham, NC: Duke University Press, 2007.

Berman, Sanford. *Prejudices and Antipathies: A Tract on the LC Subject Heads Concerning People*. Metuchen, NJ: Scarecrow Press, 1971.

Bottomore, Tom. *A Dictionary of Marxist Thought*. Malden, Mass.: Blackwell Reference, 1991.

Bowker, Geoffrey C., and Susan Leigh Star. *Sorting Things Out: Classification and Its Consequences*. Inside Technology. Cambridge, MA: MIT Press, 1999.

Caswell, Michelle. "Dusting for Fingerprints: Introducing Feminist Standpoint Appraisal." *Journal of Critical Library and Information Studies* 3, no. 2 (2021). https://doi.org/10.24242/jclis.v3i2.113.

Collins, H. M. "The TEA Set: Tacit Knowledge and Scientific Networks." In *The Science Studies Reader*, edited by Mario Biagioli, 95–109. New York: Routledge, 1999.

Collins, Patricia Hill. "Learning from the Outsider Within: The Sociological Significance of Black Feminist Thought." In *The Feminist Standpoint Reader*, edited by Sandra Harding, 103–26. New York: Routledge, 2004.

Crenshaw, Kimberlé. "Demarginalizing the Intersection of Race and Sex: A Black Feminist Critique of Antidiscrimination Doctrine, Feminist Theory and Antiracist Politics." *University of Chicago Legal Forum* 1989, no. 1 (1989): 139–67.

D'Ignazio, Catherine, and Lauren F. Klein. *Data Feminism*. Cambridge, MA: MIT Press, 2020.

Edwards, Paul N., Matthew S. Mayernik, Archer L. Batcheller, Geoffrey C. Bowker, and Christine L. Borgman. "Science Friction: Data, Metadata, and Collaboration." *Social Studies of Science* 41, no. 5 (2011): 667–90.

Feinberg, Melanie. "Hidden Bias to Responsible Bias: An Approach to Information Systems Based on Haraway's Situated Knowledges." *Information Research* 12, no. 4 (October 2007). https://d-scholarship.pitt.edu/25116/1/colis/colis07.html.

First Nations Information Governance Centre. "The First Nations Principles of OCAP." Accessed March 12, 2022. https://fnigc.ca/ocap-training/.

Fox, Melodie J., and Hope A. Olson. "Feminist Epistemologies and Knowledge Organization." In *Cultural Frames of Knowledge*, edited by Richard P Smiraglia and Hur-Li Lee, 79–97. Würzburg, Germany: Ergon Verlag, 2012.

Fullwiley, Duana. "The Molecularization of Race: Institutionalizing Human Difference in Pharmacogenetics Practice." *Science as Culture* 16, no. 1 (2007): 1–30.

Global Investigative Journalism Network. "Indigenous Data Sovereignty." GIJN/NAJA Guide for Indigenous Investigative Journalists. Accessed January 14, 2022. https://gijn.org/indigenous-data-sovereignty/.

Haraway, Donna J. "Situated Knowledges: The Science Question in Feminism and the Privilege of Partial Perspective." Chapter 9 in *Simians, Cyborgs, and Women: The Reinvention of Nature*. New York: Routledge, 1991.

Harding, Sandra G, ed. *The Feminist Standpoint Theory Reader: Intellectual and Political Controversies*. New York: Routledge, 2004.

Harding, Sandra. "'Strong Objectivity': A Response to the New Objectivity Question." *Synthese* 104, no. 3 (1995): 331–49.

Harding, Sandra G. *Whose Science? Whose Knowledge? Thinking from Women's Lives*. Ithaca, NY: Cornell University Press, 1991.

Hartsock, Nancy. *The Feminist Standpoint Revisited and Other Essays*. Boulder, CO: Westview Press, 1998.

Hegel, Georg Wilhelm Friedrich. *Phenomenology of Spirit* (1807). Translated by A. V. Miller. Oxford: Oxford University Press, 1977.

Holdren, John P. "Increasing Access to the Results of Federally Funded Scientific Research." Memorandum, Office of Science and Technology Policy, Executive Office of the President, February 22, 2013. https://obamawhitehouse.archives.gov/sites/default/files/microsites/ostp/ostp_public_access_memo_2013.pdf.

International Working Group for Indigenous Affairs. *The Indigenous World 2021: Indigenous Data Sovereignty*. Accessed January 14, 2022. https://iwgia.org/en/ip-i-iw/4268-iw-2021-indigenous-data-sovereignty.html.

Kant, Immanuel. *Critique of Pure Reason* (1781/1787). Translated by Norman Kemp Smith. Reprint, rev. ed., London: Palgrave MacMillan, 2003.

King, Katie. "Acting-Thinking One." January 11, 2022.

Kublik, Angela, Virginia Clevette, Dennis Ward, and Hope A. Olson. "Adapting Dominant Classifications to Particular Contexts." *Cataloging and Classification Quarterly* 37, no. 1 (2003): 13–31.

Kuhn, Thomas S. *The Structure of Scientific Revolutions*, 3rd ed. Chicago: University of Chicago Press, 1996.

Lee, Robert, and Tristan Ahtone. "Land-Grab Universities: Expropriated Indigenous Land Is the Foundation of the Land-Grant University System." *High Country News*, March 30, 2020. https://www.hcn.org/issues/52.4/indigenous-affairs-education-land-grab-universities.

Lukács, György. *History and Class Consciousness: Studies in Marxist Dialectics*. Cambridge, MA: MIT Press, 1971.

Marshall, Joan. "LC Labeling: An Indictment." In *Revolting Librarians*, edited by Celeste West, 45–49. San Francisco: Booklegger Press, 1972.

Marx, Karl. *Capital: A Critique of Political Economy*, vol. 1 (1867). Translated by Ben Fowkes. London: Penguin Classics, 1976.

National Science Foundation. "Data Management Guidelines for CISE Proposals and Awards." Accessed August 30, 2021. https://www.nsf.gov/cise/cise_dmp.jsp.

Nelson, Alondra. *Body and Soul: The Black Panther Party and the Fight against Medical Discrimination*. Minneapolis: University of Minnesota Press, 2011.

Olson, Hope A. "The Power to Name: Representation in Library Catalogs." *Signs* 26, no. 3 (2001): 639–68.

Olson, Hope A, and Rose Schlegl. "Standardization, Objectivity, and User Focus: A Meta-analysis of Subject Access Critiques." *Cataloging and Classification Quarterly* 32, no. 2 (2001): 61–80.

Popper, Karl. *The Logic of Scientific Discovery* (1935). London: Hutchinson, 1980.

Quinless, Jacqueline M. *Decolonizing Data: Unsettling Conversations about Social Research Methods*. Toronto: University of Toronto Press, 2022.

Radin, Joanna. "'Digital Natives': How Medical and Indigenous Histories Matter for Big Data." *Osiris* 32, no. 1 (2017): 43–64. https://doi.org/10.1086/693853.

Sandoval, Chela. *Methodology of the Oppressed*. Minneapolis: University of Minnesota Press, 2000.

Wilkinson, Mark D., Michel Dumontier, IJsbrand Jan Aalbersberg, Gabrielle Appleton, Myles Axton, Arie Baak, Niklas Blomberg, et al. "The FAIR Guiding Principles for Scientific Data Management and Stewardship." *Scientific Data* 3, no. 1 (2016): article 160018. https://doi.org/10.1038/sdata.2016.18.

Zammito, John H. *A Nice Derangement of Epistemes: Post-positivism in the Study of Science from Quine to Latour*. Chicago: University of Chicago Press, 2004.

PART III

The Labor of Librarianship

CHAPTER 6

Acting "As If"
Critical Pedagogy, Empowerment, and Labor

Rafia Mirza, Karen P. Nicholson, and Maura Seale

Introduction

In 2010, Accardi, Drabinski, and Kumbier published *Critical Library Instruction: Theories and Methods*, effectively centering both critical information literacy and critical library pedagogy within academic librarianship.[1] Critical information literacy seeks to interrogate assumptions about information literacy and "adopt an approach to teaching that recognizes that education is not itself apolitical."[2] Critical pedagogy, well established within the discipline of education, attempts to reimagine educational systems, institutions, and methods; it attends to both global and local contexts—to "institutions and ideologies" and to the needs and experiences of "particular students in a particular classroom."[3] Through the use of dialogue, reflection, and problem-posing, and relying on care work, it emphasizes empathy and relationships and seeks to increase agency and empowerment. Critical library pedagogy brings these practices to the library classroom. As a framework that requires us to reflect on and reimagine what we teach (content or curriculum) as well as how we teach (methods), critical library pedagogy has been immensely valuable in helping librarians move away from "conceptions of information literacy rooted in mechanistic notions of access and use" toward

engaging students in larger conversations about the social, economic, and political contexts in which libraries and information function.[4] As Drabinski writes, "The promise of critical pedagogy lies in its capacity to change lives as librarians try new ways of thinking and teaching that challenge systems of power that privilege some and not others."[5] Critical library pedagogy, then, has both liberatory and subversive aims. It affords opportunities for developing "an information literacy praxis" capable of resisting neoliberal imperatives and for reimagining libraries as "conceptual spaces of resistance,"[6] and also allows librarians to "question and resist the damaging effects of capital-centered education on learners, teachers, and society."[7]

The mainstreaming of critical library pedagogy, which has rendered it readily accessible in professional handbooks, guides, and programming, also means that it has become institutionalized—"managed, absorbed, and incorporated by higher education into its own logics."[8] In a recent critique, Ferretti contends that while critical library pedagogy has effectively changed our approach to teaching, it has done little to "change power relations between library colleagues."[9] Similarly, Leung and López-McKnight argue that critical librarianship has made "only incremental steps towards the necessary, vital, structural change that would fulfill the promise of social justice that we see inherent in libraries."[10] Institutionalization alone cannot account for critical librarianship's failure to challenge power and privilege beyond the library classroom, however. Building on Leung and López-McKnight's argument that critical information literacy has failed to challenge white supremacy as "a structure of domination"[11] within the profession, we contend that discourses of agency, power, and empowerment inherent in critical library pedagogy may also contribute to these shortcomings. We suggest that critical library pedagogy's emphasis on the initiative and agency of individual teachers and students risks reinscribing neoliberal subjectivities of performance and merit and exacerbating labor issues endemic to the neoliberal university, such as doing more with less, understaffing, competition, and burnout, thereby working against collective action, solidarity, and equity.

In this chapter, we explore the labor of information literacy and its devaluation in professional discourse, which lends appeal to critical library pedagogy as means to reclaim agency in the classroom.[12] We consider how discourses of agency and empowerment in critical library pedagogy fail to account for positionality, power, and context, with the result that critical pedagogy tends to center individual (heroic) efforts rather than collective action. Because critical library pedagogy emphasizes *individual* agency, it enhances, rather than diminishes, the role of the instructor; teachers "empower students both as individuals and as potential agents of social change."[13] In so doing, it positions instructors as individual actors outside of social groups, thereby sidestepping engagement with systemic oppressive structures such as racism, sexism, classism, and homophobia. Critical pedagogy thus becomes a decontextualized and disempowering fiction, a practice of "acting as if" the classroom were a safe space.[14] It becomes what Hudson refers to as "a pedagogy of the practical,"[15] a practice that reinscribes white supremacy in the library. Reframing critical library pedagogy as labor undertaken in solidarity with other workers offers another possibility for reclaiming its liberatory potential.

Information Literacy Teaching as Affective, Immaterial Labor or Care Work

Like other forms of teaching, information literacy instruction is the affective, immaterial labor of social reproduction, "the work of feeding, nurturing, soothing, educating, and ensuring that basic needs are met."[16] This intangible, often invisible work "creates and replenishes labor power," thereby "produc[ing] value under capitalism."[17] In facilitating the development of students as scholars and future knowledge workers and by smoothing information flows in the university,[18] instruction librarians not only enable knowledge production in the academy, but also serve to reproduce the academy itself.[19] Despite the value of such work in supporting "institutional goals and retention,"[20] it is often devalued as pink collar labor, a form of gendered care work associated with women and the domestic sphere.[21] In the library, "digital immaterial labor" such as coding or systems librarianship is privileged and validated as mind work largely performed by men, while the affective immaterial labor of teaching is devalued.[22] As Sloniowski and others underscore, "such valorizations have their roots in gendered divisions of labor."[23] Moreover, as is the case in higher education more broadly,[24] the burden of care work in the academic library falls disproportionately on Black and Indigenous women, and women of color.[25]

In an article that explores teaching as care work, Ismael, Lazzaro, and Ishihara identify the following "skilled dimensions" of caring education work: cultural responsiveness; acknowledging racism and other forms of discrimination; building relationships; attending to students' social, emotional, and physiological needs; and a focus on instruction and skilled pedagogy.[26] These strategies can be found throughout the critical information literacy literature. Feminist library pedagogy, which informs much critical library instruction, centers women's "experiences, voices, feelings, and ideas in educational settings" in order to raise awareness of and dismantle oppression.[27] Reflection, dialogue, problem-posing, and active learning are key methods employed by critical library teachers.[28] Douglas and Gadsby use relational-cultural theory as a lens through which to foreground "the connection and relationships between people, such as mutuality, empathy, and sensitivity to emotional contexts" that information literacy work requires.[29] Loyer describes Indigenous information literacy as a practice informed by accountability, reciprocity, relationships, and a need for awareness of students' "emotional, spiritual, and physical health" as they engage in research.[30]

At the same time, Ismael, Lazzaro, and Ishihara emphasize that the "actions and orientations" of caring teachers "represent an overwhelming individual duty."[31] In the austerity-based neoliberal university, which requires us to do more with less and prioritize efficiency in a never-ending race to the bottom, such work can be detrimental to the health of workers, pitting students' well-being against that of educators.[32] Gregg further argues that because being "emotionally invested"[33] creates a willingness to accept work intensification as the norm, it is an expectation in higher education.[34] These conditions also exist in the academic library. Like faculty, academic librarians experience work intensification (expanded responsibilities) and work acceleration (a requirement to do more work in less time).[35] Instruction librarians, already perceived as marginal educators, are further required to "modify the tempo of their own labor" to remain "'in time' with the dominant temporalities of faculty and students"[36] by providing just-in-time information literacy supports such as classes, guides, videos, and chat reference. Emotional labor undergirds this instructional work,[37] and, as Ismael, Lazzaro, and Ishihara demonstrate, "feminization, racialization, and connection to emotion make care work and care workers uniquely vulnerable to exploitation."[38]

Further exacerbating librarians' susceptibility to burnout and labor exploitation is our professional service ethic and vocational awe. Vocational awe is the "expectation that the fulfillment of job duties requires sacrifice" as a means to accomplish a "higher purpose."[39] Warner extends Ettarh's analysis of vocational awe in librarianship to the neoliberal university, identifying what he calls "institutional awe," the "belief that the institution itself is *more important* than the people it serves."[40] Institutional awe demands that we "hurl" ourselves "into the breach of austerity," sacrificing ourselves in the name of the institution lest our students be "irreparably harmed."[41] Vocational and institutional awe demand extraordinary individual efforts to sustain underfunded systems and services. When we invest in our work as critical library instructors to the detriment of our well-being by accepting last-minute requests for classes, teaching more classes than we can handle, or spending countless hours tweaking content, we reproduce vocational and institutional awe, subjecting ourselves to "relentless care without replenishment."[42]

Critical approaches to information literacy emerge in conjunction with conventional perspectives.[43] In the next section, then, we draw upon work by Hicks and Lloyd that reveals that the turn to critical library pedagogy can be understood, at least in part, as an effort by librarians to push back against professional discourses that position them as peripheral to knowledge production, powerless, and deficient.[44]

The Discourses of Information Literacy: Agency, Power, and Deficits

In an ongoing study, Hicks and Lloyd examine professional texts, including information literacy models and guidelines produced by associations such as the ACRL and ANCIL and books about information literacy itself, in order to analyze higher education discourses about information literacy, students, and librarians.[45] These texts and the stories they tell are central in shaping information literacy in higher education—what it is and how it should be taught, by whom, and under what conditions.[46]

Hicks and Lloyd's analysis reveals two mutually constitutive yet conflicting narratives about students and librarians respectively. With regard to students, an outward-facing narrative intended for external stakeholders positions information literacy within a broader category of "empowerment narratives," including critical pedagogy: "Information literacy will 'empower' learners with the skills, attitudes, behaviors and understandings that they will need to make appropriate and informed choices within both current and future endeavors."[47] At the same time, an inward-facing narrative directed at librarians themselves depicts students as "uncritical," "overwhelmed," "overloaded," "passive," "overly dependent on others," and "lacking the experience and motivation to learn and fulfil the rules of academic practice."[48] Within this narrative, nontraditional students are singled out as "problems to be solved."[49] Because this narrative positions students as deficient, and self-determination as something to be "achieved through the correction of behavior," it understands information literacy as empowering and information literacy instruction as beneficial. The result is that empowerment becomes "an individual rather than a structural problem."[50] As Hicks and Lloyd emphasize, empowerment narratives that begin with the assumption of "human inadequacy" cannot be understood as "liberatory [or] anti-oppressive."[51] Instead, liberation occurs top-down, through the "bestowal of power by benevolent authority figures rather than ideas of self-organization and social action."[52] Information literacy becomes a form of acculturation into authorized ways of knowing rather than a form of exploration or inquiry.

These texts also downplay librarians' expertise by positioning them and their labor as absent from or peripheral to information literacy teaching in higher education. In the outward-facing narrative, librarians are "othered"—marginalized, disempowered, and stigmatized—and portrayed as incapable of contributing to discussions around information literacy.[53] They are instead repeatedly blamed for the failure of the information literacy project while structural issues that might impede its success, such as status, faculty engagement, time, and understaffing, remain unacknowledged. In contrast, the inward-facing narrative centers librarians' work but simultaneously depicts librarians themselves as lacking the proficiency and capability to be effective in their role. Librarians are characterized as underprepared, unassertive, and powerless; librarians, like their students, are deficient.

Given this context, it is not difficult to see why critical library pedagogy and its focus on agency and empowerment might appeal to library educators. For example, Tewell suggests that "as an educational approach that acknowledges and emboldens learners' agency, critical information literacy has much to offer librarians"[54] And yet, since the late 1980s, feminist and antiracist educators such as Ellsworth and Gore have argued that contrary to its promise, critical pedagogy "perpetuate[s] relations of domination"[55] in the classroom. Similar critiques have recently emerged within the LIS literature.[56] In the next section, we turn our attention to these critiques. Our analysis reveals that while the allure of critical library pedagogy lies in the possibility of political engagement, its overemphasis on the agency and ability of an abstract charismatic teacher works instead to reinscribe neoliberal logics and white savior narratives in libraries, working against solidarity and collaboration.[57]

Critical Pedagogy, Agency, and Empowerment

In an influential article, "Why Doesn't This Feel Empowering? Working through the Repressive Myths of Critical Pedagogy," Ellsworth recounts her engagement with critical pedagogy as a deliberate "political intervention," intended "to clarify the structures of institutional racism underlying university practices and culture."[58] Ellsworth interrogates critical pedagogy's central "myths" as they are outlined in the literature, namely empowerment, student voice, dialogue, and critical reflection.[59] Based on her experience of trying to put critical pedagogy into practice, Ellsworth claims that one reason critical pedagogy doesn't feel empowering is because it remains abstract and utopian. While critical educators may take on concrete issues in their classrooms, "educational researchers who invoke concepts of critical pedagogy consistently strip discussions of classroom practices of historical context and political position."[60] Teachers and their students are cast as generic actors outside the space and time of specific subject formations and political struggles. Ellsworth describes this decontextualized and disempowering fiction as follows:

> Acting as if our classroom were a safe space in which democratic dialogue was possible and happening did not make it so. If we were to respond to our context and the social identities of the people in our classroom in ways that did not reproduce the oppressive formations we were trying to work against, we needed classroom practices that confronted the power dynamics inside and outside of our classroom.[61]

Ultimately, Ellsworth and her students moved away from utopian abstraction to context-specific classroom practices that acknowledged the complex interplay of "knowledge, power, and desire."[62]

Building on the work of Ellsworth, Gore examines the relationship between empowerment and pedagogy in discourses and practices of critical and feminist pedagogy.[63] Gore sees a distinction between two "strands" of critical pedagogy: the first, represented in the work of Giroux and McLaren, operates at the macro level and emphasizes "a particular (if shifting) social vision."[64] The second, represented in the work of Freire and Shor, operates at the micro level and emphasizes empowerment through instructional practices specific to their contexts.[65] Like Ellsworth, Gore contends that discourses of empowerment within critical pedagogy "attribute extraordinary abilities to the teacher, and hold a view of agency which risks ignoring the context of the teacher's work,"[66] specifically education as a patriarchal institution and site of social regulation. In positioning educators as "already empowered" agents, distinct from the not-yet-empowered student,[67] critical pedagogy oversimplifies agency, context, and power.

Critical pedagogy can also impede instructors from reflecting on their own role in perpetuating oppressive classroom practices. Gore instead argues for an intersectional understanding of empowerment that pays greater attention to context and positionality:

> More attention to contexts would help shift the problem of empowerment from dualisms of power/powerlessness, and dominant/

subordinate, that is, from purely oppositional stances, to a problem
of multiplicity and contradiction…. Context must be conceived as
filled with social actors whose personal and group histories position
them as subjects immersed in social patterns.[68]

The same uneasy tension around empowerment and authority exists in critical
library pedagogy and for library instructors; the same complex contexts frame
and constrain our work. These tensions are further complicated by librarians'
marginal status on campus and continuous pursuit of higher standing through
credentialing in the prestige hierarchy of higher education.[69] It is not surprising,
then, that related critiques of critical library pedagogy's narratives of librarians'
agency and empowerment have recently surfaced within the LIS literature as
well, although the fact that these critiques have come primarily, if not exclusively,
from BIPOC librarians is significant. For example, Loyer suggests that relationality (how we are related to each other) and reciprocity (who we are accountable
to and responsible for), concepts "informed by our relationships to the land" that
"animate the work of information as Indigenous resurgence,"[70] are largely absent
from discussions of critical librarianship and pedagogy. Loyer goes on to ask:

Is there space in critical librarianship for Indigenous kinship, for
wâhkôhtowin? The space is overwhelmingly white in many cases….
Though critical librarianship prompts us to ask who is missing from
these conversations, I still don't see my people's voices being ampli-
fied. Where are the Indigenous people in critical librarianship?[71]

Leung and López-McKnight assert that critical library pedagogy fails to
"engage …with race, power, and [w]hite [s]upremacy,"[72] rendering it "inadequate" as a liberatory framework for dismantling white supremacy within the
profession and within higher education. This failure can create a profound sense
of alienation for librarians from marginalized groups, resulting in "a destructive
separation of our identities and positionalities from our teaching selves."[73] These
authors further elaborate:

How can we share authority we never had? What does it mean for
us to share power we had to fight for with students? What do we do
when we're mistaken for the student rather than the librarian there to
teach a library workshop? What does it mean for a librarian of Color,
rather than a white librarian, to be "authentic" in the classroom, when
we aren't allowed to be anywhere else?[74]

Building on these ideas, Douglas observes that "assumptions made in critical information literacy," including the notions that "people need liberating" and "[l]ibrarians teaching information literacy hold power," make assumptions about who is doing the teaching. She goes on to note that, like many other BIPOC librarians, she finds herself at odds with critical librarianship's "loose collective."[75]

These critiques of critical library pedagogy reveal the ways that narratives of librarians' deficiency, agency, and empowerment in the classroom reinforce white savior narratives and white supremacy in librarianship.[76] Narratives that position patrons (or students) as "deficient, inherently needy, or in need of saving"[77] can also be associated with vocational awe and the archetype of the benevolent white woman in the library.[78] Like Gore before us, we conclude that advocates of critical library pedagogy should direct our energies toward "seeking ways to exercise power" that align with "our espoused aims, ways that include humility, skepticism, and self-criticism."[79] Ferretti and Leung and López-McKnight similarly call upon us to engage in critical self-reflection.[80] An important first step in this process is moving away from narratives of agency and empowerment toward narratives centered in labor and solidarity.

Conclusion

In our view, critical library pedagogy can work to advance social justice only when it is understood as a collective practice grounded in specific social and institutional contexts, namely, "the racist, misogynistic, capitalist, colonialist history and legacy of libraries."[81] Conceiving of critical library pedagogy as care work and as collaborative and contextual labor practices might provide a way forward. As Ismael, Lazzaro, and Ishihara argue, "understanding the care work of education as labor is a step toward mitigating its potential exploitation by helping workers understand what working conditions will sustain the kind of care work that our students deserve."[82] Likewise, Chaput contends that one way to live through the complex subjectivity of "oppositional thinkers [such as critical librarians] in the university" is "to reappropriate our professional embodiedness" through a "working-class professionalism"[83] in which professionals identify as laborers. Similarly, reframing critical library pedagogy as an ongoing process of higher education reform undertaken collaboratively and in solidarity with other workers offers another possibility for reclaiming its liberatory potential, as Elmborg argues.

> Being a literacy worker involves something other than imparting
> skills. It involves connecting daily work with students, colleagues,

and institutions to larger ideological questions about who belongs
in higher education and how to make higher education as accessible
as possible to everyone.[84]

In this chapter, we have considered how we might reenvision critical library
pedagogy as caring work undertaken in solidarity with our colleagues. Such
reframing requires us to interrogate the assumptions of the content and methods
of library instruction. It requires us to acknowledge teaching as caring work, as
immaterial affective labor, and to critically examine discourses of critical pedagogy and critical library pedagogy, particularly their understandings of agency
and empowerment. It requires us to attend to the structures and conditions that
shape contemporary higher education and academic libraries and to establish
boundaries, expectations, and policies that push back against vocational and
institutional awe, creating a more equitable workload for library instructors.[85]
It requires us to "explore our teaching and learning experiences against, and
through, white supremacy—while interrogating, and responding to critical
library instruction."[86] This chapter represents a partial effort forward, in the framing of Sara Ahmed, and we hope other librarians will help make the path clearer.[87]

Notes

1. Maria T. Accardi, Emily Drabinski, and Alana Kumbier, eds., *Critical Library Instruction: Theories and Methods* (Duluth, MN: Library Juice Press, 2010).
2. Patti Ryan and Lisa Sloniowski, "The Public Academic Library: Friction in the Teflon Tunnel," in *Information Literacy and Social Justice*, ed. Lua Gregory and Shana Higgins (Sacramento, CA: Library Juice Press, 2013), 276.
3. Emily Drabinski, "Toward a *Kairos* of Library Instruction," *Journal of Academic Librarianship* 40, no. 5 (September 2014): 484, https://doi.org/10.1016/j.acalib.2014.06.002.
4. Eamon Tewell, "The Practice and Promise of Critical Information Literacy: Academic Librarians' Involvement in Critical Library Instruction," *College and Research Libraries* 79, no. 1 (2018): 11, https://doi.org/https://doi.org/10.5860/crl.79.1.10.
5. Emily Drabinski, "A Kairos of the Critical: Teaching Critically in a Time of Compliance," *Communications in Information Literacy* 11, no. 1 (2017): 76.
6. Ryan and Sloniowski, "The Public Academic Library," 275.
7. Eamon Tewell, "A Decade of Critical Information Literacy: A Review of the Literature," *Communications in Information Literacy* 9, no. 1 (2015): 25–26, https://doi.org/10.15760/comminfolit.2015.9.1.174.
8. Maura Seale, "Critical Library Instruction, Causing Trouble, and Institutionalization," *Communications in Information Literacy* 14, no. 1 (2020) 79.
9. Jennifer M. Ferretti, "Building a Critical Culture: How Critical Librarianship Falls Short in the Workplace," *Communications in Information Literacy* 14, no. 1 (2020): 134.
10. Sofia Y. Leung and J. R. López-McKnight, "Dreaming Revolutionary Futures: Critical Race's Centrality to Ending White Supremacy," *Communications in Information Literacy* 14, no. 1 (2020): 14, https://doi.org/10.15760/comminfolit.2020.14.1.2.
11. Leung and López-McKnight, "Dreaming Revolutionary Futures," 15.
12. Alison Hicks and Annemaree Lloyd, "Relegating Expertise: The Outward and Inward Positioning of Librarians in Information Literacy Education," *Journal of Librarianship and Information Science* 54, no. 3 (September 2022): 415–26, https://doi.org/10.1177/09610006211020104; Alison Hicks and

Annemaree Lloyd, "Deconstructing Information Literacy Discourse: Peeling Back the Layers in Higher Education," *Journal of Librarianship and Information Science* 53, no. 4 (December 2021): 559–71, https://doi.org/10.1177/0961000620966027.

13. Peter McLaren, *Life in Schools: An Introduction to Critical Pedagogy in the Foundation of Education* (New York: Longman, 1989), 221, quoted in Jennifer M. Gore, "What Can We Do For You! What Can 'We' Do for 'You'? Struggling over Empowerment in Critical and Feminist Pedagogy," *Journal of Educational Foundations* 4, no. 3 (1990): 8.

14. Elizabeth Ellsworth, "Why Doesn't This Feel Empowering? Working through the Repressive Myths of Critical Pedagogy," *Harvard Educational Review* 59, no. 3 (August 1989): 315.

15. David James Hudson, "On Critical Librarianship & Pedagogies of the Practical." Keynote, Critical Librarianship and Pedagogy Symposium, Tucson, AZ, February 25, 2016, https://youtu.be/cP--V1oSllE.

16. Julia Ismael, Althea Eannace Lazzaro, and Brianna Ishihara, "It Takes Heart: The Experiences and Working Conditions of Caring Educators," *Radical Teacher* 119 (2021): 32, https://doi.org/10.5195/rt.2021.707.

17. Ismael, Lazzaro, and Ishihara, "It Takes Heart," 32.

18. Lisa Sloniowski, "Affective Labor, Resistance, and the Academic Librarian," *Library Trends* 64, no. 4 (2016): 645–66, https://doi.org/10.1353/lib.2016.0013; Stacy Allison-Cassin, "Bodies, Brains, and Machines: An Exploration of the Relationship between the Material and Affective States of Librarians and Information Systems," *Library Trends* 68, no. 3 (Winter 2020): 409–30, https://doi.org/10.1353/lib.2020.0009.

19. Sloniowski, "Affective Labor."

20. Ismael, Lazzaro, and Ishihara, "It Takes Heart," 32.

21. Veronica Arellano Douglas and Joanna Gadsby, "Gendered Labor and Library Instruction Coordinators: The Undervaluing of Feminized Work," In *At the Helm: Leading Transformation: The Proceedings of the ACRL Conference*, ed. Dawn M. Mueller (Chicago: Association of College and Research Libraries, 2017) 266–74, https://alair.ala.org/bitstream/handle/11213/17739/GenderedLaborandLibraryInstructionCoordinators.pdf?sequence=1&isAllowed=y; Veronica Arellano Douglas and Joanna Gadsby, "All Carrots, No Sticks: Relational Practice and Library Instruction Coordination," *In the Library with the Lead Pipe*, July 10, 2019, https://www.inthelibrarywiththeleadpipe.org/2019/all-carrots-no-sticks-relational-practice-and-library-instruction-coordination/; Rafia Mirza and Maura Seale, "Dudes Code, Ladies Coordinate: Gendered Labor in Digital Scholarship" (presentation, Digital Library Forum. Pittsburgh, PA, October 23–25, 2017), https://osf.io/hj3ks/; Sloniowski, "Affective Labor"; Ismael, Lazzaro, and Ishihara, "It Takes Heart."

22. Sloniowski, "Affective Labor," 651; see also Mirza and Seale, "Dudes Code, Ladies Coordinate."

23. Sloniowski, "Affective Labor," 653; see also Mirza and Seale, "Dudes Code, Ladies Coordinate."; Douglas and Gadsby, 2017.

24. Alison Mountz et al., "For Slow Scholarship: A Feminist Politics of Resistance through Collective Action in the Neoliberal University," *ACME: An International Journal for Critical Geographies* 14, no. 4 (2015): 1235–59, https://acme-journal.org/index.php/acme/article/view/1058; Ismael, Lazzaro, and Ishihara, "It Takes Heart."

25. Kawanna Bright, "A Woman of Color's Work Is Never Done: Intersectionality, Emotional and Invisible Labor in Reference and Information Work," in *Pushing the Margins: Women of Color and Intersectionality in LIS*, ed. Rose L. Chou and Annie Pho (Sacramento, CA: Library Juice Press, 2018), 163–96; Amy VanScoy and Kawanna Bright, "Articulating the Experience of Uniqueness and Difference for Librarians of Color," *Library Quarterly: Information, Community, Policy* 89, no. 4 (October 2019): 285–97, https://doi.org/10.1086/704962.

26. Ismael, Lazzaro, and Ishihara, "It Takes Heart," 33.

27. Maria T. Accardi, *Feminist Pedagogy for Library Instruction* (Sacramento, CA: Library Juice Press, 2013), 25.

28. James K. Elmborg, "Critical Information Literacy: Implications for Instructional Practice," *Journal of Academic Librarianship* 32, no. 2 (March 2006): 192–99, https://doi.org/10.1016/j.acalib.2005.12.004; Heidi L. M. Jacobs, "Information Literacy and Reflective Pedagogical Praxis," *Journal of Academic Librarianship* 34, no. 3 (May 2008): 256–62, https://doi.org/10.1016/j.acalib.2008.03.009; Accardi,

Drabinski, and Kumbier, eds., *Critical Library Instruction*; Accardi, *Feminist Pedagogy for Library Instruction*; Annie Downey, *Critical Information Literacy: Foundations, Inspiration, and Ideas* (Duluth, MN: Library Juice Press, 2016); Tewell, "Practice and Promise."

29. Douglas and Gadsby, "All Carrots, No Sticks."
30. Jessie Loyer, "Indigenous Information Literacy: nêhiyaw Kinship Enabling Self-Care in Research," in *The Politics of Theory and the Practice of Critical Librarianship*, ed. Karen P. Nicholson and Maura Seale (Sacramento, CA: Library Juice Press, 2018), 151.
31. Ismael, Lazzaro, and Ishihara, "It Takes Heart," 33.
32. Ismael, Lazzaro, and Ishihara, "It Takes Heart," 31.
33. Melissa Gregg, *Counterproductive* (Durham, NC: Duke University Press, 2018), 189.
34. Gregg, *Counterproductive*, 187.
35. Karen P. Nicholson, "'Being in Time': New Public Management, Academic Librarians, and the Temporal Labor of Pink-Collar Public Service Work," *Library Trends* 68, no. 2 (Fall 2019): 130–52, https://doi.org/10.1353/lib.2019.0034.
36. Nicholson, "Being in Time," 130.
37. Sherianne Shuler and Nathan Morgan, "Emotional Labor in the Academic Library: When Being Friendly Feels like Work," *Reference Librarian* 54, no. 2 (2013): 118–33, https://doi.org/10.1080/02763877.2013.756684; Celia Emmelhainz, Erin Pappas, and Maura Seale, "Behavioral Expectations for the Mommy Librarian: The Successful Reference Transaction as Emotional Labor," in *The Feminist Reference Desk: Concepts, Critiques, and Conversations*, ed. Maria Accardi (Sacramento: Library Juice Press, 2017), 27-45.; Miriam L. Matteson, Sharon Chittock, and David Mease, "In Their Own Words: Stories of Emotional Labor from the Library Workforce," *Library Quarterly: Information, Community, Policy* 85, no. 1 (January 2015): 85–105, https://doi.org/10.1086/679027; Douglas and Gadsby, "Gendered Labor"; Douglas and Gadsby, "All Carrots, No Sticks"; Sloniowski, "Affective Labor, Resistance, and the Academic Librarian."
38. Ismael, Lazzaro, and Ishihara, "It Takes Heart," 32.
39. Fobazi Ettarh, "Vocational Awe and Librarianship: The Lies We Tell Ourselves," *In the Library with the Lead Pipe*, January 10, 2018, https://www.inthelibrarywiththeleadpipe.org/2018/vocational-awe/.
40. John Warner, "'Institutional Awe' Makes for Bad Leadership," Inside Higher Ed, August 19, 2020, https://www.insidehighered.com/blogs/just-visiting/institutional-awe-makes-bad-leadership; emphasis in the original.
41. Warner, "'Institutional Awe' Makes for Bad Leadership."
42. Ismael, Lazzaro, and Ishihara, "It Takes Heart," 31.
43. Drabinski, "A Kairos of the Critical,"83.
44. Hicks and Lloyd, "Deconstructing Information Literacy Discourse."
45. Hicks and Lloyd, "Deconstructing Information Literacy Discourse."
46. Hicks and Lloyd, "Deconstructing Information Literacy Discourse."
47. Hicks and Lloyd, "Deconstructing Information Literacy Discourse." 564.
48. Hicks and Lloyd, "Deconstructing Information Literacy Discourse." 564-5.
49. Hicks and Lloyd, "Deconstructing Information Literacy Discourse." 561.
50. Hicks and Lloyd, "Deconstructing Information Literacy Discourse." 566.
51. Hicks and Lloyd, "Deconstructing Information Literacy Discourse." 565.
52. Hicks and Lloyd, "Deconstructing Information Literacy Discourse." 566.
53. Hicks and Lloyd, "Relegating Expertise." 421.
54. Tewell, "Practice and Promise." 10.
55. Ellsworth, "Why Doesn't This Feel Empowering?" 289.
56. Leung and López-McKnight, "Dreaming Revolutionary Futures"; Douglas, "WILU Closing Plenary Session."
57. Lauren Gail Berlant, "Feminism and the Institutions of Intimacy," in *The Politics of Research*, ed. E. Ann Kaplan and George Levine (New Brunswick, NJ: Rutgers University Press, 1997), 143.
58. Ellsworth, "Why Doesn't This Feel Empowering?" 299.
59. Ellsworth, "Why Doesn't This Feel Empowering?" 289.
60. Ellsworth, "Why Doesn't This Feel Empowering?" 300.
61. Ellsworth, "Why Doesn't This Feel Empowering?" 315.

62. Ellsworth, "Why Doesn't This Feel Empowering?" 316.
63. Gore, "What Can We Do for You!"
64. Gore, "What Can We Do for You!" 7.
65. Gore, "What Can We Do for You!" 7.
66. Gore, "What Can We Do for You!" 9.
67. Gore, "What Can We Do for You!" 14.
68. Gore, "What Can We Do for You!" 13.
69. Cathy Eisenhower and Dolsy Smith, "The Library as 'Stuck Place': Critical Pedagogy in the Corporate University," in *Critical Library Instruction: Theories and Methods*, ed. Maria T. Accardi, Emily Drabinski, and Alana Kumbier (Duluth, MN: Library Juice Press, 2010), 305–17; Maura Seale and Rafia Mirza, "Empty Presence: Library Labor, Prestige, and the MLS," *Library Trends* 68, no. 2 (2019): 252–68, https://doi.org/10.1353/lib.2019.0038.
70. Loyer, "Indigenous Information Literacy," 154.
71. Loyer describes wâhkôhtowin as "a life philosophy, worldview and way of life" that foregrounds "the kinship connections …to all of creation" in Michif culture. Loyer, "Indigenous Information Literacy," 151, 154.
72. Leung and López-McKnight, "Dreaming Revolutionary Futures," 15.
73. Leung and López-McKnight, "Dreaming Revolutionary Futures," 17.
74. Leung and López-McKnight, "Dreaming Revolutionary Futures," 19.
75. Veronica Arellano Douglas, "WILU Closing Plenary Session," *Libraries + Inquiry* (blog), June 25, 2021. https://veronicaarellanodouglas.com/information-literacy-2/wilu-closing-plenary-session/.
76. Ettarh, "Vocational Awe"; Christine Pawley, "Unequal Legacies: Race and Multiculturalism in the LIS Curriculum," *Library Quarterly: Information, Community, Policy* 76, no. 2 (2006): 149–68, https://doi.org/10.1086/506955; Gina Schlesselman-Tarango, "The Legacy of Lady Bountiful: White Women in the Library," *Library Trends* 64, no. 4 (Spring 2016): 667–86, https://doi.org/10.1353/lib.2016.0015.
77. Pawley, "Unequal Legacies," 159.
78. Ettarh, "Vocational Awe"; Pawley, "Unequal Legacies"; Schlesselman-Tarango, "The Legacy of Lady Bountiful."
79. Gore, "What Can We Do for You!" 21.
80. Ferretti, "Building a Critical Culture," 134; Leung and López-McKnight, "Dreaming Revolutionary Futures," 22.
81. Leung and López-McKnight, "Dreaming Revolutionary Futures," 22.
82. Ismael, Lazzaro, and Ishihara, "It Takes Heart," 32.
83. Catherine Chaput, *Inside the Teaching Machine* (Tuscaloosa: University of Alabama Press, 2015), 2.
84. James K. Elmborg, "Critical Information Literacy: Definitions and Challenges," in *Transforming Information Literacy Programs: Intersecting Frontiers of Self, Library Culture, and Campus Community*, ed. Carroll Wetzel Wilkinson and Courtney Bruch (Chicago: Association of College and Research Libraries, 2012), 94.
85. Anne Helen Petersen, "Imagine Your Flexible Office Work Future," *Culture Study*, March 1, 2021, https://annehelen.substack.com/p/imagine-your-flexible-office-work.
86. Leung and López-McKnight, "Dreaming Revolutionary Futures," 22.
87. Gore, "What Can We Do for You!" 15; Sara Ahmed, *What's the Use? On the Uses of Use* (Durham, NC: Duke University Press, 2019).

Bibliography

Accardi, Maria T. *Feminist Pedagogy for Library Instruction*. Sacramento, CA: Library Juice Press, 2013.
Accardi, Maria T., Emily Drabinski, and Alana Kumbier, eds. *Critical Library Instruction: Theories and Methods*. Duluth, MN: Library Juice Press, 2010.
Ahmed, Sara. *What's the Use? On the Uses of Use*. Durham, NC: Duke University Press, 2019.
Allison-Cassin, Stacy. "Bodies, Brains, and Machines: An Exploration of the Relationship between the Material and Affective States of Librarians and Information Systems." *Library Trends* 68, no. 3 (Winter 2020): 409–30. https://doi.org/10.1353/lib.2020.0009.

Berlant, Lauren Gail. "Feminism and the Institutions of Intimacy." In *The Politics of Research*, edited by E. Ann Kaplan and George Levine, 143–61. New Brunswick, NJ: Rutgers University Press, 1997.

Bright, Kawanna. "A Woman of Color's Work Is Never Done: Intersectionality, Emotional and Invisible Labor in Reference and Information Work." In *Pushing the Margins: Women of Color and Intersectionality in LIS*, edited by Rose L. Chou and Annie Pho, 163–96. Sacramento, CA: Library Juice Press, 2018.

Chaput, Catherine. *Inside the Teaching Machine: Rhetoric and the Globalization of the U.S. Public Research University*. Tuscaloosa: University of Alabama Press, 2015.

Douglas, Veronica Arellano. "WILU Closing Plenary Session." *Libraries + Inquiry* (blog), June 25, 2021. https://veronicaarellanodouglas.com/information-literacy-2/wilu-closing-plenary-session/.

Douglas, Veronica Arellano, and Joanna Gadsby. "All Carrots, No Sticks: Relational Practice and Library Instruction Coordination." *In the Library with the Lead Pipe*. July 10, 2019. https://www.inthelibrarywiththeleadpipe.org/2019/all-carrots-no-sticks-relational-practice-and-library-instruction-coordination/.

———. "Gendered Labor and Library Instruction Coordinators: The Undervaluing of Feminized Work." In *At the Helm: Leading Transformation: The Proceedings of the ACRL Conference*, edited by Dawn M. Mueller, 266–74. Chicago: Association of College and Research Libraries, 2017. https://alair.ala.org/bitstream/handle/11213/17739/GenderedLaborandLibraryInstructionCoordinators.pdf?sequence=1&isAllowed=y .

Downey, Annie. *Critical Information Literacy: Foundations, Inspiration, and Ideas*. Duluth, MN: Library Juice Press, 2016.

Drabinski, Emily. "A Kairos of the Critical: Teaching Critically in a Time of Compliance." *Communications in Information Literacy* 11, no. 1 (2017): 76–94.

———. "Toward a *Kairos* of Library Instruction." *Journal of Academic Librarianship* 40, no. 5 (September 2014): 480–85. https://doi.org/10.1016/j.acalib.2014.06.002.

Eisenhower, Cathy, and Dolsy Smith. "The Library as 'Stuck Place': Critical Pedagogy in the Corporate University." In *Critical Library Instruction: Theories and Methods*, edited by Maria T. Accardi, Emily Drabinski, and Alana Kumbier, 305–17. Duluth, MN: Library Juice Press, 2010.

Ellsworth, Elizabeth. "Why Doesn't This Feel Empowering? Working through the Repressive Myths of Critical Pedagogy." *Harvard Educational Review* 59, no. 3 (August 1989): 297–325.

Elmborg, James K. "Critical Information Literacy: Definitions and Challenges." In *Transforming Information Literacy Programs: Intersecting Frontiers of Self, Library Culture, and Campus Community*, edited by Carroll Wetzel Wilkinson and Courtney Bruch, 75–95. Chicago: Association of College and Research Libraries, 2012.

———. "Critical Information Literacy: Implications for Instructional Practice." *Journal of Academic Librarianship* 32, no. 2 (March 2006): 192–99. https://doi.org/10.1016/j.acalib.2005.12.004.

Emmelhainz, Celia, Erin Pappas, and Maura Seale. "Behavioral Expectations for the Mommy Librarian: The Successful Reference Transaction as Emotional Labor." In *The Feminist Reference Desk: Concepts, Critiques, and Conversations*, edited by Maria Accardi, 27-45. Sacramento: Library Juice Press, 2017.

Ettarh, Fobazi. "Vocational Awe and Librarianship: The Lies We Tell Ourselves." *In the Library with the Lead Pipe*, January 10, 2018. https://www.inthelibrarywiththeleadpipe.org/2018/vocational-awe/.

Ferretti, Jennifer A. "Building a Critical Culture: How Critical Librarianship Falls Short in the Workplace." *Communications in Information Literacy* 14, no. 1 (2020): 134–52.

Gore, Jennifer M. "What Can We Do for You! What Can 'We' Do for 'You'? Struggling over Empowerment in Critical and Feminist Pedagogy." *Journal of Educational Foundations* 4, no. 3 (1990): 5–26.

Gregg, Melissa. *Counterproductive: Time Management in the Knowledge Economy*. Durham, NC: Duke University Press, 2018.

Hicks, Alison, and Annemaree Lloyd. "Deconstructing Information Literacy Discourse: Peeling Back the Layers in Higher Education." *Journal of Librarianship and Information Science* 53, no. 4 (December 2021): 559–71. https://doi.org/10.1177/0961000620966027.

———. "Relegating Expertise: The Outward and Inward Positioning of Librarians in Information Literacy Education." *Journal of Librarianship and Information Science* 54, no. 3 (September 2022): 415–26. https://doi.org/10.1177/09610006211020104.

Hudson, David James. "On Critical Librarianship & Pedagogies of the Practical." Keynote, Critical Librarianship and Pedagogy Symposium, Tucson, AZ, February 25, 2016, https://youtu.be/cP--V1oSllE.

Ismael, Julia, Althea Eannace Lazzaro, and Brianna Ishihara. "It Takes Heart: The Experiences and Working Conditions of Caring Educators." *Radical Teacher* 119 (2021): 30–40. https://doi.org/10.5195/rt.2021.707.

Jacobs, Heidi L. M. "Information Literacy and Reflective Pedagogical Praxis." *Journal of Academic Librarianship* 34, no. 3 (May 2008): 256–62. https://doi.org/10.1016/j.acalib.2008.03.009.

Leung, Sofia Y., and J. R. López-McKnight. "Dreaming Revolutionary Futures: Critical Race's Centrality to Ending White Supremacy." *Communications in Information Literacy* 14, no. 1 (2020): 12–26. https://doi.org/10.15760/comminfolit.2020.14.1.2.

Loyer, Jessie. "Indigenous Information Literacy: nêhiyaw Kinship Enabling Self-Care in Research." In *The Politics of Theory and the Practice of Critical Librarianship*, edited by Karen P. Nicholson and Maura Seale, 145–56. Sacramento, CA: Library Juice Press, 2018.

Matteson, Miriam L., Sharon Chittock, and David Mease. "In Their Own Words: Stories of Emotional Labor from the Library Workforce." *Library Quarterly: Information, Community, Policy* 85, no. 1 (January 2015): 85–105. https://doi.org/10.1086/679027.

McLaren, Peter. *Life in Schools: An Introduction to Critical Pedagogy in the Foundations of Education*. New York: Longman, 1989,

Mirza, Rafia, and Maura Seale. "Dudes Code, Ladies Coordinate: Gendered Labor in Digital Scholarship." Presentation, Digital Library Forum, Pittsburgh, PA, October 23–25, 2017. https://osf.io/hj3ks/.

Mountz, Alison, Anne Bonds, Becky Mansfield, Jenna Loyd, Jennifer Hyndman, Margaret Walton-Roberts, Ranu Basu, Risa Whitson, Roberta Hawkins, Trina Hamilton, and Winifred Curran. "For Slow Scholarship: A Feminist Politics of Resistance through Collective Action in the Neoliberal University." *ACME: An International Journal for Critical Geographies* 14, no. 4 (2015): 1235–59. https://acme-journal.org/index.php/acme/article/view/1058.

Nicholson, Karen P. "'Being in Time': New Public Management, Academic Librarians, and the Temporal Labor of Pink-Collar Public Service Work." *Library Trends* 68, no. 2 (Fall 2019): 130–52. https://doi.org/10.1353/lib.2019.0034.

Pawley, Christine. "Unequal Legacies: Race and Multiculturalism in the LIS Curriculum." *Library Quarterly: Information, Community, Policy* 76, no. 2 (2006): 149–68. https://doi.org/10.1086/506955.

Petersen, Anne Helen. "Imagine Your Flexible Office Work Future." *Culture Study*, March 1, 2021. https://annehelen.substack.com/p/imagine-your-flexible-office-work.

Ryan, Patti, and Lisa Sloniowski. "The Public Academic Library: Friction in the Teflon Tunnel." In *Information Literacy and Social Justice*, edited by Lua Gregory and Shana Higgins, 275–300. Sacramento, CA: Library Juice Press, 2013.

Schlesselman-Tarango, Gina. "The Legacy of Lady Bountiful: White Women in the Library." *Library Trends* 64, no. 4 (Spring 2016): 667–86. https://doi.org/10.1353/lib.2016.0015.

Seale, Maura. "Critical Library Instruction, Causing Trouble, and Institutionalization." *Communications in Information Literacy* 14, no. 1 (2020): 75–85.

Seale, Maura, and Rafia Mirza. "Empty Presence: Library Labor, Prestige, and the MLS." *Library Trends* 68, no. 2 (2019): 252–68. https://doi.org/10.1353/lib.2019.0038.

Shuler, Sherianne, and Nathan Morgan. "Emotional Labor in the Academic Library: When Being Friendly Feels like Work." *Reference Librarian* 54, no. 2 (2013): 118–33. https://doi.org/10.1080/02763877.2013.756684.

Sloniowski, Lisa. "Affective Labor, Resistance, and the Academic Librarian." *Library Trends* 64, no. 4 (2016): 645–66. https://doi.org/10.1353/lib.2016.0013.

Tewell, Eamon. "A Decade of Critical Information Literacy: A Review of the Literature." *Communications in Information Literacy* 9, no. 1 (2015): 24–43. https://doi.org/10.15760/comminfolit.2015.9.1.174.

———. "The Practice and Promise of Critical Information Literacy: Academic Librarians' Involvement in Critical Library Instruction." *College and Research Libraries* 79, no. 1 (2018): 10–34. https://doi.org/https://doi.org/10.5860/crl.79.1.10.

VanScoy, Amy, and Kawanna Bright. "Articulating the Experience of Uniqueness and Difference for Librarians of Color." *Library Quarterly: Information, Community, Policy* 89, no. 4 (October 2019): 285–97. https://doi.org/10.1086/704962.

Warner, John. "'Institutional Awe' Makes for Bad Leadership." *Inside Higher Ed*, August 19, 2020. https://www.insidehighered.com/blogs/just-visiting/institutional-awe-makes-bad-leadership.

CHAPTER 7

Beyond Sustainability and Self-Care

Veronica Arellano Douglas, Emily Deal, and Carolina Hernandez

Introduction

In *Teaching to Transgress,* bell hooks introduced the concept of engaged pedagogy, a model of education that "does not seek to simply empower students …[but] will also be a place where teachers grow and are empowered by the [learning] process."[1] It's a feminist expansion of critical pedagogy that takes into account the personhood of the teacher as well as the student, creating a co-learning environment rooted in mutual respect where intellectual and personal development can flourish. As critical pedagogy has become more widely accepted in academic librarianship, many teaching librarians have adopted educational practices that embolden students and seek to expand the concept of critical consciousness. We downplay our authority in the classroom to create a space in which our students can learn from one another, we acknowledge the strengths our students bring to the classroom and the lives they have outside of it, and we want students to feel a sense of agency in their education. However, in doing so, we often neglect to think about what we may need from the classroom experience: a sense of community, a feeling of mattering in the educational context, and a connection

to learners. How can we sustain such an intensive practice of teaching without caring for ourselves as well as students?

In this chapter, we will examine what we can do as a profession to create a critical, engaged, and emotionally sustainable practice of teaching in libraries. We will acknowledge the problematic values that frequently accompany teaching librarianship and discuss the attempts critical pedagogy practices have made to ameliorate those harmful experiences. There is also a need to critique the typically accepted approaches to cultivating sustainable teaching programs in academic libraries—self-care and standardization—which either place the responsibility for well-being on librarians or create business-like models for "efficient" teaching practices. Instead, we will set engaged pedagogy as a foundation for all teaching practices. In doing so we return to the roots of self-care as described by Audre Lorde, as a political act by and for BIPOC women; build off the principles of community care to push against ideas of sustainability; and work toward empowerment for everyone involved in learning experiences.

The Work of Teaching in Libraries + Critical Pedagogy

Teaching is an inherently relational act, dependent on the interactions and relationships between teachers, students, and in the case of teaching librarians, faculty as well. Harriett Schwartz describes "relationship as the site and source of learning," the place where ideas and affect meet and are exchanged.[2] Yet so often in academic libraries, those in instruction-related roles exist in a state of tension. We are asked to teach more, show value, prove worth, and do more with less, all at the expense of cultivating relationships and care within those interactions.[3] The focus is not on why we do what we do but rather on what we do and how often we do it.[4] The work of teaching librarians is feminized, but not feminist and is undervalued within structures of academic libraries that focus on new technologies, return on investment, and shiny new projects.[5] Under these circumstances, teaching becomes an extractive practice, one where instruction librarians give of themselves until they are left with only stress, demotivation, and burnout.[6] Students become an afterthought to delivery of content, teaching statistics, and institutional value initiatives. There is nothing reciprocal or fulfilling about this kind of work, and in the end it becomes rote.

Critical pedagogy broadly, and critical library instruction and critical information literacy in particular, attempt to push back on the value-laden neoliberal approach to teaching in academic libraries. In *The Critical Library Pedagogy*

Handbook, Nicole Pagowsky and Kelly McElroy define critical pedagogy as "engaging in the theory and practice (or praxis) of inclusive and reflective teaching in order to broaden students' understanding of power structures within the education system and in society."[7] Through critical pedagogy, teachers and students participate in a learning partnership by which students develop a critical consciousness that will serve them in all facets of life and encourage action in the face of injustice.[8] Within critical librarianship there is a tendency to conflate critical information literacy and critical pedagogy, and although the two are distinct (one is content, one is praxis), it's difficult to teach critical information literacy without a critical pedagogical approach. Eamon Tewell's "The Practice and Promise of Critical Information Literacy" looks at both method and content of critical instruction among academic librarians and shows that teaching librarians find a better sense of learning community, student engagement, and personal meaning through critical information literacy and critical pedagogy.[9] Yet academic teaching librarians who embrace critical pedagogy are continuously challenged by institutional pressures to quantify learning, make teaching more efficient, reach more students, and stick to teaching methods and content that emphasize assignment needs, research skills, and transferability to the workplace.[10] Critical pedagogy in library instruction needs a supportive underpinning to be able to exist within increasingly neoliberal academic contexts. Simply encouraging academic librarians to pursue critical pedagogy and critical information literacy does not make it a possible or sustainable practice. So what can help us create meaningful, engaged, critically conscious learning experiences for students in a long-term, continuous way? To answer this question, we must examine the discourse of sustainable teaching practices in libraries.

Efforts at Sustainability

Academic library teaching programs often suffer from issues of scale and sustainability. They operate on a reactive model: teaching librarians or liaison librarians solicit requests for one- (or two- or three-) shot information literacy workshops and then accommodate these classes as best as they can with existing personnel and resources. This often leads to unpredictable demand—overwhelming requests for in-person classes that may or may not be curricularly relevant—and an inability to meet the needs of students and course instructors.[11] This leaves instruction librarians and coordinators in the precarious position of being victims of their own successes, so to speak, where they are able to point to increased teaching numbers and instruction requests but individual teaching librarians suffer from overwork and stress. Rather than change the approach to teaching in libraries, emphasis is often placed on two methods of sustainability for long-term work in instruction programs: self-care and standardization.

Self-care is a concept with radical origins. There is an oft-quoted statement from Audre Lorde, from her book *A Burst of Light*: "Caring for myself is not self-indulgence; it is self-preservation, and that is an act of political warfare."[12] This conceptualization of self-care is still relevant and important today, particularly for BIPOC women, who are often left to fend for themselves. However, self-care has also been co-opted through capitalism, which has made it more of an individualistic and performative practice.[13] It has become about uncritical consumption that fails to actually address any root issue or problem. Instead, in the context of the workplace, self-care has become about taking care of oneself not so much for the sake of personal mental health concerns, but for the sake of being able to maintain a sustainable and efficient workload.

In librarianship broadly, we see that self-care is often presented as a way to mediate the negative effects of being overworked.[14] We can also see this sort of messaging extend to teaching librarians in particular. ACRL's Immersion Program, which provides a week of training on information literacy instruction, recently included a session on avoiding burnout in one's teaching practice. While some of the advice given certainly provides helpful guidance on how to manage one's work-life balance healthily, it often puts the onus on the individual to take care of themself. In focusing on and encouraging self-care as the antidote to burnout, we are ignoring the root cause of the problem: that academic libraries are toxic work environments.

It also absolves organizations and those in charge from making any substantive change to work culture and expectations. For example, one piece of advice that pops up frequently for library workers is to establish healthy boundaries between home life and work. However, this advice does not help much if someone's employer expects them to be available at all times or has established an environment where they are always expected to go above and beyond. There is no acknowledgment of the labor practices that can lead to burnout, and there is not the same push or support for managers and administrators to help their employees avoid burnout. Instead, managers should be the ones setting healthy expectations and modeling proper work-life balance so that employees feel less pressure to overwork themselves. Looking at ACRL's LibGuide "Pandemic Resources for Academic Libraries" demonstrates this disparity in expectations. While this guide does feature a section on self-care and how individuals can manage their work from home, the guide has no similar section that offers guidance to managers looking to support their employees.[15]

In addition to pushing an individualistic, depoliticized version of self-care, standardization of teaching is another commonly proposed solution to the question of sustainability in library instruction. Teaching librarians build LibGuides, online modules and tutorials, and standardized lesson plans in an effort to save time and conserve energy, but this kind of standardization only makes teachers interchangeable, dehumanizes teaching librarians, and invisibilizes the labor of teaching. Karen P. Nicholson and others refer to this kind of standardization as part of the "McDonaldization" of academic libraries, which Nicholson argues "reflects the growing influence of corporate aims and values …in the public sector."[16] It is part of the neoliberal agenda of the corporate university, in which information literacy is seen as workforce preparation, students are viewed as customers, and librarians are transformed into trainers rather than educators. These efficiencies in teaching take us away from critical pedagogy, and away from what Nicholson refers to as "feminist slow scholarship," which, as she writes, "seeks to re-envision the university itself by challenging structures of power and inequality and calling attention to the value (and toil) of academic labour."[17]

The technology we rely on to standardize our teaching—from online guides and tutorials to learning management systems—is also an example of *solutionism*, a term used to describe the focus on technology as a solution to complex social problems,[18] and what is teaching if not a complex social problem? In their book chapter "Who Killed the World? White Masculinity and the Technocratic Library of the Future," Rafia Mirza and Maura Seale describe how there is "a continual push for technological interventions to replace even that small amount of interaction between librarians and patrons: tutorials, library guides, badges, FAQs, flipped learning, connected learning, and gamification."[19] And, as they argue, because technocratic ideology is "inextricably bound up in white supremacy and patriarchy,"[20] the so-called technological solutions we use to standardize our teaching further invisibilize and devalue the feminized labor of library instruction.

Community Care

One countermeasure for issues of sustainability is the idea of community care. Rather than turn to capitalist versions of self-care and standardization of education programs at the expense of the people involved in the learning exchange, engaging in community care offers a possible way forward for teaching librarians and library instruction programs. This concept was first introduced in LIS literature by Jessica Schomberg in their chapter titled, "Disability at Work: Libraries, Built to Exclude." Using critical disability theory as a frame, Schomberg posits how we can better support library employees with disabilities and improve the workplace for all. One way is through this idea of community care, which involves providing care for each other and pushing against harmful workplace norms.[21] It is intended to work in stark contrast to the "toxic individualism" that can often take hold in libraries and encourages library employees to work themselves to the bone.[22] Some of Schomberg's suggested approaches for fostering community care at work include allowing flexibility in working from home, hosting potluck gatherings, and acknowledging that some disabilities remain invisible.

Schomberg's application of community care to librarianship was expanded by Dianne N. Brown and Leo Settoducato at a LOEX workshop and subsequent essay, "Caring for Your Community of Practice: Collective Responses to Burnout."[23] Acknowledging that the concept of community care is deeply rooted in the longtime practices of BIPOC communities (especially BIPOC women) outside of library spaces, they argue that "individual action is not a sustainable response to structural issues" that produce library burnout, such as "unstable working conditions, a culture of individualism, and expectations of resilience."[24] Brown and Settoducato define community care as "giving and receiving care in ways that support shared well-being and connectedness, particularly amidst shared struggles."[25] They offer examples of what community care can look like in practice in libraries, from publicly celebrating colleagues' successes, to building a workplace culture in which colleagues regularly check in on each other's well-being. "Ultimately, community care recognizes that we are all people, and caring for/being cared for by people holistically can improve our work life immensely."[26] This sentiment was further echoed by Miriame Kaba and Dean Spade at the ACRL President's Program at the 2021 ALA Annual conference. Spade emphasized the importance of mutual aid within and outside of work environments, asking us all to consider, "What is needed in the communities and spaces I'm in?"[27] If we apply this question to our work as teaching librarians and the impact we can have on one another, it's about finding collective solutions to problems that are frequently seen as individual deficits. We are not letting our organizations off the hook, so to speak, but rather we are seeking means of supporting one another as we work to facilitate change.

While community care is generally an effective strategy in ensuring we as employees can support each other and unite to remedy potentially toxic work environments, it falls short of including students in the conversation. It is a practice that is difficult to extend into the classroom because we cannot obligate students to care about us, the people who are getting paid to do this work. This is a power dynamic we cannot completely undo. However, students are not immune to experiencing burnout and feeling stretched thin. This is the reason that around every finals week, we espouse messages of self-care, encouraging students to take breaks and providing them with therapy dogs, never acknowledging the real stressor of juggling multiple exams while dealing with private problems like food insecurity or mental health. What moves community care into the realm of engaged pedagogy is bringing students into the conversation around collective care, introducing our needs and boundaries and helping them identify their own.

Engaged Pedagogy

To ensure students are also cared for and considered in the development of their learning, the teaching process needs to be a collaborative one that values the input of the learner just as much as that of the teacher. This is the hallmark of engaged pedagogy.

Origins of Engaged Pedagogy

In developing the concept of engaged pedagogy, bell hooks drew inspiration from the critical pedagogy of Paolo Freire as well as the work of Buddhist monk Thich Nhat Hanh, whose philosophy of engaged Buddhism emphasized a "focus on practice in conjunction with contemplation,"[28] similar to Freire's idea of praxis, or "action and reflection upon the world in order to change it."[29] hooks was particularly inspired by Thich Nhat Hanh's holistic approach to education, one that united "mind, body, and spirit"[30] and informed her ideas about engaged pedagogy. According to hooks, what distinguishes engaged pedagogy from critical or feminist pedagogy is its emphasis on well-being for both students and teachers.[31] for both students and teachers. To practice engaged pedagogy, "teachers must be actively committed to a process of self-actualization that promotes their own well-being if they are to teach in a manner that empowers students."[32]

Engaged pedagogy empowers students because it affirms their voices and experiences both in and outside the classroom, but hooks argues that engaged pedagogy benefits teachers as well. She writes, "Any classroom that employs a holistic model of learning will also be a place where teachers grow, and are empowered by the process" but that "empowerment cannot happen if we refuse to be vulnerable while encouraging students to take risks."[33] A kind of mutual (though not coercive) vulnerability between students and teachers is key to hooks's concept of engaged pedagogy and requires most teachers to "practice being vulnerable in the classroom, being wholly present in mind, body, and spirit."[34] Being wholly present in the classroom may feel like an intimidating or uncomfortable prospect for many teachers, but hooks argues that those teachers who "embrace the challenge of self-actualization will be better able to create pedagogical practices that engage students, providing them with ways of knowing that enhance their capacity to live fully and deeply."[35]

Classroom/Learning Environment

Much of what has been written about engaged pedagogy comes from the perspective of the traditional for-credit course or within the context of a larger academic program.[36] In part, this is because teaching a semester- or quarter-length class allows for more time to foster relationships and generate engagement from students. Although most teaching librarians do not teach credit-bearing courses, engaged pedagogy can still apply to information literacy instruction as it is conducted through the guest-lecture/workshop model, frequently called the one-shot (or two- or three-shot!). When considering what engaged pedagogy looks like in practice, it is important to remember that it is not simply a checklist. Instead, it is an approach that will vary depending on your context. For example, while listening to your students and not just talking at them can be an important part of engaged pedagogy, what that looks like in practice within the classroom may differ. It may involve allowing time and space for students to bring up topics and questions that you may not have planned to address originally. Or it could mean ditching your usual script and simply engaging the students in conversation, letting them lead the discussion.

There is also a certain level of vulnerability that is involved with engaged pedagogy. Most of the time, we ask students to participate in class in ways that may leave them feeling exposed to criticism without reciprocating that same level of vulnerability, such as when we prompt them with questions to generate participation in discussions. Instead of putting them on the spot, though, we should also make sure we are sharing our own experiences and perspectives, without dominating the conversation. As hooks points out, this helps us avoid seeming like "all-knowing, silent interrogators."[37] For example, in an activity where you ask students to outline their research process, it can help to share your own process with them, while emphasizing that it's only one way to approach research. Essentially, we should be willing to participate in the same ways that we expect our students to do.

Programs and Structures

To create lasting, systemic change we need to expand engaged pedagogy beyond the actions of individual teaching librarians to the structures and programs that shape information literacy education in academic libraries. In practice, engaged pedagogy requires that those with positional authority and influence create a supportive library, department, or program with boundaries, flexibility, and care for both the learners and teaching librarians. Doing so means treating teaching librarians not as interchangeable cogs in a standardized education machine but as people who bring unique experiences and perspectives to the act of teaching. Rather than creating inflexible or unchangeable activities or lesson plans that all librarians must follow, programs can create templates or suggestions for classes that can be easily modified depending on the needs of the librarian or learners. These teaching materials should be revisited regularly (at the end of the year or semester) to ensure that they are still meeting the needs and interests of the librarians responsible for teaching. Yes, some measure of structure and organization is needed to maintain not only good teaching but also good working conditions; however, there needs to be room for flexibility, change, and an openness to acknowledging what isn't working.

From a structural perspective, rather than focusing on creating information literacy teaching programs that reach as many students as possible in a scaffolded, sequential way (which is often not possible because of major requirements, transfer credits, and other factors out of our control), we should recenter what we value as librarians and educators. We value "learners, whoever they may be and in whatever context they exist; learning, via open minds and integration of past experience and connection; and our relationship with learners and their learning."[38] If our focus is on "the learner, learning, and the learning relationship, then we [as teaching librarians] matter, too."[39] Rather than focus on learning sequences and outcomes, we can build programs that have high impact by focusing on where there are opportunities to build significant learning relationships with students and faculty. For example, rather than viewing an undergraduate major sequence of classes as an opportunity to teach basic, essential, and advanced information literacy skills, we can look at courses within the major to determine where students may need the most support and where we as librarians can make a positive impact, without the restrictions of having to teach only specific skills at set times.

Engaged pedagogy that centers our values also values us as teachers. To do so, individuals who are responsible for shaping teaching programs in libraries should consider the working conditions under which we can best foster a collaborative, engaging learning environment. What would it look like to have an instruction program where librarians aren't just getting through this extremely busy part of the semester to be able to do real work? Instead of reacting to or accepting all teaching requests (however problematic), we could create a program with boundaries that reinforce the important relational nature of teaching and learning. This means setting limits on the amount of teaching we do, saying no to problematic teaching requests, and finding teaching opportunities, both in and out of the classroom, that are fulfilling, enriching, and empowering for both learners and teaching librarians.

It also means facilitating a program that can grow and change with the librarian and learner. In overfocusing on standardization, we lose the ability to respond to the needs of our learners and teacher librarians. Rather than centering content, an information literacy or library instruction program that adopts an engaged pedagogy approach would center the people involved in the learning process. Instead of focusing on acquisition of skills or measurable learning outcomes and assessment that proves worth or value, an engaged pedagogy *program* would reinforce connectedness, relational work, and mutual respect. It would not center the kinds of statistics collected for ACRL or ARL reporting purposes—number of sessions, number of students—but the act of connected learning. Students and teachers alike would engage in an iterative, reflective practice, where students share (verbally, in writing, or through other means) how their thinking has changed or what they've learned in a particular context. Teaching librarians would consistently reflect on not just what they teach but how they teach and how students engage with one another, the ideas, and the teacher. There may not be room in professional or institutional reporting structures for this kind of work, but those of us who manage and lead teaching programs and libraries can reinforce our value on this work through making it a part of annual review, promotion, and feedback processes. A library teaching program can be a site of generative work and holistic education, but it must be an intentional creation on the part of those who lead these programs alongside teaching librarians.

Conclusion

At the core of engaged pedagogy is the idea that the learner and teacher grow and change together through the learning process. The relationship is mutually respectful, as authentic as it can be while maintaining healthy boundaries, and fulfilling for all involved. We recognize that engaged pedagogy in practice may encounter resistance or pushback from those who work in unsupportive library environments, those of us suffering from lack of time or bandwidth, or those who have a more rigid approach to teaching and learning. However, we do believe that there is an opportunity for engaged pedagogy in most academic library contexts. We can identify where we can care for and support one another in small ways as an act of resistance while still pushing for broader systemic change within our organizations. Our teaching programs are not going to be transformed overnight or even in a year, but we can begin to look for spaces where engaged pedagogy can take hold. Small tactics in response to capitalist sustainability narratives can create a model and room for more caring, supportive, and even radical approaches to teaching and learning. As adrienne maree brown states, "what we practice at the small scale sets the patterns for the whole system," so we must work within roles we inhabit to create change in education.[40]

Notes

1. bell hooks, *Teaching to Transgress* (New York: Routledge, 1994), 21.
2. Harriet L. Schwartz, *Connected Teaching* (Sterling, VA: Stylus, 2019), 14.
3. Karen Nicholson, "'Taking Back' Information Literacy: Time and the One-Shot in the Neoliberal University," in *Critical Library Pedagogy Handbook*, vol. 1, ed. Nicole Pagowsky and Kelly McElroy (Chicago: Association of College and Research Libraries, 2016), 25–39; Megan Oakleaf, *The Value of Academic Libraries* (Chicago: Association of College and Research Libraries, 2010), https://www.ala.org/acrl/sites/ala.org.acrl/files/content/issues/value/val_report.pdf; Jacob Berg, Angela Galvan, and Eamon Tewell, "Responding to and Reimagining Resilience in Academic Libraries," *Journal of New Librarianship* 3, no. 1 (2018): 1–4, https://doi.org/10.21173/newlibs/4/1.
4. David James Hudson, "The Whiteness of Practicality," in *Topographies of Whiteness: Mapping Whiteness in Library and Information Studies*, ed. Gina Schlesselman-Tarango (Sacramento, CA: Library Juice Press, 2017), 203–34.
5. Veronica Arellano Douglas and Joanna Gadsby, "Gendered Labor and Library Instruction Coordinators: The Undervaluing of Feminized Work," in *At the Helm: Leading Transformation: The Proceedings of the ACRL 2017 Conference*, ed. Dawn M. Mueller (Chicago: Association of College and Research Libraries, 2017), 266–74, https://alair.ala.org/bitstream/handle/11213/17739/GenderedLaborandLibraryInstructionCoordinators.pdf?sequence=1&isAllowed=y; Maura Seale, "Critical Library Instruction, Causing Trouble, and Institutionalization," *Communications in Information Literacy* 14, no. 1 (2020): 75–85, https://doi.org/10.15760/comminfolit.2020.14.1.6.
6. Mary Ann Affleck, "Burnout among Bibliographic Instruction Librarians," *Library and Information Science Research* 18, no. 2 (Spring 1996): 165–83, https://doi.org/10.1016/S0740-8188(96)90018-3; Deborah F. Sheesley, "Burnout and the Academic Teaching Librarian: An Examination of the Problem and Suggested Solutions," *Journal of Academic Librarianship* 27, no. 6 (November 2001): 447–51.
7. Nicole Pagowsky and Kelly McElroy, "Introduction," in *Critical Library Pedagogy Handbook*, vol. 1, ed. Nicole Pagowsky and Kelly McElroy (Chicago: Association of College and Research Libraries, 2016), xvii.
8. Pagowsky and McElroy, "Introduction"; Eamon Tewell, "The Practice and Promise of Critical Information Literacy: Academic Librarians' Involvement in Critical Library Instruction," *College and Research Libraries* 79, no. 1 (January 2018): 10–32, https://doi.org/10.5860/crl.79.1.10.
9. Tewell, "Practice and Promise."
10. Tewell, "Practice and Promise"; Jason Coleman and Lis Pankl, "Rethinking the Neoliberal University: Critical Library Pedagogy in an Age of Transition," *Communications in Information Literacy* 14, no. 1 (June 2020): 66–74, https://doi.org/10.15760/comminfolit.2020.14.1.5.
11. Angela Bridgland and Martha Whitehead, "Perspectives On …Information Literacy in the 'E' Environment: An Approach for Sustainability," *Journal of Academic Librarianship* 31, no. 1 (January 2005): 54–59, https://doi.org/10.1016/j.acalib.2004.09.010; Jody Nelson, Joan Morrison, and Lindsey Whitson, "Piloting a Blended Model for Sustainable IL Programming," *Reference Services Review* 43, no. 1 (2015): 137–51, https://doi.org/10.1108/RSR-09-2014-0040.
12. Audre Lorde, *A Burst of Light and Other Essays*, reprint (Mineola, NY: Ixia Press, 2017), 130.
13. Ester Bloom, "How 'Treat Yourself' Became a Capitalist Command," *Atlantic*, November 19, 2015, https://www.theatlantic.com/business/archive/2015/11/

how-treat-yourself-became-a-consumerist-command/416664/; Aisha Harris, "A History of Self-Care," *Slate*, April 5, 2017, http://www.slate.com/articles/arts/culturebox/2017/04/the_history_of_self_care.html.

14. Tina Chan, "Self-Care Strategies for a Healthy Work-Life Balance," *Intersections: A Blog on Diversity, Literacy, and Outreach*, October 30, 2020, https://www.ala.org/advocacy/diversity/odlos-blog/self-care-strategies; Melanie Kletter, "Self-Care for Stressful Times," *Library Journal*, June 1, 2021, https://www.libraryjournal.com?detailStory=self-care-for-stressful-times-your-home-librarian; Bill Sannwald, "Self-Care for Librarians: Journaling," *Intersections: A Blog on Diversity, Literacy, and Outreach,* December 17, 2018, https://www.ala.org/advocacy/diversity/odlos-blog/self-care-journaling.

15. Association of College and Research Libraries, "Pandemic Resources for Academic Libraries: Home," LibGuide, accessed July 30, 2021, https://acrl.libguides.com/pandemic/home.

16. Karen P. Nicholson, "The McDonaldization of Academic Libraries and the Values of Transformational Change," *College and Research Libraries* 76, no. 3 (2015): 330, https://doi.org/10.5860/crl.76.3.328.

17. Nicholson, "'Taking Back' Information Literacy," 31.

18. Rafia Mirza and Maura Seale, "Who Killed the World? White Masculinity and the Technocratic Library of the Future," in *Topographies of Whiteness: Mapping Whiteness in Library and Information Science*, ed. Gina Schlesselman-Tarango (Sacramento, CA: Library Juice Press, 2017), 171–97.

19. Mirza and Seale, "Who Killed the World?" 185.

20. Mirza and Seale, "Who Killed the World?" 172.

21. Jessica Schomberg, "Disability at Work: Libraries, Built to Exclude," in *The Politics and Theory of Critical Librarianship*, ed. Karen P. Nicholson and Maura Seale (Sacramento, CA: Library Juice Press, 2018), 119.

22. Schomberg, "Disability at Work," 120.

23. Dianne N. Brown and Leo Settoducato, "Caring for Your Community of Practice: Collective Responses to Burnout," *LOEX Quarterly* 45, no. 4 (2019): article, 5, pp. 10–12, https://commons.emich.edu/loexquarterly/vol45/iss4/5.

24. Brown and Settoducato, "Caring for Your Community," 11.

25. Brown and Settoducato, "Caring for Your Community," 11.

26. Brown and Settoducato, "Caring for Your Community," 11.

27. Emily Drabinski, Miriame Kabe, and Dean Spade, "Making Change: Organizing for Action While Caring for Each Other" (President's Program, ALA Annual conference, online, June 24, 2021), https://www.eventscribe.net/2021/ALA-Annual/fsPopup.asp?Mode=presInfo&PresentationID=891440 (page discontinued).

28. hooks, *Teaching to Transgress*, 14.

29. hooks, *Teaching to Transgress*, 14.

30. hooks, *Teaching to Transgress*, 14.

31. hooks, *Teaching to Transgress*, 15.

32. hooks, *Teaching to Transgress*, 15.

33. hooks, *Teaching to Transgress*, 21.

34. hooks, *Teaching to Transgress*, 21.

35. hooks, *Teaching to Transgress*, 22.

36. Theodorea Regina Berry, "Engaged Pedagogy and Critical Race Feminism," *Educational Foundations* 24, no. 3/4 (2010): 20; Mary Ann Danowitz and Frank Tuitt, "Enacting Inclusivity through Engaged Pedagogy: A Higher Education Perspective," *Equity and Excellence in Education* 44, no. 1 (2011): 41, https://doi.org/10.1080/10665684.2011.539474; hooks, *Teaching to Transgress*, 10.

37. hooks, *Teaching to Transgress*, 21.

38. Veronica Arellano Douglas, "Innovating against a Brick Wall: Rebuilding the Structures That Change Our Teaching" (presentation, Innovative Library Classroom Conference, Williamsburg, VA, June 6–7, 2019).

39. Arellano Douglas, "Innovating against a Brick Wall."

40. adrienne maree brown, *Emergent Strategy* (Chico, CA: AK Press, 2017), 53.

Bibliography

Affleck, Mary Ann. "Burnout among Bibliographic Instruction Librarians." *Library and Information Science Research* 18, no. 2 (Spring 1996): 165–83. https://doi.org/10.1016/S0740-8188(96)90018-3.

Arellano Douglas, Veronica. "Innovating against a Brick Wall: Rebuilding the Structures That Change Our Teaching." Presentation, Innovative Library Classroom Conference, Williamsburg, VA, June 6–7, 2019.

Arellano Douglas, Veronica, and Joanna Gadsby. "Gendered Labor and Library Instruction Coordinators: The Undervaluing of Feminized Work." In *At the Helm: Leading Transformation: The Proceedings of the ACRL 2017 Conference*, edited by Dawn M. Mueller, 266–74. Chicago: Association of College and Research Libraries, 2017. https://alair.ala.org/bitstream/handle/11213/17739/GenderedLaborandLibraryInstructionCoordinators.pdf?sequence=1&isAllowed=y.

Association of College and Research Libraries. "Pandemic Resources for Academic Libraries: Home." LibGuide. Accessed July 30, 2021. https://acrl.libguides.com/pandemic/home.

Berg, Jacob, Angela Galvan, and Eamon Tewell. "Responding to and Reimagining Resilience in Academic Libraries." *Journal of New Librarianship* 3, no. 1 (2018): 1–4. https://doi.org/10.21173/newlibs/4/1.

Berry, Theodorea Regina. "Engaged Pedagogy and Critical Race Feminism." *Educational Foundations* 24, no. 3/4 (2010): 19–26.

Bloom, Ester. "How 'Treat Yourself' Became a Capitalist Command." *Atlantic*, November 19, 2015. https://www.theatlantic.com/business/archive/2015/11/how-treat-yourself-became-a-consumerist-command/416664/.

Bridgland, Angela, and Martha Whitehead. "Perspectives On …Information Literacy in the 'E' Environment: An Approach for Sustainability." *Journal of Academic Librarianship* 31, no. 1 (January 2005): 54–59. https://doi.org/10.1016/j.acalib.2004.09.010.

brown, adrienne maree. *Emergent Strategy: Shaping Change, Changing Worlds*. Chico, CA: AK Press, 2017.

Brown, Dianne N., and Leo Settoducato. "Caring for Your Community of Practice: Collective Responses to Burnout." *LOEX Quarterly* 45, no. 4 (2019): article 5. https://commons.emich.edu/loexquarterly/vol45/iss4/5.

Chan, Tina. "Self-Care Strategies for a Healthy Work-Life Balance." *Intersections: A Blog on Diversity, Literacy, and Outreach*, October 30, 2020. https://www.ala.org/advocacy/diversity/odlos-blog/self-care-strategies.

Coleman, Jason, and Lis Pankl. "Rethinking the Neoliberal University: Critical Library Pedagogy in an Age of Transition." *Communications in Information Literacy* 14, no. 1 (June 2020): 66–74. https://doi.org/10.15760/comminfolit.2020.14.1.5.

Danowitz, Mary Ann, and Frank Tuitt. "Enacting Inclusivity through Engaged Pedagogy: A Higher Education Perspective." *Equity and Excellence in Education* 44, no. 1 (2011): 40–56. https://doi.org/10.1080/10665684.2011.539474.

Drabinski, Emily, Miriame Kabe, and Dean Spade. "Making Change: Organizing for Action While Caring for Each Other." Presentation, ALA Annual Conference, online, June 24, 2021. https://www.eventscribe.net/2021/ALA-Annual/fsPopup.asp?Mode=presInfo&PresentationID=891440 (page discontinued).

Harris, Aisha. "A History of Self-Care." *Slate*, April 5, 2017. http://www.slate.com/articles/arts/culturebox/2017/04/the_history_of_self_care.html.

hooks, bell. *Teaching to Transgress: Education as the Practice of Freedom*. New York: Routledge, 1994.

Hudson, David James. "The Whiteness of Practicality." In *Topographies of Whiteness: Mapping Whiteness in Library and Information Studies*, edited by Gina Schlesselman-Tarango, 203–34. Sacramento, CA: Library Juice Press, 2017. https://atrium.lib.uoguelph.ca/xmlui/bitstream/handle/10214/11619/Hudson_Whiteness_Of_Practicality_IR_r1.pdf?sequence=6&isAllowed=y.

Kletter, Melanie. "Self-Care for Stressful Times." *Library Journal*, June 1, 2021. https://www.libraryjournal.com?detailStory=self-care-for-stressful-times-your-home-librarian.

Lorde, Audre. *A Burst of Light and Other Essays*. Reprint. Mineola, NY: Ixia Press, 2017.

Mirza, Rafia, and Maura Seale. "Who Killed the World? White Masculinity and the Technocratic Library of the Future." In *Topographies of Whiteness: Mapping Whiteness in Library and Information Science*, edited by Gina Schlesselman-Tarango, 171–97. Sacramento, CA: Library Juice Press, 2017.

Nelson, Jody, Joan Morrison, and Lindsey Whitson. "Piloting a Blended Model for Sustainable IL Programming." *Reference Services Review* 43, no. 1 (2015): 137–51. https://doi.org/10.1108/RSR-09-2014-0040.

Nicholson, Karen P. "The McDonaldization of Academic Libraries and the Values of Transformational Change." *College and Research Libraries* 76, no. 3 (2015): 328–38. https://doi.org/10.5860/crl.76.3.328.

———. "'Taking Back' Information Literacy: Time and the One-Shot in the Neoliberal University." In *Critical Library Pedagogy Handbook*, vol. 1, edited by Nicole Pagowsky and Kelly McElroy, 25–39. Chicago: Association of College and Research Libraries, 2016.

Oakleaf, Megan. *The Value of Academic Libraries: A Comprehensive Research Review and Report.* Chicago: Association of College and Research Libraries, 2010. https://www.ala.org/acrl/sites/ala.org.acrl/files/content/issues/value/val_report.pdf.

Pagowsky, Nicole, and Kelly McElroy. "Introduction." In *Critical Library Pedagogy Handbook*, vol. 1, edited by Nicole Pagowsky and Kelly McElroy, xvii–xxi. Chicago: Association of College and Research Libraries, 2016.

Sannwald, Bill. "Self-Care for Librarians: Journaling." *Intersections: A Blog on Diversity, Literacy, and Outreach*, December 17, 2018. https://www.ala.org/advocacy/diversity/odlos-blog/self-care-journaling.

Schomberg, Jessica. "Disability at Work: Libraries, Built to Exclude." In *The Politics and Theory of Critical Librarianship*, edited by Karen P. Nicholson and Maura Seale, 111–23. Sacramento, CA: Library Juice Press, 2018.

Schwartz, Harriet L. *Connected Teaching: Relationship, Power, and Mattering in Higher Education.* Sterling, VA: Stylus, 2019.

Seale, Maura. "Critical Library Instruction, Causing Trouble, and Institutionalization." *Communications in Information Literacy* 14, no. 1 (2020): 75–85. https://doi.org/10.15760/comminfolit.2020.14.1.6.

Sheesley, Deborah F. "Burnout and the Academic Teaching Librarian: An Examination of the Problem and Suggested Solutions." *Journal of Academic Librarianship* 27, no. 6 (November 2001): 447–51.

Tewell, Eamon. "The Practice and Promise of Critical Information Literacy: Academic Librarians' Involvement in Critical Library Instruction." *College and Research Libraries* 79, no. 1 (January 2018): 10–32. https://doi.org/10.5860/crl.79.1.10.

PART IV
Practices of Care

CHAPTER 8

Academic Library Labor as Community Care Work

Siân Evans and Amanda Meeks

I am a student of complexity. I am learning complexity from the inside out.

—*adrienne maree brown*[1]

Situating Ourselves

In the summer of 2020—in the middle of a global pandemic, political uprising, and climate crisis—the authors began meeting to learn about disability justice and how to address ableism in our work. The community of practice we formed with another colleague, Linden How, was born from recent experiences the authors had wherein accessibility was an afterthought in our workplaces, especially during the rapid move to online engagement. In April of 2020, one of the authors and cofounder of Art+Feminism, Siân Evans, presented on the organization's Safe, Brave Space policy at the Common Field Convening.[2] The workshop

focused on building safer and more accessible spaces and was organized with Kira Wisniewski, executive director of Art+Feminism, Shawna Potter (frontwoman of feminist punk band War on Women and author of *Making Spaces Safer*), and Tyde Courtney-Edwards of Baltimore-based activist organizations, FORCE: Upsetting Rape Culture and Ballet after Dark.[3] All the presenters worked in activist communities that exist primarily outside of academic institutions. Conversations with attendees throughout the workshop made clear that the most holistic, radical work around inclusion and accessibility was happening *outside* of these institutional spaces and that institutions have a lot to learn from activists.

In March of 2020, Meeks, the other author of this chapter, was making parallel observations while serving on the Critical Library and Pedagogy Symposium (CLAPS) organizing committee at the University of Arizona in Tucson. The organizers made the difficult decision to postpone the in-person gathering just days before it was scheduled. CLAPS was among the first library conferences to postpone in-person gathering, so with little guidance or precedent, CLAPS organizers surveyed the small community of attendees. Although many people were still willing to travel, there were also attendees who expressed concern, disclosed chronic illness and disability, and urged the committee to move the conference online. In response the committee decided to prioritize these accessibility needs. Almost six months after the in-person conference was postponed, CLAPS was hosted online. This opened registration to many more people, but as the committee navigated hosting such a large event online for the first time, additional accessibility concerns bubbled up. The organizers were unable to get live captioning integrated with Zoom due to platform limitations and budget constraints and found the internal workings of the campus disability resource center opaque and unhelpful. The committee settled for recommending resources and best practices to the individual presenters and added closed captions to the recorded sessions after the fact. Placing the onus on individual presenters meant inconsistency and a lack of reliability in terms of which sessions would actually be accessible. Without dedicated expertise and institutional support, the committee was not able to confidently support people with disabilities.

These two experiences shaped our community of practice because they illustrated how little care institutions generally display for disabled people. In this chapter we attempt to explore how the radical activist model of care work within a disability justice framework can be applied to the labor of academic librarians. We will survey recent library and information science (LIS) literature on disability, discuss how we define care work, and offer practical solutions for how to enact care in our communities. Because we are writing about building community, we want to start with the assertion that there is always a relationship between the author and the reader, although it often goes unacknowledged. Drawing on adrienne maree brown's practice of naming herself, and in the spirit of relational care, we want to begin our analysis of care work in libraries by positioning our experiences so that the reader can make an informed decision about how they choose to relate to our work.[4] Both authors identify as white and able-bodied and, at the time of writing, both are employed at academic libraries. Amanda identifies as queer, nonbinary, and working-class, while Siân identifies as a cisgender, heterosexual feminist socialist. Both Siân and Amanda experience mental health–related disabilities including depression and complicated grief. Our practice as library workers is also informed by an insider-outsider dynamic that reflects our positionality as authors of this chapter. Together, we bring ten-plus years of experience with grassroots community and labor organizing, activism, and creative practices into our teaching and library work. Our personal experiences of depression and grief, alongside our respective work in grassroots organizations and libraries such as Art+Feminism, the Occupy Wall Street Archives Working Group, the Portland Q-Center, and Chicago's Read/Write Library built the foundation of our understanding of what a library *could* and *should* be: a creative, radical, accessible, safe/brave space and a site for healing through mutual aid and community care work. As we explore the library's radical potential, we want to address, via our literature review, our colleagues' critical voices on where libraries so often fail disabled people because we believe that thoughtful criticism sets the stage for meaningful change.

Disability in Academic Librarianship: A Literature Review

Drawing on Kelsey George's chapter, "DisService: Disabled Library Staff and Service Expectations" in *Deconstructing Service in Libraries: Intersections of Identities and Expectations*, we'd like to open our literature review with the reflection that identifying as disabled is a complex and political act. George writes that it is her "way of acknowledging that there is an entire community with history, activism, and people who have shared lived experiences due to their disability status."[5] Following George, we also want to acknowledge that while some people prefer identity-first language (*disabled person*), others may opt for person-first language (*people with disabilities*). In another chapter in the same volume, Siân also noted the complications of language people use to self-identify, ranging from catchalls like *disabled* to using their diagnoses as a primary identifier.[6] As students of complexity ourselves, we will use these terms interchangeably throughout the chapter to respect multiple perspectives.

We do not wish to replicate George's thorough literature review of disability in LIS, so we will call out some relevant aspects of her research, while drawing on more recently published literature. George highlights that there has been an increase in library literature on the experiences of disabled workers in recent years.[7] Indeed, several studies have delved into how libraries reinforce systemic and social barriers for disabled folks, create precarity for disabled library workers, and are in need of deep and critical self-reflection.[8] George cites a 2013 article by Heather Hill as the most recent content analysis on disability in the field.[9] In 2021, Amelia Gibson, Kristen Bowen, and Dana Hanson coauthored an article that continued in a vein similar to Hill's research. In reviewing LIS research between 1978 and 2018, they found a field that has an "unprioritized and short-sighted understanding of disability."[10] Gibson, Bowen, and Hanson also argued that very few studies use an intersectional lens to center the experiences of Black, Indigenous, and People of Color (BIPOC) or lesbian, gay, bisexual, queer, intersex, asexual, and more (LGBTQIA+) people with disabilities.[11] In her 2017 article, Stephanie Rosen articulates how a focus on disability alone in libraries "is not enough to understand disability for what it is: always an intersectional identity."[12]

Gibson, Bowen, and Hanson also point out that "like whiteness, ableism protects itself by building social, political, and economic structures (policies, norms, institutions, etc.) that reinforce systems of privilege and exclusion."[13] During the pandemic these systems were laid bare for all of society, as everything from medical rationing of critical life-saving equipment and hospital beds to work-from-home policies was debated. Yet as libraries returned to in-person work, the discussions about disability accommodations to allow remote work were similar to those that existed before the pandemic, with nondisabled managers and administrators deciding that "an employee is not disabled 'enough' to warrant accommodations, or that an accommodation is an 'undue burden,'" despite many of us having successfully worked remotely for over a year.[14]

Since this chapter is focused on academic libraries, we also need to address how disability has been theorized in higher education in general. In our professional careers and activist work, the authors have found that moving between grassroots organizations or community-centered efforts and academic libraries has been a jarring process at times. This is largely because academia itself has racist, ableist, and eugenicist roots that are at odds with community building. In *Academic Ableism: Higher Education and Disability*, J. Timothy Dolmage details a long history of disabled people being studied and abused in academic institutions.[15] He argues that higher education was instrumental in "inventing and enforcing" the label of *disabled* as abnormal and justifying inequality not only for disabled people but also for other marginalized groups by attributing disability to them.[16] He also notes that although the field of disability studies (which theorizes disability as socially constructed, in opposition to the traditional medical model of definition) emerges in higher education, "this emergence cannot overwrite the activist, community-based roots of the disability rights movement, even when these connections and roots are often ignored."[17]

Dolmage goes on to explore how the neoliberalization of higher education since the 1970s has continued to oppress and exploit disabled people who work and learn within the universities' hallowed halls. In the neoliberal college, we are all encouraged to become "middle managers" running our classrooms "like corporations."[18] We are awash in institutionally sanctioned diversity committees that don't solve equity issues and encouraged to develop information literacy initiatives guided toward the development of a workforce.[19] Dolmage argues that neoliberal higher education is not only hostile to care work, but it is also "a system that powerfully masks inequalities and readily co-opts concerns like diversity, tolerance, and democracy."[20] We see how neoliberalism co-opts concepts coming out of disability studies and disability rights movements in the recent explosion of literature on universal design (UD) and Universal Design for Learning (UDL). UD began as an architectural movement to make physical spaces more accessible, but has expanded into a number of other fields, including UDL, which focuses on multimodal learning in the classroom to better support disabled students. Dolmage warns that as UD concepts are co-opted by neoliberal institutions they become mere "marketing tools" because the neoliberal university is designed to maximize profits and exploit available resources.[21] We will return to UDL later in this chapter as an avenue for care work provided we remain aware of its potential to be a way for institutions to promise "everything while not doing much of anything" and to place the onus on individual students to manage their own access levels.[22]

Disability studies is as diverse as the population of disabled people who make it up. George cites three recent theoretical frameworks that have emerged to address the experiences of people with disabilities: critical disability theory, the social justice model, and disability justice. In this chapter, we will focus on the latter.[23] Disability justice invokes a movement stemming from the Disability Justice Collective, which was founded by a number of Black, brown, queer, and trans disabled organizers in Oakland in 2005. It is also a broader ethic of community care that involves informal "care webs" for caretaking disabled folks outside of the medical industrial complex, which so often fails them, and mutual aid.[24] Disability justice is inherently intersectional in that it recognizes ableism as intrinsically connected to other systems of oppression. Disability justice activists don't seek just to address disability in a vacuum, but see it as a means to challenge and dismantle all systems of oppression. In the words of disabled activist Mia Mingus,

> Disability is not monolithic. Ableism plays out very differently for wheelchair users, deaf people or people who have mental, psychiatric and cognitive disabilities. None of these are mutually exclusive, and are all complicated by race, class, gender, immigration, sexuality, welfare status, incarceration, age and geographic location.[25]

It is from within the framework of disability justice that we want to explore how we talk about care and how we build community in academic libraries, taking some first steps into community care work in academic libraries. As George and Gibson, Bowen, and Hanson have demonstrated, the field of LIS has a long way to go in terms of being a safe and accessible place for disabled patrons and workers. It was during our community of practice that the authors realized that our teachers in disability justice have primarily been folks outside of the library community, particularly BIPOC, queer, and trans people who are also disabled, chronically ill, or neurodivergent. It was this community, not our own professional context, that had helped us redefine disability as a social issue—versus a medical issue—that embraces interdependence, intersectionality, and cross-movement organizing.[26]

What We Talk about When We Talk about Care Work

It would be impossible for us to discuss care work in libraries without acknowledging the ways that our experience in community organizing has shaped our understanding of what care work constitutes. Specifically, when we talk about care work, we're talking about an idea that comes out of the disability justice movement. In *Care Work: Dreaming Disability Justice*, disability justice activist Leah Lakshmi Piepzna-Samarasinha defines care work as "a place where disability justice and queer femme emotional labor intersect."[27] She notes that this work is often underdocumented and private—consisting of the emotional labor of talking to friends through their chronic pain or writing and recording their own experiences as disabled people—and therefore often not seen as "real activism."[28] Further, in Piepzna-Samarasinha's words, at the very center of care work is an ethic of love:

At the risk of seeming like a Christian, or a Che Guevara poster, love is bigger, huger, more complex, and more ultimate than petty fucked-up desirability politics. We all deserve love. Love as an action verb. Love in full inclusion, in centrality, in not being forgotten. Being loved for our disabilities, our weirdness, not despite them.[29]

At its core, care work implies that we are all deserving of care and that it might look different in practice, depending on our varied needs. Disability justice also asserts that "ableism helps make racism, christian supremacy, sexism, and queer- and transphobia possible, and that all those systems of oppression are locked up tight."[30] In other words, care work through a disability justice lens must take into account the ways in which all forms of oppression intersect and serve each other.

The COVID-19 pandemic raised the visibility of people with disabilities and the challenges they face every day. Suddenly, the general public was thrust into a new reality in which they too faced challenges around health, safety, isolation, and an unsettling uncertainty. Disability justice activists responded to the COVID-19 crisis with protest and critique, mutual aid, and creative world-making; they have tirelessly fought for and reimagined a more equitable post-pandemic society.[31] As Alice Wong, the founder of the activist group Disability Visibility, notes in the quotation below, the world we live in was never designed for people with disabilities. Perhaps if it were, society would have been better prepared for the public health crisis that COVID-19 presented.

It is a strange time to be alive as an Asian American disabled person who uses a ventilator. The coronavirus pandemic in the United States has disrupted and destabilized individual lives and institutions. For many disabled, sick, and immunocompromised people like myself, we have always lived with uncertainty and are skilled in adapting to hostile circumstances in a world that was never designed for us in the first place. Want to avoid touching door handles by hitting the automatic door opener with your elbow? You can thank the Americans with Disabilities Act and the disabled people who made it happen.[32]

So, as we shift now to talking about care work in academic libraries, we want to keep the activist roots of our understanding of care work at the forefront of our discussion. In LIS literature, *care* and *service* are often used in the same breath. There are many chapters in Veronica Arellano Douglas and Joanna Gadsby's aforementioned edited volume, *Deconstructing Service in Libraries*, dedicated to exploring how both service and care work are gendered and racialized, as well as how they negatively affect workers who are marginalized.[33] Similarly, in their interviews with fifty-four academic librarian women of color, Tarida Anantachai and Camille Chesley demonstrate the ways in which racialized identity adds an additional dimension of "cultural taxation" to the "burden of care" that takes a very real emotional toll in feminized fields, like librarianship, that center around caregiving.[34]

Using the lens of critical race theory (CRT), Anne Cong-Huyen and Kush Patel have argued we need more spaces of "radical care" in libraries, specifically for BIPOC librarians.[35] Shana Higgins has also used CRT, in conjunction with a feminist ethic of care, to "revalue feminized labor that is often the infrastructure of our library work and lives."[36] She specifically defines care as work: "Care is work, care is a disposition by choice, care is a cultivated skill, and care is an orientation that motivates action."[37] Like Cong-Huyen and Patel, she advocates for care work that is intersectional and takes into account the overwhelming whiteness of our field, with over 86 percent of librarians identifying as white. And, drawing on the concept of "vocational awe," she argues that we need to critically engage the "nice white lady inertia" that upholds library work as "inherently good."[38] Ultimately, she states that we need care work that supports our students while also uplifting our library workers: "We must find ways to offer and shape inclusive, anti-oppressive services in academic libraries that are also anti-oppressive for staff."[39]

Thus far, we have discussed how care work affects library workers, but as Higgins mentions, how do we conceptualize care work as it relates to our patrons? There have been a few recent studies that compare care work in the medical field to care work in libraries. In a 2020 article, Arellano Douglas stressed the need for an ethic of care in libraries with a call for us to move from a critical model of library assessment to one based in care. Like Higgins, she makes the point that care work—often entailing "soft skills" or "emotional labor"—is not innate, but is something that can be taught and practiced.[40] Arellano Douglas defines care in library assessment through the lens of bell hooks' "engaged pedagogy." Care, she argues, is both "mutual and relational."[41] Arellano Douglas goes on to highlight the ways in which other service-oriented professions, specifically nursing and midwifery, incorporate a holistic approach to patient assessment that is centered in care. In nursing, for example,

> Assessment is done "with rather than on patients" and is "a process of evaluating a patient's ...needs ...and of identifying the patient's wishes." These needs go beyond the medical and physical and

encompass a patient's "life world" or all of the social, cultural, relational and experiential aspects of a patient's life.[42]

Although medical assessment is, indeed, different from information literacy assessment, she argues that our field could learn from educational practices in the similarly feminized fields of nursing and midwifery. She concludes that an assessment of care would value students as "whole people who bring all of themselves and all of life's complications and joys with them into the classroom," while also valuing ourselves holistically in relation to our students.[43] Similarly, Elizabeth Galoozis draws on research from the field of midwifery to argue that LIS should adopt a feminist ethic of care that "requires that professionals care about what their clients/users/students are subjectively feeling and connect to it."[44] We certainly acknowledge that the stakes are different in an ICU than in a library classroom, but still believe the context of feminized service-oriented work offers a productive avenue for exploration. We would like to extend Arellano Douglas's and Gazoolis's analyses and return to care work through a disability justice lens: as centered in an ethic of love and existing to challenge the institutional structures that so often dehumanize people with disabilities.

Community Building

That care work is relational has been implicit in so much of the writing we've discussed so far. Both Higgins and Cong-Huyen and Patel stress community as a place to situate care. They cite We Here in LIS[45] as an example of a group that coheres "would-be marginalized individuals into radical loving, caring communities that help underrepresented researchers, librarians, teachers, and activists sustain each other through community building."[46] Similarly, Anantachai and Chesley argued that in order to retain women librarians of color on the tenure track, peer networks and communities of practice are necessary.[47] Moore and Estrellado also connect self-care and community care, arguing that "having community helps women of color navigate whiteness in the profession."[48]

However, Cong-Huyen and Patel note that community building centered around care requires significant labor that is rarely recognized or compensated by our institutions:

> For some of us, though, this is pleasurable, life-sustaining labor. This is how we care for each other and ourselves. It is the kind of labor that keeps us in our jobs and as part of our professions. We are always reminded that the neoliberal academy will prioritize

efficiency-centered interventions over lived and structurally transformative relationships. In spite of that, we nurture our relationships,
even when they may slow down the system. It is relationships that
will always serve as the organization's nurturing core.[49]

Evans's interviews with library workers about their experiences of mental
illness highlighted a similar trend toward care work. Although many of the interviewees did not disclose their diagnoses publicly, they felt that their experiences
of disability made them more caring, better librarians and better colleagues.[50]
However, they often found themselves in hostile work environments. According to George's survey of ninety-nine disabled library workers, fifty-six of them
had experienced "microaggressions or overt aggression" in the workplace. And
these experiences were pretty evenly distributed among patrons, colleagues, and
supervisors.[51] All of this highlights a need and desire for greater care within our
library communities.

We want to acknowledge that *community* is a tricky term because it implies
both inclusion and exclusion. It is often associated with a kind of "uncomplicated
goodness," but we cannot forget that exclusion "is what creates the conceptual
coherence of a community."[52] That said, as is the case for a community like We
Here, which is open only to BIPOC library workers, "thoughtful exclusion" can
be both "generous" and "defining."[53] Building communities for disabled library
workers has another added layer of complexity in that, as we noted earlier, how
an individual defines their own relationship to disability is often a personal and
private matter. Further, as George notes, "disability is something that affects
every group of people, and it is a fluctuating status that a person can fall into at
any time."[54]

Toward Communities of Care

In academic libraries, we might define our communities pretty broadly:
the students, faculty, and in some cases publics we serve; other cocurricular
colleagues we collaborate with; and our colleagues and supervisors in the library.
George's interviewees have already stressed the importance of organization-
al-level changes to better support disabled workers, including flexible scheduling,
remote work options, and ergonomic workstations, as well as Americans with
Disabilities Act (ADA) and Family and Medical Leave Act (FMLA) training for
supervisors.[55]

George also argues that we must go beyond merely addressing legal issues of
accessibility and take a human-centered approach. She outlines the workplace

culture recommendations of Jennifer Gillies and Shelley L. Dupuis from the research study they conducted on their college campus: provide access for all; value diversity and uniqueness of all; value interdependence and social responsibility; value diverse knowledge, bases, voices, and perspectives; value the power of learning and education as tools for growth and change; and value the whole person.[56] While we believe institutional change is necessary in supporting communities of care, especially because it alleviates the burden placed on already marginalized people to do care work, we want to end this chapter with some practical starting points to help build a community of care in our individual workplaces. We will use examples that emerge from our own grassroots community organizing efforts to highlight how this work, even when applied in academic settings, comes from activist roots.

Universal Design For Learning

As we noted earlier in this chapter, UDL is a mode of designing lesson plans and classroom spaces to support diverse learners. A thorough exploration of UDL is beyond the scope of this chapter, but there are plenty of examples in LIS literature that view accessibility through a UDL lens.[57] We want to heed Dolmage's warning that checklists can move UDL from its radical roots and defeat its rhetorical purpose. Although Dolmage cautions against this practice, he concedes that if there's one checklist UDL teachers and organizers could use, it would be this one:

- Multiple means of representation, to give learners various ways of acquiring information and knowledge,

- Multiple means of expression, to provide learners alternatives for demonstrating what they know,

- Multiple means of engagement, to tap into learners' interests, offer appropriate challenges, and increase motivation.[58]

Dolmage argues that UD is action—"a patterning of engagement and effort."[59] Below, we offer three examples of this radical, multimodal engagement in practice.

Drawing on the design thinking techniques of empathy mapping and personas, Amanda has used a reflective instructional design process since 2015 to consider how library work reproduces or reinforces structural barriers. In order "to consciously work against the values and habits and biases of mainstream design practices," librarians can start with acknowledging one's own positionality and then develop affirming learning environments or approaches to reduce harm and address aforementioned barriers, including considering the effects of overstimulating group work for folks who are neurodivergent and language barriers for international students.[60] The process of analyzing and redesigning our practice to make it responsive to student experiences and identities is an intentionally anti-oppressive approach. As we do this, we may notice the myriad ways our institutions were not designed for, *or with*, marginalized groups within our society and how this design flaw has had a greater impact.[61]

Multimodal engagement translates well to cocurricular activities as well as classroom instruction. In March 2020, the Tucson Art+Feminism Edit-a-Thon collective moved our event online. We learned several lessons during this shift: (1) Breaking up a longer event into multiple sessions allows people to rest and recharge in between. (2) Working in small groups on specific projects that attendees choose from gives them agency over how they engage with what is being taught. (3) Providing short presentations and activities, as well as self-guided working time, increases interest and motivation. These lessons also helped inform the event design of other community-based projects Amanda would host later that year.

Following the murder of George Floyd, Amanda felt it was critical to create and hold open a container within the Tucson community, sparking the idea for the Movement/Rest Quilting Bee, which she co-facilitated alongside her colleague and history faculty member Dr. Marya McQuirter. The police brutality inflicted on the Black community in America is intersectional in nature. While there is no official reporting system for this, it is estimated that between 30 and 50 percent of all victims of police brutality are people with disabilities *and* Black.[62] The goal of the #MoveRestBee was to come together to make and learn in the midst of COVID-19 and a crisis of white supremacy and ableism, while focusing on the traditional craft of quilting, which has been historically and is currently used to support Black American freedom from oppression. Invited speakers included scholars, activists, artists, and educators who shared their experiences and knowledge of quilting as a form of resistance. Events were intended to hold space for listening, learning, and supporting one another as a way to honor Black life and envision a future without police brutality. #MoveRestBee resulted in multiple means of expression through sometimes uncomfortable conversations between participants, two collaborative quilts, and many notes and letters about what was learned over the course of the semester, showing the power of cultivating joy alongside grief as a form of care.

This brings us back to the discussion of UDL and its place in academic libraries. None of the above examples followed a rubric, checklist, or guide; how we enacted accessibility looked different for each one, per the lens of disability justice. We encourage teachers and event organizers to follow Dolmage's radical "patterning of engagement and effort"[63] in thinking about how they could leverage UDL to enact care in their own communities.

Safe, Brave Spaces

Our advice to library workers interested in making their spaces—be they classrooms or departmental meetings—more accessible is to look to radical collectives (at a local, global, or national level) and see what types of safe, brave space language they've developed. It's a first step toward a culture of relational accountability within communities.

In 2013, Siân cofounded Art+Feminism, a nonprofit devoted to building a global community of activists that is committed to closing information gaps related to gender, feminism, and the arts, beginning with Wikipedia. As events proliferated around the world, it became clear that the leadership collective needed to be explicit about our values and what we would not tolerate in our physical and virtual spaces.[64] Amanda codeveloped Art+Feminism's safe, brave space agreement, drawing on examples from a number of grassroots organizations, including FemTechNet, Allied Media Projects, Emergent Strategy, Movement Killing Behaviors by Njimie Dzurinko, Rooted in Rights, Ideas for Ears, and the Queer Futures Collective.

If you've never created a safe or brave space document before, there are many examples available online. Below you will find an abbreviated version of Art+Feminism's Safe, Brave Space Policy. There is also a longer version available on Art+Feminism's website and Wikipedia:

> We Believe in Brave, Friendly Spaces. The goal of this session is to create an encouraging space for collective learning. This requires intentional behavior, wherein participants are conscious of and accountable for the effect of their statements and actions on others. We respect our experiences and the experiences of others and recognize that we can't do this work without one another. We agree to hold each other accountable to foster a Brave, Friendly Space. Review the whole Brave, Friendly Spaces agreement here: bit.ly/AFBraveSpace https://en.wikipedia.org/wiki/Wikipedia:Meetup/ArtandFeminism/Safespacepolicy[65]

It is important to acknowledge that a safe, brave space agreement is only a first step and that it is also only as effective as its enforcement. Ideally, it should be a philosophy that permeates every interaction within a community.

Restorative Practices

Restorative practices have a long history in education, and libraries could easily adopt restorative practices and restorative justice models to repair and reduce harm within their working environments. Given the experiences of BIPOC and disabled librarians that have been discussed in this chapter and documented elsewhere, we would argue that this practice is pivotal if we want our libraries to support a cultural shift toward community care. Below, we'll discuss how the Art+Feminism leadership team adopted restorative practices.

Building a large body of organizers and editors working to shift the content and culture of Wikipedia—a community that can be hostile to new editors and particularly female editors—necessitated a significant investment in care work within the Art+Feminism leadership collective.[66] In 2019, the team engaged in a restorative practices seminar with a Baltimore-based practitioner, Joyell Arvella. Restorative practices is a social science rooted in restorative justice, which is a framework for criminal justice that focuses on repairing harm as opposed to merely punishing offenders.[67] While restorative justice is often attributed to a movement centered around mediation between victims and perpetrators of crime beginning in the 1970s, it also has much deeper roots in Indigenous practices from around the world.[68] Restorative practices reflect a deceptively simple framework for maintaining "social norms and behavioral boundaries:" the underlying principle is for teachers, parents, leaders, organizers to do things *with* instead of *to* or *for* their community.[69]

Restorative practitioners believe that participatory learning and decision-making are key to building healthy communities. Arvella's approach is also founded on an intersectional understanding of the ways in which power dynamics play out in communities. Our leadership team began our two-part workshop with a power mapping exercise, in which we charted the ways in which we held privilege over each other as colleagues, in terms of race, gender, ethnicity, ability, and other vectors of identity, as well as professional roles. This work was centered around the idea that the leadership collective needed to be consistent and thoughtful in the ways we enacted care for our community. In Art+Feminism's section of our 2020 Common Field presentation, we stated, "it's one thing to say we support brave, friendly spaces, but it's another thing to put it into practice." We then went on to highlight some of the direct outcomes of our research into care work, including creating online meeting accessibility documentation for our organizers as our events moved online during a global pandemic and working directly with the Wikimedia Foundation to reduce online harassment and harm at not only Art+Feminism events, but all Wikipedia-related events.[70]

Where Do We Go from Here?

We began this chapter with the acknowledgment that this piece of writing came out of a small community of practice. It feels fitting to end with a reminder that although this group was a space of learning and growing together professionally, it was also a space of care. We took things slowly and intentionally; we made room for discussions about the pain points we were feeling at our workplaces—including overwork, underwork, and furloughs. We also talked about our dogs (shout out to Dottie, Pickle, and Willie!) and the various things we were doing to radically care for ourselves and others and to cultivate joy in the face of a global pandemic.

Returning to Dolmage's vision of UD as action and Piepzna-Samarasinha's understanding of care work as acts of love, we would like to end with the acknowledgment that what we have proposed above are mere starting points. If we want our institutions to be loving, caring, radical spaces, we are looking for a seismic shift in the culture of neoliberal academia, and such a shift requires action: a repeated, concerted "patterning of engagement and effort"[71] to build community. This might include incorporating power mapping into your library meetings or UDL into your teaching, but it also necessarily requires advocating for larger structural change. This might look different, based on the local community, but could include trauma-informed care or collective bargaining power to support those most vulnerable.

Notes

1. adrienne maree brown, *We Will Not Cancel Us and Other Dreams of Transformative Justice* (Chico, CA: AK Press, 2020), 3.
2. McKensie Mack and Amanda Meeks, "Safe, Brave Space Policy," Art+Feminism, accessed July 26, 2021, https://artandfeminism.org/resources/safety/safe-space-brave-space/.
3. Tyde-Courtney Edwards et al., "Building Safer Spaces in Creative Communities" (workshop, Common Field Convening, April 23, 2020), accessed July 26, 2021, https://www.commonfield.org/convenings/3248/program/4020/building-safer-spaces-in-creative-communities; Shawna Potter, *Making Spaces Safer* (Chico, CA: AK Press, 2019).
4. brown, *We Will Not Cancel Us*, 23.
5. Kelsey George, "DisService: Disabled Library Staff and Service Expectations," in *Deconstructing Service in Libraries: Intersections of Identities and Expectations*, ed. Veronica Arellano Douglas and Joanna Gadsby (Sacramento, CA: Litwin Books, 2020), 95.
6. Siân Evans, "The Weight of Service: Librarianship and Mental Health," in *Deconstructing Service in Libraries: Intersections of Identities and Expectations*, ed. Veronica Arellano Douglas and Joanna Gadsby (Sacramento, CA: Litwin Books, 2020), 147.
7. George, "DisService," 97.
8. Amelia Gibson, Kristen Bowen, and Dana Hanson, "We Need to Talk about How We Talk about Disability: A Critical Quasi-systematic Review," *In the Library with the Lead Pipe*, February 24, 2021, https://www.inthelibrarywiththeleadpipe.org/2021/disability/; Joanne Oud, "Systemic Workplace Barriers for Academic Librarians with Disabilities," *College and Research Libraries* 80, no. 2 (March

2019): 169–94, https://doi.org/10.5860/crl.80.2.169; Alana Kumbier and Julia Starkey, "Access Is Not Problem Solving: Disability Justice and Libraries," *Library Trends* 64, no. 3 (Winter 2016): 468–91, https://doi.org/10.1353/lib.2016.0004; Christine M. Moeller, "Disability, Identity, and Professionalism: Precarity in Librarianship," *Library Trends* 67, no. 3 (Winter 2019): 455–70, https://doi.org/10.1353/lib.2019.0006.

9.   Heather Hill, "Disability and Accessibility in the Library and Information Science Literature: A Content Analysis," *Library and Information Science Research* 35, no. 2 (April 2013): 142, https://doi.org/10.1016/j.lisr.2012.11.002.

10. Gibson, Bowen, and Hanson, "We Need to Talk About."

11. Gibson, Bowen, and Hanson, "We Need to Talk About."

12. Stephanie Rosen, "Accessibility for Justice: Accessibility as a Tool for Promoting Justice in Librarianship," *In the Library with the Lead Pipe*, November 29, 2017, https://www.inthelibrarywiththeleadpipe.org/2017/accessibility-for-justice/.

13. Gibson, Bowen, and Hanson, "We Need to Talk About."

14. Gibson, Bowen, and Hanson, "We Need to Talk About."

15. Jay T. Dolmage, *Academic Ableism* (Ann Arbor: University of Michigan Press, 2017), 4.

16. Dolmage, *Academic Ableism*, 6.

17. Dolmage, *Academic Ableism*, 9.

18. Dolmage, *Academic Ableism*, 139. For the purposes of this paper, we are defining *neoliberalism*, especially as it relates to higher education, as an overarching social and economic philosophy rooted in free-market capitalism and policies grounded in economic austerity, privatization, and globalization. In the neoliberal university, education is understood in its financial terms as a commodity.

19. Frank Dobbin and Alexandra Kalev, "Why Diversity Programs Fail," *Harvard Business Review*, July–August 2016. https://hbr.org/2016/07/why-diversity-programs-fail.

20. Dobbin and Kalev, "Why Diversity Programs Fail," 140.

21. Dobbin and Kalev, "Why Diversity Programs Fail," 140.

22. Dobbin and Kalev, "Why Diversity Programs Fail," 131–40.

23. George, "DisService," 99.

24. Leah Lakshmi Piepzna-Samarasinha, *Care Work* (Vancouver, BC: Arsenal Pulp Press, 2018), 15, EBSCOhost.

25. Mia Mingus, "Changing the Framework: Disability Justice," *Leaving Evidence* (blog), February 12, 2011, https://leavingevidence.wordpress.com/2011/02/12/changing-the-framework-disability-justice/.

26. Sins Invalid, "Ten Principles of Disability Justice," *Sins Invalid* (blog) September 17, 2015, https://www.sinsinvalid.org/blog/10-principles-of-disability-justice; Piepzna-Samarasinha, *Care Work*.

27. Piepzna-Samarsinha, *Care Work*, 24.

28. Piepzna-Samarsinha, *Care Work*, 19

29. Piepzna-Samarsinha, *Care Work*, 78

30. Piepzna-Samarsinha, *Care Work*, 22

31. Faye Ginsburg, Mara Mills, and Rayna Rapp, "From Quality of Life to Disability Justice: Imagining a Post-Covid Future," *Somatosphere* (blog), June 2, 2020, http://somatosphere.net/2020/from-quality-of-life-to-disability-justice.html/.

32.   Alice Wong, "I'm Disabled and Need a Ventilator to Live. Am I Expendable during This Pandemic?" Vox, April 4, 2020, https://www.vox.com/first-person/2020/4/4/21204261/coronavirus-covid-19-disabled-people-disabilities-triage.

33. For example, see Shana Higgins, "Situating Service: Care and Equity in Academic Libraries," in *Deconstructing Service in Libraries: Intersections of Identities and Expectations*, ed. Veronica Arellano Douglas and Joanna Gadsby (Sacramento, CA: Litwin Books, 2020), 271–92; Evans, "Weight of Service"; George, "DisService."

34. Tarida Anantachai and Camille Chesley, "The Burden of Care: Cultural Taxation of Women of Color Librarians on the Tenure-Track," in *Pushing the Margins: Women of Color and Intersectionality in LIS*, ed. Rose L. Chou and Annie Pho (Sacramento, CA: Library Juice Press, 2018), 301–27.

35. Anne Cong-Huyen and Kush Patel, "Precarious Labor and Radical Care in Libraries and Digital Humanities," in *Knowledge Justice: Disrupting Library and Information Studies through Critical Race Theory*, ed. Sofia Leung and Jorge R. López-McKnight (Cambridge, MA: MIT Press, 2021), 277.

36. Higgins, "Situating Service," 272–74.

37. Higgins, "Situating Service," 275.

38. Higgins, "Situating Service," 276–78.

39. Higgins, "Situating Service," 281.

40. Veronica Arellano Douglas, "Moving from Critical Assessment to Assessment as Care," *Communications in Information Literacy* 14, no. 1 (2020): 46–65.

41. Arellano Douglas, "Moving from Critical Assessment," 52.

42. Arellano Douglas, "Moving from Critical Assessment," 54.

43. Arellano Douglas, "Moving from Critical Assessment," 57.

44. Elizabeth Galoozis, "You Know How to Do This: Caring Service in Librarianship and Midwifery," in *Deconstructing Service in Libraries: Intersections of Identities and Expectations*, ed. Veronica Arellano Douglas and Joanna Gadsby (Sacramento, CA: Litwin Books, 2020), 263.

45. We Here is a community and LLC composed of Black and Indigenous Folks and People of Color working in library and information science that seeks to "recognize, discuss, and intervene in systemic social issues" inherent in the profession. "About Us," We Here, accessed January 5, 2022, https://www.wehere.space/about.

46. Cong-Huyen and Patel, "Precarious Labor," 277.

47. Anantachai and Chesley, "Burden of Care," 301.

48. Moore and Estrellado, "Identity, Activism, Self-Care, And Women of Color Librarians," 381.

49. Cong-Huyen and Patel, "Precarious Labor," 277.

50. Evans, "Weight of Service," 152–53.

51. George, "DisService," 114.

52. Siân Evans, Jacqueline Mabey, and Michael Mandiberg, "What We Talk about When We Talk about Community," in *Wikipedia @ 20: Stories of an Incomplete Revolution*, ed. Jackie Koerner and Joseph Reagle (Cambridge, MA: MIT Press, 2020), 224.

53. Priya Parker, *The Art of Gathering* (New York: Riverhead Books, 2018), 41.

54. George, "DisService," 115.

55. George, "DisService," 116–17.

56. George, "DisService," 199.

57. For example, see Jennifer Turner and Jessica Schomberg, "Inclusivity, Gestalt Principles, and Plain Language in Document Design," *In the Library with the Lead Pipe*, June 29, 2016, https://www.inthelibrarywiththeleadpipe.org/2016/accessibility/.

58. Dolmage, *Academic Ableism*, 145.

59. Dolmage, *Academic Ableism*, 145.

60. Dolmage, *Academic Ableism*, 132.

61. Amanda Meeks, "More than a Thought Experiment: Designing Anti-oppressive Events and Instruction," LibGuide, ACRL 2019 President's Program, April 15, 2019, https://acrl.libguides.com/c.php?g=899144&p=6468942&t=36708.

62. WNYC Studios, "The Overlooked Reality of Police Violence against Disabled Black Americans," The Takeaway, June 15, 2020, https://www.wnycstudios.org/podcasts/takeaway/segments/police-violence-disabled-black-americans.

63. Dobbin and Kalev, "Why Diversity Programs Fail," 140.

64. Evans, Mabey, and Mandiberg, "What We Talk About."

65. Mack and Meeks, "Safe, Brave Space Policy."

66. Evans, Mabey, and Mandiberg, "What We Talk About."

67. Ted Wachtel, "Defining Restorative," International Institute of Restorative Practices Graduate School, November 2016, https://www.iirp.edu/images/pdf/Defining-Restorative_Nov-2016.pdf.

68. Laura Mirsky, "Restorative Justice Practices of Native American, First Nation and Other Indigenous People of North America: Part One," Restorative Practices eForum, April 27, 2004, https://www.iirp.edu/pdf/natjust1.pdf.

69. Wachtel, "Defining Restorative."

70. Edwards et al., "Building Safer Spaces."

71. Dolmage, *Academic Ableism*, 145.

Bibliography

Anantachai, Tarida, and Camille Chesley. "The Burden of Care: Cultural Taxation of Women of Color Librarians on the Tenure-Track." In *Pushing the Margins: Women of Color and Intersectionality in LIS*, edited by Rose L. Chou and Annie Pho, 301-327. Series on Critical Race Studies and Multiculturalism in LIS. Sacramento, CA: Library Juice Press, 2018. EBSCOhost.

Arellano Douglas, Veronica. "Moving from Critical Assessment to Assessment as Care." *Communications in Information Literacy* 14, no. 1 (2020): 46–65.

brown, adrienne maree. *We Will Not Cancel Us and Other Dreams of Transformative Justice.* Chico, CA: AK Press, 2020.

Cong-Huyen, Anne, and Kush Patel. "Precarious Labor and Radical Care in Libraries and Digital Humanities." In *Knowledge Justice: Disrupting Library and Information Studies through Critical Race Theory*, edited by Sofia Y. Leung and Jorge R. López-McKnight, 263–82. Cambridge, MA: MIT Press, 2021.

Dobbin, Frank, and Alexandra Kalev. "Why Diversity Programs Fail." *Harvard Business Review*, July–August 2016. https://hbr.org/2016/07/why-diversity-programs-fail.

Dolmage, Jay T. *Academic Ableism: Disability and Higher Education.* Ann Arbor: University of Michigan Press, 2017.

Edwards, Tyde-Courtney, Siân Evans, Shawna Potter, and Kira Wisniewski. "Building Safer Spaces in Creative Communities." Online workshop, Common Field Convening, April 23, 2020. https://www.commonfield.org/convenings/3248/program/4020/building-safer-spaces-in-creative-communities (site discontinued).

Evans, Siân. "The Weight of Service: Librarianship and Mental Health." In *Deconstructing Service in Libraries: Intersections of Identities and Expectations*, edited by Veronica Arellano Douglas and Joanna Gadsby, 141–58. Sacramento, CA: Litwin Books, 2020.

Evans, Siân, Jacqueline Mabey, and Michael Mandiberg. "What We Talk about When We Talk about Community." In *Wikipedia @ 20: Stories of an Incomplete Revolution*, edited by Jackie Koerner and Joseph Reagle, 221–38. Cambridge, MA: MIT Press, 2020. https://wikipedia20.pubpub.org/pub/llx97ml5/release/2.

Galoozis, Elizabeth. "You Know How to Do This: Caring Service in Librarianship and Midwifery." In *Deconstructing Service in Libraries: Intersections of Identities and Expectations*, edited by Veronica Arellano Douglas and Joanna Gadsby, 255–70. Sacramento, CA: Litwin Books, 2020.

George, Kelsey. "DisService: Disabled Library Staff and Service Expectations." In *Deconstructing Service in Libraries: Intersections of Identities and Expectations*, edited by Veronica Arellano Douglas and Joanna Gadsby, 95–124. Sacramento, CA: Litwin Books, 2020.

Gibson, Amelia, Kristen Bowen, and Dana Hanson. "We Need to Talk about How We Talk about Disability: A Critical Quasi-systematic Review." *In the Library with the Lead Pipe*, February 24, 2021. https://www.inthelibrarywiththeleadpipe.org/2021/disability/.

Ginsburg, Faye, Mara Mills, and Rayna Rapp. "From Quality of Life to Disability Justice: Imagining a Post-Covid Future." *Somatosphere* (blog), June 2, 2020. http://somatosphere.net/2020/from-quality-of-life-to-disability-justice.html/.

Higgins, Shana. "Situating Service: Care and Equity in Academic Libraries." In *Deconstructing Service in Libraries: Intersections of Identities and Expectations*, edited by Veronica Arellano Douglas and Joanna Gadsby, 271–92. Sacramento, CA: Litwin Books, 2020.

Hill, Heather. "Disability and Accessibility in the Library and Information Science Literature: A Content Analysis." *Library and Information Science Research* 35, no. 2 (April 2013): 137–42. https://doi.org/10.1016/j.lisr.2012.11.002.

Kumbier, Alana, and Julia Starkey. "Access Is Not Problem Solving: Disability Justice and Libraries." *Library Trends* 64, no. 3 (Winter 2016): 468–91. https://doi.org/10.1353/lib.2016.0004.

Mack, McKensie, and Amanda Meeks. "Safe, Brave Space Policy." Art+Feminism. Accessed July 26, 2021. https://artandfeminism.org/resources/safety/safe-space-brave-space/.

Meeks, Amanda. "More than a Thought Experiment: Designing Anti-oppressive Events and Instruction." LibGuide, ACRL 2019 President's Program, April 15, 2019. https://acrl.libguides.com/c.php?g=899144&p=6468942&t=36708.

Mingus, Mia. "Changing the Framework: Disability Justice." *Leaving Evidence* (blog), February 12, 2011. https://leavingevidence.wordpress.com/2011/02/12/changing-the-framework-disability-justice/.

Mirsky, Laura. "Restorative Justice Practices of Native American, First Nation and Other Indigenous People of North America: Part One." Restorative Practices eForum, April 27, 2004. https://www.iirp.edu/pdf/natjust1.pdf.

Moeller, Christine M. "Disability, Identity, and Professionalism: Precarity in Librarianship." *Library Trends* 67, no. 3 (Winter 2019): 455–70. https://doi.org/10.1353/lib.2019.0006.

Moore, Alanna Aiko and Estrellado, Jan E., "Identity, Activism, Self-Care, and Women of Color Librarians." In *Pushing the Margins Women of Color and Intersectionality in LIS*, edited by Rose L. Chou and Annie Pho, 349-389. Sacramento, CA: Library Juice Press, 2018

Oud, Joanne. "Systemic Workplace Barriers for Academic Librarians with Disabilities." *College and Research Libraries* 80, no. 2 (March 2019): 169–94. https://doi.org/10.5860/crl.80.2.169.

Parker, Priya. *The Art of Gathering: How We Meet and Why It Matters.* New York: Riverhead Books, 2018.

Piepzna-Samarasinha, Leah Lakshmi. *Care Work: Dreaming Disability Justice.* Vancouver, BC: Arsenal Pulp Press, 2018. EBSCOhost.

Potter, Shawna. *Making Spaces Safer: A Guide to Giving Harassment the Boot Wherever You Work, Play, and Gather.* Chico, CA: AK Press, 2019.

Rosen, Stephanie. "Accessibility for Justice: Accessibility as a Tool for Promoting Justice in Librarianship." *In the Library with the Lead Pipe*, November 29, 2017. https://www.inthelibrarywiththeleadpipe.org/2017/accessibility-for-justice/.

Sins Invalid. "Ten Principles of Disability Justice." *Sins Invalid* (blog), September 17, 2015. https://www.sinsinvalid.org/blog/10-principles-of-disability-justice.

Turner, Jennifer, and Jessica Schomberg. "Inclusivity, Gestalt Principles, and Plain Language in Document Design." *In the Library with the Lead Pipe*, June 29, 2016. https://www.inthelibrarywiththeleadpipe.org/2016/accessibility/.

Wachtel, Ted. "Defining Restorative." International Institute of Restorative Practices Graduate School, November 2016. https://www.iirp.edu/images/pdf/Defining-Restorative_Nov-2016.pdf.

We Here. "About Us." Accessed January 5, 2022. https://www.wehere.space/about.

Wong, Alice. "I'm Disabled and Need a Ventilator to Live. Am I Expendable during This Pandemic?" Vox, April 4, 2020. https://www.vox.com/first-person/2020/4/4/21204261/coronavirus-covid-19-disabled-people-disabilities-triage.

WNYC Studios. "The Overlooked Reality of Police Violence Against Disabled Black Americans." The Takeaway, June 15, 2020. https://www.wnycstudios.org/podcasts/takeaway/segments/police-violence-disabled-black-americans.

CHAPTER 9

A Practice of Connection

Applying Relational-Cultural Theory to Librarianship

Anastasia Chiu, Veronica Arellano Douglas, Joanna Gadsby, Alana Kumbier, and Lalitha Nataraj

Introduction

In this chapter we apply relational-cultural theory (RCT) to librarianship through community storytelling and autoethnography. Autoethnography is a "qualitative, reflexive, ethnographic method where the researcher is also the subject of inquiry."[1] It is a relational method of research, helping us "understand knowledge in terms of relationships, in context, and not abstracted through the lens of borrowed theory."[2] What follows is a brief primer on RCT and a series of stories generated through conversation and linked through theory and collective reflection. This chapter models a way of building relational competence, "the capacity to effect change [through] relationship,"[3] which is how we hope to create positive transformation through connection and help others realize that possibility in their work lives. We first publicly shared our experiences with RCT at the

2018 Critical Librarianship and Pedagogy Symposium (CLAPS) and the Association for College and Research Libraries' (ACRL) 2019 "Recasting the Narrative" conference and were heartened to hear how RCT tenets that had helped us make sense of our own work resonated with LIS workers' and students' experiences, values, and praxes. This chapter is a continuation of that conversation, honoring the work of RCT theorists by sharing applications of RCT to librarianship.

What Is RCT?

RCT is a model of human development that posits that "connection is at the core of human growth and development."[4] It has developed and expanded through a series of meetings, papers, conferences, and books held between and written by Jean Baker Miller, Judith V. Jordan, Alexandra G. Kaplan, Irene P. Stiver, Janet L. Surrey, Maureen Walker, and Linda M. Hartling. As clinicians, supervisors, and teachers, these women observed that dominant models of human development which stressed autonomy and independence had a detrimental impact on clients of all genders, but particularly women, who were pathologized as underdeveloped or overly dependent. They questioned the "usefulness of a psychology that elevates and celebrates the separate self"[5] and rightly characterized it as a tool of dominant white, cis male, middle-class, heterosexual culture. In RCT the "path of human development is through movement to increasingly differentiated and growth-fostering connection."[6] We all grow through and toward relationship, and those relationships are positioned within a larger sociocultural context where race, ethnicity, class, gender, and sexual orientation all complicate connection.[7] RCT is a way of understanding our growth as people, our relationships to others, and the primacy of connection in our lives.

The central tenets of RCT have evolved over the years but are generally agreed to be the following:

Mutuality or *intersubjective mutuality* is an "appreciation of the wholeness of the other person" with whom you are in relationship.[8] It's a reciprocal acknowledgment and respect of the other person's humanity and unique, subjective life experience.

Empathy is a complex cognitive and affective process that requires "a well-differentiated sense of self," as well as an appreciation for the other person. It is a "temporary identification with the other's state" in order to better understand the other person and create growth in the relationship.[9]

Vulnerability is a person's ability to represent themselves more fully in a relationship. It is more accurately described as *relational authenticity*, which is "not the same thing as total honesty ...it is about quality of presence."[10] It's about being genuinely engaged in the relationship, however brief.

Openness is not synonymous with a lack of boundaries. Boundaries are essential for self-protection, self-differentiation, "respect, clarity, and responsibility" in relationship. However, it is about using boundaries as meeting places to "open ourselves to being known, to being moved, and to moving another person."[11]

Power with, NOT power over is a frequent refrain within RCT. Within Western cultures, we tend to think of power as synonymous with authority, something to be wielded while lording over others, making people do as we say. Within RCT, Miller describes power as "the capacity to produce a change."[12] This can mean "moving one's own thoughts or emotions" or creating movement in relationship.[13] Power is about mutual empowerment rather than power hoarding, ensuring that all individuals in the relationship benefit.[14]

Growthful conflict is highly valued within RCT. It is a "necessary part of relationships, essential for the changes that must be made so that the relationship and each person in it can change and grow."[15] When conflict happens, we have an opportunity to learn from the disconnection and to do our best to move back into connection with one another.

RCT has been applied outside of the mental health therapeutic context to understanding workplace dynamics, higher education, teaching, assessment, and, most recently, librarianship.[16] The work of three of the chapter authors and Symphony Bruce, Torie Quiñonez, and Antonia Olivas has looked at reference work, teaching, instruction coordination, and librarianship as a whole through an RCT lens.[17]

Why Stories?

As we contemplated how to share the ways in which RCT has enriched our professional practice, we turned to both our interactions as a community of practice and the models of scholarship set by the originators of RCT. So much of our learning and processing of RCT took place through conversation. We shared experiences, related them to our reading, and found connections between theory and practice. This method was modeled after the originating RCT theorists, who practiced collaborative writing, conversational tone, and use of clinical examples and narrative in their essays. Their process of community knowledge building broadened our perspective on the forms scholarship can take. Each of our stories connects different aspects of academic librarianship to facets of RCT. Where there is overlap is where we come together as practitioners and scholars to further our understanding of the primacy of connection and relationship in our work.

Power with/Establishing Boundaries—Joanna Gadsby

My engagement with RCT, particularly the idea of *power with* rather than *power over*, has taken place primarily through teaching and learning. To share power is to create energy and movement in learning, which serves the essential goal of teaching.[18] When we examine power sharing from the perspective of instruction librarians in the classroom, we often reveal a lack of agency. Teaching faculty typically set the tone and determine the content for their class, even those sessions that involve library instruction, without consultation or collaboration. Our efforts end up feeling disconnected or dropped in. We need more narratives surrounding what it looks like for faculty and librarians to contribute equally to instruction in the classroom, and this requires intentional effort to move toward mutually empowering relationships. If the work we do together is built on mutual respect, this enhances the experience for everyone involved. There is relational work to be done before the lesson planning even begins, particularly in how the program is structured.

My library's instruction department often starts this relational work through setting boundaries via policy. One such policy is a requirement for two weeks' notice from faculty in order to schedule a class. The lead time exists as a general courtesy to the librarians with busy calendars, but it also allows time for planning and thoughtful integration of the library session into the course's curriculum. Unofficially, in the past, many of our department's more seasoned librarians, myself included, would honor a last-minute request from a faculty member to work with their students the next day or after another length of time shorter than two weeks. The librarians who chose to schedule these classes did so due to their own comfort level with teaching as well as an interest in accommodating faculty and their students. This created inconsistencies with the librarians who chose to enforce the department's policy.

As the department's instruction coordinator, I could have decided to either discard this policy or insist on its enforcement. However, we do our best work together when we function as a community of practice; utilizing the principles of relational-cultural theory would help us reach community agreement. A unilateral decision on my part would reduce the strength and power of our group,[19] so I organized a meeting for us to work through these inconsistencies. We agreed that everyone would remain consistent on the two weeks' notice as a way of drawing a clear boundary. In doing so, we create space for those who need the additional time without them having to ask for it.

This conversation led to discussion about other scheduling policies that would help our teaching librarians feel more empowered as a unit and allow us to do our best work without risking burnout. We developed a policy that states that all classes must be scheduled and on the calendar by the midpoint of the semester; sessions can take place later in the semester, but the teaching faculty need to make the request before midterms. After that deadline, classes cannot be added. We felt that continuing to add classes later in the semester did a disservice to our department and did not allow us to do our best teaching. It is easier to get through what can be an exhausting time line when you know what lies ahead, which becomes more difficult when responsibilities are continually added to the pile.

This process allowed members of our teaching team to be vulnerable by asking for consistency in policy, to show support for one another and give the program greater strength in solidarity, and to set some clear boundaries for our time and energy. These boundaries "potentially include the capacity to authentically represent one's needs and feelings in a context that holds some promise of mutuality."[20] Although our new policies were not a definitive guarantee that instructors would enter into a professional relationship with teaching librarians from a place of mutual respect and openness, it did set a necessary foundation for mutuality and relational authenticity.

Onboarding Is Relational—Lalitha Nataraj

Four years ago, I started reflecting on how collegial and validating relationships could contribute to a sense of empowerment within the workplace. I had just made the transition to academic librarianship after working as a public librarian for over a decade; this was largely motivated by a desire for greater agency and autonomy in my work. I also wanted to leave behind dysfunctionality, which included incivility, mission creep, and resilience narratives[21]—these problems were systemic issues in the public libraries in which I worked, exacerbated by dwindling budgets. Staff felt pressured to demonstrate value by increasing productivity despite dwindling resources, which led to burnout.

Many of the aforementioned issues, particularly resilience narratives, stem from entrenched bureaucratic practices in libraries[22] that compound fundamental organizational problems.[23] Bureaucracies withhold information to maintain power structures and force employees to manage their expectations and emotions around work, as well as adopting a scarcity mentality of doing more with less.[24]

Norms were often unstated, and I frequently learned the "correct" way to do (or be) after committing gaffes and being on the receiving end of judgment and criticism from my coworkers. Such feelings lead to low morale and manifest as "work dread …reduced professional confidence, reduced ability to concentrate, self-censorship, and depression."[25]

In each job where I had such discomfiting experiences, I observed that onboarding processes were minimal, poorly defined, or nonexistent. During onboarding, a new employee is "introduced to the organization, its work culture, and its mission and values. Much of the tone of new staff members' supervisory, departmental, and administrative relationships is struck in this period."[26] When it's done properly, the onboarding process allows an employee to fully realize what Morandin, Russo, and Bergami refer to as the future relational self, which encompasses the types of relationships one hopes to foster and sustain with colleagues in the workplace.[27] Research has shown that affective experiences at work contribute to positive outcomes for the employee and the organization. The onboarding process potentially forecasts a person's capacity to "adjust to the social dynamics of the new workplace …and to develop a clear understanding of the expectations associated with their new role."[28] But when it's done poorly, onboarding is an aspect of what Kendrick refers to as an overall *enabling system* within the organization that reifies low morale.[29]

I vividly recall my very first day of work as a public librarian; I arrived just before the library opened, but I didn't have my card key yet, so I waited for my coworkers to let me into the building. Two passed by, and when I smiled and tried to make eye contact with them, they hurried into the library while I ended up walking in with our patrons. Later, those colleagues admitted that they didn't realize who I was; this minor interaction, as well as the fact that my direct supervisor was unavailable to meet me, cast a pall on that day. I was also scheduled for a solo shift on the reference desk and expected to intuitively figure out the catalog and shelving system while delivering stellar service to our library patrons.

Jordan writes that the "need to connect, and the need to contribute in a meaningful way, to be competent, productive, and creative, optimally flow together."[30] This stark lack of an onboarding process was one manifestation of "power-over" dynamics in this library. In a power-over relationship, one person (or specific group) sets the "rules for discourse and the direction that the relationship will take."[31] In that first month, I was told by several colleagues (including managers) about previous employees who had not passed probation, and no one knew why. These pointed disclosures unnerved me such that in the first twelve months of this job, I spent a lot of time feeling as if I had to engage in preemptive damage control. Onboarding is part and parcel of a psychological contract between the new employee and the employer where formalized socialization impacts a person's capacity to develop enduring relationships and be successful in their job.[32]

While my career in public librarianship was replete with such experiences, I found a supportive environment in the academic library. But here also, the formal onboarding process was somewhat lacking; my office space was not set up appropriately—I used a conference room chair for several weeks as my desk chair—and it took me several months to understand the campus governance structure. Interdependence between various library units is vital to relationship building and collegiality, and that took me a while to understand. The crucial difference between this job and my previous ones was that my colleagues in the academic library did not judge me harshly for the mistakes I inevitably made; on the contrary, they encouraged me to lean into discomfort and to forgo self-consciousness for the sake of improving my skills. I learned that the teaching and learning department had a relational awareness, or attentiveness to others' needs,[33] and prioritized the collective well-being of its members. As an adjunct lecturer librarian, and later a tenure-track librarian, I was acknowledged as a fully contributing member of the department, helping to shape norms and teaching practices. However, these contexts were clear only after I spent significant time within the department. Several of us agreed that we needed a more explicit onboarding process for new lecturers.

During the COVID-19 pandemic, one of my colleagues, April Ibarra Siqueiros, drafted a relational onboarding document that extended beyond a "transactional and informational onboarding …to make space for the existing expertise and skills of a new librarian to share with the department."[34] This document describes our current anti-racism efforts, our reflective teaching philosophies, and even the Black, Indigenous, and People of Color (BIPOC) affinity groups we have formed in our library. Here, we have a "power-with" dynamic, where the primary focus is on creating connections to enhance existing relationships and empower one another.[35]

Navigating Workplace Conflict—Alana Kumbier

RCT has helped me, as a white person who was socialized to "avoid, ignore, and deny conflict,"[36] learn to navigate—and even welcome—growthful conflict in the workplace. The conflict that shines brightest in my memory is the one where I felt the greatest sense of disappointment in myself. I was in charge of a hiring process to expand a cohort of alumni fellows working with the library. The cohort included multiple Black, queer, transgender, and nonbinary people. In order to give prospective hires a sense of what the fellowship involved, I asked current fellows to meet with the candidates for question-and-answer conversation time. I envisioned the meetings as nonevaluative, as the cohort members would not be on the hiring committee.

I didn't realize, until a fellow spoke with me about the process, that I'd basically created a situation of fake inclusion. The fellow, a Black queer person, shared their experience of meeting with candidates for several hours of their workweek, acting as a workplace representative, and developing a stake in the hiring process without having structural agency or decision-making power in the outcome. This was especially hard for the cohort members because they cared deeply about their work, the future of the project they were supporting, and the students who these candidates would support. I had included BIPOC fellows in the process in ways that benefited the candidates and the organization, but by excluding them from the decision-making process, I reproduced racialized and role-contingent structures of power and value in the library.[37] For BIPOC, this practice of fake inclusion and racialized exclusion can contribute to traumatic stress and the experience of a work environment as unsafe.[38]

As we moved into our conversation, I reminded myself of the RCT perspective that these moments can be generative and that they are normal. As Bergman and Surrey argue,

> Constructive conflict and *struggling with difference* are inevitable in relationships. They stimulate growth when the creative tension of *staying with the differences* is supported by the relational context. What Miller has called 'waging good conflict' (1976) can lead to growth and enlargement of relationships.[39]

Approaching a conflict with this perspective allowed me to focus on listening with openness and empathy, for understanding.

I appreciated that this was a moment for building our connection: as the cohort member shared their experience, I better understood how the situation made them feel and what it meant to them. I also maintained awareness of the cultural contexts for our conversation. As a white supervisor and person in solidarity with BIPOC coworkers, I am responsible for interrupting histories of racial violence that result in harm, separation, and disconnection. When white coworkers dismiss or otherwise disrespect BIPOC coworkers' experiences and perspectives, BIPOC coworkers have reason to withdraw from connection (in the present and in the future) because their authentic expression has resulted in "isolation, devaluation, and disconnection."[40] By listening with openness and empathy, I followed psychotherapist Roseann Adams's guidance to "[take] responsibility for the co-creation of a context of safety within a racially unsafe culture."[41]

As I listened to the fellow and heard what they shared, some of my familiar conflict feelings surfaced: strong disappointment in myself for creating the situation, anger that I was having to navigate a conflict, panic about not having a solution, dread at the thought of sharing my faults with my supervisor, and defensiveness. My emotional responses resonated with a larger set of power-over moves I'd witnessed and experienced in my work with other white managers: reasserting the status quo ("that's just how it is"), trying to name a deficiency on the coworker's part, minimizing the situation ("we all experience that"), or encouraging them to calm down as a way to foreclose authentic sharing. These are all common ways power-over culture shows up in conflicts, including cross-cultural or interracial conflict. As I noticed what was coming up internally, I was also aware that these intense feelings, and my disappointment at having them, made me want to cry.

I knew, as a white person, that my crying in response to feedback from a Black person about racist actions would be (intentionally or not) a power-over move: white people may employ our tears to signal our status as the hurt or victimized party in a conflict, to dodge accountability, and to garner empathy that might otherwise be directed to a Black person sharing a grievance or experience. I couldn't stop my physiological response, but I could own it and acknowledge where it was coming from: my anger and disappointment at myself—not the fellow's feedback. The fellow and I had been in our relationship long enough that they knew I was prone to expressing all kinds of big feelings through tears, but still: recognizing the power dynamics that could play out in this particular crying moment was essential to maintaining mutuality. As we continued our conversation, I acknowledged the harm the fellow experienced and shared my heartfelt appreciation for their trusting me with their story. I asked if we could spend the rest of our meeting time talking through their ideas for what should happen so I could gather information to bring to others involved in the process. We didn't come up with a solution to the problem in that meeting, but we left the conversation having grown our mutual respect, trust, and empathy.

What's Legal Advice Anyway?— Anastasia Chiu

As a scholarly communications librarian, I staff an informational consultation service on copyright and fair use in research and teaching. One of my first consultations was with a team of instructional designers building an online course for faculty members. I had just transitioned from cataloging and metadata to scholarly communications, and the work was a big change in terms of relationship building and interpersonal dynamics. Although I wasn't new to talking about copyright and fair use with colleagues and library users, it was my first time reinforcing the line between an informational consultation and legal advice.

The team I spoke with in this consultation sought to understand whether they could rely on fair use, a commonly used exception to copyright, to provide access to copyrighted materials in various ways and for various class uses on the course site. My goal in the conversation was to give general information about how to think through fair use. As we moved through the conversation, many of the team's questions became more specific and began to range into legal advice territory, including questions like "Is it fair use to do X or not?" or "How much legal risk is there in doing Y?"

Although I am not a lawyer and it's impossible for anything I say to be legal advice, my manager *is* licensed as a lawyer but is not positioned to provide legal advice in this role. It is important that both of us provide consultations with similar openness and boundaries. Therefore, I began reframing some of the team's questions to speak more generally about fair use. When team members insisted that I answer their question specifically as framed, I expressed that the question required legal advice. I could help them understand copyright and fair use, but decisions about whether and how to use copyrighted materials were theirs to make based on their own knowledge of the materials and the course needs. In most of my consultations, which are usually with faculty members, this is generally met with acceptance, if tinged with slight disappointment. In this case, it was met with gently expressed but unmistakable frustration and tiredness. Members of the team emphasized their positionality as staff members and expressed their frustration in being responsible for seamless course design, but they did not consider themselves institutionally empowered to take risks of any kind in doing so.

Although I expected that the team might experience vulnerability in asking for help, I did not anticipate their range of sentiments. Our consultation service's goal is to build power with scholars and teachers, but it seemed clear that they were not experiencing our interaction as mutual, and my overtures toward openness in the conversation were not aligned with where they experienced need or desire for openness. From a relational-cultural perspective, I understood that the instructional design team members emphasized their positionality in part because they wanted reciprocally authentic responsiveness—"movement into fuller and deeper connection with the feeling-thoughts of the moment."[42] At first, I struggled to do this within my boundary of providing general information without entering legal advice territory. I saw from the team members' frustration that simply stating "I can't give legal advice" in response to a question, especially after they had given voice to vulnerability, was understood as a refusal to meet them with mutuality. I sought to build more openness into my responses, sometimes by providing further examples and analysis and sometimes by pointing them to a source that provided further clarity. Eventually, over the course of many follow-ups, we began to establish a less stumbling rhythm of conversation with a stronger sense of how to ask questions of each other and answer each other's questions.

In reflection, and over the course of more consultations like this one, I came to realize that I could insist upon my boundary while also explaining it more clearly. It is not always self-evident what kinds of questions require legal advice and how they can be reframed to empower all parties to engage. Many people, including myself, often navigate the legal advice boundary by bumping up against it more than once. Although having this particular boundary bumped into does not harm me, the memory of this interaction reminds me that it can be frustrating for library users to move through a consultation with the sense that they have to navigate an important boundary through trial and error. Since that consultation, I have worked on providing explanations around what kinds of questions I can speak to most directly and on building the skill of framing questions and answers in ways that ensure that both users and I can engage in an open conversation together about copyright and fair use.

Connection in the Classroom— Veronica Arellano Douglas

In February 2021 winter storm Uri hit Texas, pushing the state's aging power grid to a breaking point and leaving much of the population without power and water in freezing temperatures. Classes at the University of Houston, already held virtually in response to COVID-19 pandemic precautions, were canceled, as students and instructors struggled to meet basic needs for the week. When we all finally returned to our virtual workplaces and classrooms, we were weary, a little jittery anytime the lights flickered, and thankful that we were lucky enough to get through the storm when we all knew that some folks did not.[43]

My first class after the storm was a research workshop for a psychology research methods course. It was scheduled at a time when the instructor expected all students to have selected a research topic so that they could begin to engage with the research literature in support of a final research proposal. Not surprisingly, none of us were in the curricular, emotional, or cognitive state we thought we would be in when I first scheduled the workshop with the instructor. We'd all just been through a traumatic event, one we could not just ignore and push past during a sixty-minute class. Instead we took time at the beginning of the workshop to check in with one another and offer words of affirmation and care. I began with the following:

> I'm glad we're all here today. Are you doing ok? How is your house? Any burst pipes? Do you need anything? I know, it was awful. We aren't where we thought we'd be in the semester and that is totally OK. We will just work with where we are right now. I'm so happy to see you all here today.

Some students really wanted to dig into research, but most were still trying to gather their thoughts after an incredibly stressful week. The instructor herself was frazzled and off schedule. It was a rare moment of almost instantaneous trust in the classroom fueled by a shared experience and need to connect. More than anything we all wanted to come together that day to regain a sense of connection and routine during an already stressful time made even more intense by an unexpected winter snowstorm. It was a moment of what Judith V. Jordan refers to as "supported vulnerability."[44] We all, in that moment, experienced a need for emotional acknowledgment. We wanted to be seen and briefly share what we had all been through. In doing so we were quite vulnerable, as we were "letting people directly know about our need."[45] Yet by expressing and maintaining a sense of openness to one another—a mutual desire to speak, listen, be heard, and connect—we were able to honor that vulnerability and support one another through the process. The conversation was not without boundaries, as even in supported vulnerability boundaries are a necessary method of cultivating trust. No one was asked to share anything. No one was made to express anything they weren't able or willing to express, and some people did choose to remain silent. Yet those who needed to discuss the events of the last week were able to come together at their boundary, their place of meeting, and move forward together by acknowledging a shared event.[46]

One thing I take from that event and the sharing that took place in the classroom after it is the way in which mutuality was at the center of healing and connection. Students later expressed, as they brainstormed ideas for research topics, that they were anxious, unable to sleep, nervous, and stressed out. These were all very normal reactions to an acute moment of trauma in a year of pandemic isolation. In "Relational Resilience," Jordan states that as a society we "cannot continue to pathologize individual adaptations to socially destructive patterns."[47] Rather than pathologize students whose ideas around research were being informed by an event caused by government, economic, and infrastructure failings, we as a class decided to validate those feelings and explore them as nuanced ideas for research informed by experience.

In that moment we were relationally authentic, present "with the thoughts and feelings occurring in the relationship."[48] There was a sense of mutual empathy, of openness and willingness to engage with one another. Without that trust and confidence it was highly unlikely that any kind of learning could have occurred in that workshop. Irene Stiver states that "authenticity is a process in movement."[49] By moving together we were all able to create a learning space where we could set our own boundaries, express a need for help when it was needed, and maintain a sense of openness to learn and grow. Although this particular instance of connection, trust, and relational authenticity was born out of a shared experience, it continues to inspire me to seek moments of connection and relational authenticity in all of my teaching opportunities. As teacher librarians we need to ask ourselves how we can create a safe haven for supported vulnerability in our classes and how we can foster confidence in the relationships we create in our learning environments. "Relationship [is] the site and source of learning"[50]—so how can we make sure these relationships are healthy, connected, and capable of creating change?

Conclusion

Centering relationships and connection in library work, though complex and difficult, can be a transformative practice. RCT can provide an important framework for critically thinking through how our work affects ourselves and others. It stresses the development of significant skills to be able to hold relational priorities of mutuality, empathy, openness, vulnerability/authenticity, power with, and growthful conflict, all in balance with other goals for our work. In a broader political economy that values productivity above all, and values relationality only insofar as it encourages productivity, these relational skills are rarely intentionally cultivated. And because library work is a part of this broader system of ideals around labor, the work that goes into relational aspects of library work is often made invisible or labeled as "the soft stuff" despite the centrality of relationships and connection to library services. Much of the connection that we, as a community of practice, have forged with each other has grown by illuminating the invisibilized relational aspects of our work together. Through our shared reading and conversations, we learned to articulate the acts of moving through relationships within our work—with our students, our colleagues, and our organizations—and seek ways to build the types of relationships that we aspire toward with each other. The wideness and variety of ways in which we have already begun to apply RCT consciously in our work indicates that there are many nooks, crannies, and crevices for this framework to show up in LIS. As this thread of scholarship and practice grows, we eventually hope to see the field develop practices and priorities acknowledging that, in fact, the soft stuff *is* the real stuff.

Notes

1. Anne-Marie Deitering, "Introduction: Why Autoethnography?" in *The Self as Subject: Autoethno-graphic Research into Identity, Culture and Academic Librarianship*, ed. Anne-Marie Deitering, Robert Schroeder, and Richard Stoddart (Chicago: ACRL Publications, 2017), 2.
2. Deitering, "Introduction," 10.
3. Judith V. Jordan, "Toward Competence and Connection," in *The Complexity of Connection: Writings from the Stone Center's Jean Baker Miller Training Institute*, ed. Judith V. Jordan, Maureen Walker, and Linda M. Hartling (New York: Guilford Press, 2004), 15.
4. Judith V. Jordan and Maureen Walker, "Introduction," in *The Complexity of Connection: Writings from the Stone Center's Jean Baker Miller Training Institute*, ed. Judith V. Jordan, Maureen Walker, and Linda M. Hartling (New York: Guilford Press, 2004), 2.
5. Jordan and Walker, "Introduction," 2.
6. Jordan and Walker, "Introduction," 2.
7. Jordan and Walker, "Introduction," 4–5.
8. Judith V. Jordan, "The Meaning of Mutuality," in *Women's Growth in Connection: Writings from the Stone Center*, by Judith V. Jordan et al. (New York: Guilford Press, 1991), 82.
9. Judith V. Jordan et al., "Empathy and Self Boundaries," in *Women's Growth in Connection: Writings from the Stone Center* (New York: Guilford Press, 1991), 69.
10. Jean Baker Miller et al., "Therapists' Authenticity," in *The Complexity of Connection: Writings from the Stone Center's Jean Baker Miller Training Institute*, ed. Judith V. Jordan, Maureen Walker, and Linda M. Hartling (New York: Guilford Press, 2004), 67.
11. Miller et al., "Therapists' Authenticity," 69–71.
12. Jean Baker Miller, "Women and Power," in *Women's Growth in Connection: Writings from the Stone Center*, by Judith V. Jordan et al. (New York: Guilford Press, 1991), 198.
13. Miller, "Women and Power," 198.
14. Nikki M. Fedele, "Relationships in Groups," in *The Complexity of Connection: Writings from the Stone Center's Jean Baker Miller Training Institute*, ed. Judith V. Jordan, Maureen Walker, and Linda M. Hartling (New York: Guilford Press, 2004), 201.
15. Alexandra G. Kaplan, Rona Klein, and Nancy Gleason, "Women's Self Development in Late Adolescence," in *Women's Growth in Connection: Writings from the Stone Center*, by Judith V. Jordan et al. (New York: Guilford Press, 1991), 125.
16. Harriet Schwartz, "Sometimes It's about More Than the Paper: Assessment as Relational Practice," *Journal on Excellence in College Teaching* 28, no. 2 (2017): 5–28; Joyce K. Fletcher, *Disappearing Acts* (Cambridge, MA: MIT Press, 1999); Sharon Freedberg, *Relational Theory for Social Work Practice* (New York: Routledge, 2009); Harriet Schwartz, *Connected Teaching* (Sterling, VA: Stylus, 2019).
17. Veronica Arellano Douglas and Joanna Gadsby, "All Carrots, No Sticks: Relational Practice and Library Instruction Coordination," *In the Library with the Lead Pipe*, July 10, 2019, https://www.inthelibrary-withtheleadpipe.org/2019/all-carrots-no-sticks-relational-practice-and-library-instruction-coor-dination/; Symphony Bruce, "Teaching with Care: A Relational Approach to Individual Research

Consultations," *In the Library with the Lead Pipe*, February 5, 2020, https://www.inthelibrarywiththe-leadpipe.org/2020/teaching-with-care/. Torie Quiñonez, Lalitha Nataraj, and Antonia Olivas, "The Praxis of Relation, Validation, and Motivation: Articulating LIS Collegiality through a CRT Lens," in *Knowledge Justice: Disrupting Library and Information Studies through Critical Race Theory*, edited by Sofia Y. Leung and Jorge R. López-McKnight (Cambridge, MA: MIT Press, 2021), 241-261.

18. Schwartz, *Connected Teaching*, 87.

19. Jordan and Walker, "Introduction," 5.

20. Miller et al., "Therapists' Authenticity," 69.

21. Kaetrena Davis Kendrick, "The Public Librarian Low-Morale Experience: A Qualitative Study," *Partnership: The Canadian Journal of Library and Information Practice and Research* 15, no. 2 (2020): 1–32, https://doi.org/10.21083/partnership.v15i2.5932.

22. Lalitha Nataraj et al., "'Nice White Meetings': Unpacking Absurd Library Bureaucracy through a Critical Race Theory Lens," *Canadian Journal of Academic Librarianship/Revue Canadienne de Bibliothéconomie Universitaire* 6 (2020): 1–15, https://doi.org/10.33137/cjal-rcbu.v6.34340.

23. Kendrick, "Public Librarian Low-Morale Experience."

24. Kendrick, "Public Librarian Low-Morale Experience."

25. Kendrick, "Public Librarian Low-Morale Experience," 12.

26. Lorelei Rutledge et al., "Onboarding: Setting the Stage," in *Developing a Residency Program: A Practical Guide for Librarians* (Lanham, MD: Rowman & Littlefield, 2019), 75.

27. Gabriele Morandin, Marcello Russo, and Massimo Bergami, "Imagining the Newcomer–Supervisor Relationship: Future Relational Self in the Workplace," *Human Resource Management Journal* 31, no. 4 (November 2021): 1010–24, https://doi.org/10.1111/1748-8583.12340.

28. Morandin, Russo, and Bergami, "Imagining the Newcomer–Supervisor Relationship," 1012.

29. Kendrick, "Public Librarian Low-Morale Experience."

30. Jordan, "Toward Competence and Connection," 11.

31. Judith V. Jordan, "Relational Resilience," in *The Complexity of Connection: Writings from the Stone Center's Jean Baker Miller Training Institute*, ed. Judith V. Jordan, Maureen Walker, and Linda M. Hartling (New York: Guilford Press, 2004), 35.

32. Lorelei Rutledge et al., "Onboarding: Resident's Arrival and Beyond," in *Developing a Residency Program: A Practical Guide for Librarians* (Lanham, MD: Rowman & Littlefield, 2019), 93–111.

33. Jordan, "Toward Competence and Connection."

34. April Ibarra Siqueiros, "Teaching and Learning Relational Onboarding" (unpublished internal document, California State University San Marcos, January 2021).

35. Ibarra Siqueiros, "Relational Onboarding."

36. Cynthia García Coll, Robin Cook-Nobles, and Janet L. Surrey, "Building Connection through Diversity," in *Women's Growth in Diversity: More Writings from the Stone Center*, ed. Judith V. Jordan (New York: Guilford Press, 1997), 187.

37. David James Hudson, "On 'Diversity' as Anti-racism in Library and Information Studies: A Critique," *Journal of Critical Library and Information Studies* 1, no. 1 (January 31, 2017), https://doi.org/10.24242/jclis.v1i1.6.

38. Pratyusha Tummala-Narra, *Psychoanalytic Theory and Cultural Competence in Psychotherapy* (Washington, DC: American Psychological Association, 2016), 149.

39. Stephen J. Bergman and Janet L. Surrey, "Woman-Man Relationship: Impasses and Possibilities," in *Women's Growth in Diversity: More Writings from the Stone Center*, ed. Judith V. Jordan (New York: Guilford Press, 1997), 261 (italics in the original).

40. Roseann Adams, "The Five Good Things in Cross-cultural Therapy," in *How Connections Heal: Stories from Relational Cultural Therapy*, ed. Maureen Walker and Wendy B. Rosen (New York: Guilford Press, 2004), 152.

41. Adams, "Five Good Things," 153.

42. Maureen Walker, "Walking a Piece of the Way: Race, Power, and Therapeutic Movement," in *How Connections Heal: Stories from Relational Cultural Therapy*, ed. Maureen Walker and Wendy B. Rosen (New York: Guilford Press, 2004), 50.

43. Kara Norton, "Why Texas Was Not Prepared for Winter Storm Uri," *NOVA*, PBS Education, March 25, 2021, https://www.pbs.org/wgbh/nova/article/texas-winter-storm-uri/.

44. Jordan, "Relational Resilience," 33.
45. Jordan, "Relational Resilience," 34.
46. Miller et al., "Therapists' Authenticity," 70.
47. Jordan, "Relational Resilience," 43.
48. Miller et al., "Therapists' Authenticity," 65.
49. Miller et al., "Therapists' Authenticity," 73.
50. Schwartz, *Connected Teaching*, 14.

Bibliography

Adams, Roseann. "The Five Good Things in Cross-cultural Therapy." In *How Connections Heal: Stories from Relational Cultural Therapy*, edited by Maureen Walker and Wendy B. Rosen, 151–73. New York: Guilford Press, 2004.

Arellano Douglas, Veronica, and Joanna Gadsby. "All Carrots, No Sticks: Relational Practice and Library Instruction Coordination." *In the Library with the Lead Pipe*, July 10, 2019. https://www.inthelibrarywiththeleadpipe.org/2019/all-carrots-no-sticks-relational-practice-and-library-instruction-coordination/.

Bergman, Stephen J., and Janet L. Surrey. "Woman-Man Relationship: Impasses and Possibilities." In *Women's Growth in Diversity: More Writings from the Stone Center*, edited by Judith V. Jordan, 260–88. New York: Guilford Press, 1997.

Bruce, Symphony. "Teaching with Care: A Relational Approach to Individual Research Consultations." *In the Library with the Lead Pipe*, February 5, 2020. https://www.inthelibrarywiththeleadpipe.org/2020/teaching-with-care/.

Deitering, Anne-Marie. "Introduction: Why Autoethnography?" In *The Self as Subject: Autoethnographic Research into Identity, Culture and Academic Librarianship*, edited by Anne-Marie Deitering, Robert Schroeder, and Richard Stoddart, 1-22. Chicago: ACRL Publications, 2017.

Fedele, Nikki M. "Relationships in Groups." In *The Complexity of Connection: Writings from the Stone Center's Jean Baker Miller Training Institute*, edited by Judith V. Jordan, Maureen Walker, and Linda M. Hartling, 194–219. New York: Guilford Press, 2004.

Fletcher, Joyce K. *Disappearing Acts: Gender, Power and Relational Practice at Work*. Cambridge, MA: MIT Press, 1999.

Freedberg, Sharon. *Relational Theory for Social Work Practice: A Feminist Perspective*. New York: Routledge, 2009.

García Coll, Cynthia, Robin Cook-Nobles, and Janet L. Surrey. "Building Connection through Diversity." In *Women's Growth in Diversity: More Writings from the Stone Center*, edited by Judith V. Jordan, 176–98. New York: Guilford Press, 1997.

Hudson, David James. "On 'Diversity' as Anti-racism in Library and Information Studies: A Critique." *Journal of Critical Library and Information Studies* 1, no. 1 (January 31, 2017). https://doi.org/10.24242/jclis.v1i1.6.

Ibarra Siqueiros, April. "Teaching and Learning Relational Onboarding." Unpublished internal document. California State University, San Marcos, January 2021.

Jordan, Judith V. "The Meaning of Mutuality." In *Women's Growth in Connection: Writings from the Stone Center*, by Judith V. Jordan, Alexandra G. Kaplan, Jean Baker Miller, Irene P. Stiver, and Janet L. Surrey, 81–96. New York: Guilford Press, 1991.

———. "Relational Resilience." In *The Complexity of Connection: Writings from the Stone Center's Jean Baker Miller Training Institute*, edited by Judith V. Jordan, Maureen Walker, and Linda M. Hartling, 28–46. New York: Guilford Press, 2004.

———. "Toward Competence and Connection." In *The Complexity of Connection: Writings from the Stone Center's Jean Baker Miller Training Institute*, edited by Judith V. Jordan, Maureen Walker, and Linda M. Hartling, 11–27. New York: Guilford Press, 2004.

Jordan, Judith V., Alexandra G. Kaplan, Jean Baker Miller, Irene P. Stiver, and Janet L. Surrey. "Empathy and Self Boundaries." In *Women's Growth in Connection: Writings from the Stone Center*, 67–80. New York: Guilford Press, 1991.

Jordan, Judith V., and Maureen Walker. "Introduction." In *The Complexity of Connection: Writings from the Stone Center's Jean Baker Miller Training Institute*, edited by Judith V. Jordan, Maureen Walker, and Linda M. Hartling, 1–8. New York: Guilford Press, 2004.

Kaplan, Alexandra G., Rona Klein, and Nancy Gleason. "Women's Self Development in Late Adolescence." In *Women's Growth in Connection: Writings from the Stone Center*, by Judith V. Jordan, Alexandra G. Kaplan, Jean Baker Miller, Irene P. Stiver, and Janet L. Surrey, 122–42. New York: Guilford Press, 1991.

Kendrick, Kaetrena Davis. "The Public Librarian Low-Morale Experience: A Qualitative Study." *Partnership: The Canadian Journal of Library and Information Practice and Research* 15, no. 2 (2020): 1–32. https://doi.org/10.21083/partnership.v15i2.5932.

Miller, Jean Baker. "Women and Power." In *Women's Growth in Connection: Writings from the Stone Center*, by Judith V. Jordan, Alexandra G. Kaplan, Jean Baker Miller, Irene P. Stiver, and Janet L. Surrey, 197–205. New York: Guilford Press, 1991.

Miller, Jean Baker, Judith V. Jordan, Irene P. Stiver, Maureen Walker, Janet L. Surrey, and Natalie S. Eldridge. "Therapists' Authenticity." In *The Complexity of Connection: Writings from the Stone Center's Jean Baker Miller Training Institute*, edited by Judith V. Jordan, Maureen Walker, and Linda M. Hartling, 64–89. New York: Guilford Press, 2004.

Morandin, Gabriele, Marcello Russo, and Massimo Bergami. "Imagining the Newcomer–Supervisor Relationship: Future Relational Self in the Workplace." *Human Resource Management Journal* 31, no. 4 (November 2021): 1010–24. https://doi.org/10.1111/1748-8583.12340.

Nataraj, Lalitha, Holly Hampton, Talitha R. Matlin, and Yvonne Nalani Meulemans. "'Nice White Meetings': Unpacking Absurd Library Bureaucracy through a Critical Race Theory Lens." *Canadian Journal of Academic Librarianship/Revue Canadienne de Bibliothéconomie Universitaire* 6 (2020): 1–15. https://doi.org/10.33137/cjal-rcbu.v6.34340.

Norton, Kara. "Why Texas Was Not Prepared for Winter Storm Uri." *NOVA*, PBS Education, March 25, 2021. https://www.pbs.org/wgbh/nova/article/texas-winter-storm-uri/.

Quiñonez, Torie, Lalitha Nataraj, and Antonia Olivas. "The Praxis of Relation, Validation, and Motivation: Articulating LIS Collegiality through a CRT Lens." In *Knowledge Justice: Disrupting Library and Information Studies through Critical Race Theory*, edited by Sofia Y. Leung and Jorge R. López-McKnight, 241-61. Cambridge, MA: MIT Press, 2021.

Rutledge, Lorelei, Jay L. Colbert, Anastasia Chiu, and Jason Alston. "Onboarding: Resident's Arrival and Beyond." In *Developing a Residency Program: A Practical Guide for Librarians*, 93–111. Lanham, MD: Rowman & Littlefield, 2019.

———. "Onboarding: Setting the Stage." In *Developing a Residency Program: A Practical Guide for Librarians*, 75–91. Lanham, MD: Rowman & Littlefield, 2019.

Schwartz, Harriet. *Connected Teaching: Relationship, Power, and Mattering in Higher Education*. Sterling, VA: Stylus, 2019.

———. "Sometimes It's about More Than the Paper: Assessment as Relational Practice." *Journal on Excellence in College Teaching* 28, no. 2 (2017): 5–28.

Tummala-Narra, Pratyusha. *Psychoanalytic Theory and Cultural Competence in Psychotherapy*. Washington, DC: American Psychological Association, 2016.

Walker, Maureen. "Walking a Piece of the Way: Race, Power, and Therapeutic Movement." In *How Connections Heal: Stories from Relational Cultural Therapy*, edited by Maureen Walker and Wendy B. Rosen, 35–52. New York: Guilford Press, 2004.

PART V

Community Archives

CHAPTER 10

Community-Based Archives and Their Pedagogies

Jamie A. Lee, Kristen Suagee-Beauduy (Cherokee Nation), and Samantha Montes

Introduction

Over the past two decades, community archives have become increasingly recognized as rich sites of research and as integral to the greater archival studies discipline and profession.[1] This chapter introduces our research that begins in the acknowledgment of the limited and limiting, top-down naming practices that are oftentimes adhered to in institutional archival contexts. In our research, we are interested in understanding the practices and the power of naming in community archives as spaces that can accommodate multiple histories, voices, and modalities. Such an approach can function to disrupt oppressive archival practices that re-center white, ethnically European, bourgeois, Christian, cis, citizen, heterosexual, able-bodied men (WEBCCCHAM).[2]

Community archives emerge in our research as spaces for dynamic pedagogies and innovative practices including around description and naming. We highlight these as emergent pedagogical understandings that can contribute to archival studies education.

This chapter introduces preliminary insights from the Community-Based Archives: Considering the Power of Naming Practices research project that seeks to answer these questions:[3]

- How are naming practices—those related to archival appraisal and description—understood, deployed, and, importantly, differently consequential for distinct communities?

- How can archival description practices be reimagined to account for the incommensurable ontologies and epistemologies within and among communities?

- And how can these reimagined practices be applicable across the spectrum of community-based archives to be relevant, to empower, and to respectfully establish new historical narratives from and about underrepresented communities?

We share elements of the research process and center the term *community-based archives* (CBA), which encompass the spectrum of community-centered archival projects ranging from autonomous and independent community archives to those that have emerged within institutional contexts. As coauthors, we purposely write from our individual locations as queer, Indigenous, and Latinx (respectively), action-oriented researchers, scholars, and archivists. We shift registers to write as a collective "we" and then, where appropriate, as individuals. We have deliberately and respectfully named Kristen as she has carefully crafted her culturally relevant method for doing this work. We write this way so as not to conflate our voices, our experiences, and our lived locations. With this writing style, we mean to explicitly acknowledge ourselves as differently positioned with regard to power in the larger institution from which we write but also in the research project and in our differing roles as students and professor. We share insights into our early research and focus on our inquiry into the ways CBA describe and name themselves and their collections. By *naming practices*, we mean those practices and standards of vocabularies that are produced and called upon to describe records and collections. Naming practices have traditionally reflected universalized standards developed and utilized without full regard for diverse community perspectives, histories, and contributions. To avoid further marginalization that can be reproduced in top-down descriptions and other valuation standards, we designed our research through a pluralistic, relational, and critical framework. Such a framework recognizes the urgent need to acknowledge that underrepresented peoples exist and must meaningfully inform, participate in, and even oversee the ways their histories are collected, preserved, described, and remembered. This is, to us, what makes CBA exciting sites of telling, teaching, and learning.

The pedagogical potential in CBA demands a closer look at relationships. We introduce the concept of *contextual relationality* to acknowledge particular archival contexts and practices, including naming and description, as methods of storytelling and relating to stories that, in turn, offer an interactive, relational exchange.[4] Engaging the practice of storytelling as critical and pedagogical in our research has elucidated multiplicities. CBA are collections of multilayered, historical, and experiential events. They are storytelling spaces that introduce new histories and historical actors. Such multiplicities in CBA make for robust, contradictory, complex, and (always) incomplete collections that can tell many stories. They are open-ended *stories so far*.[5]

Our work focuses on the relational and incorporates the importance of intergenerational dialogues that archivists, communities, teachers, and students may have when they work together. Our research is attentive to the *doing* of archives as a practice of teaching, learning, and theory making across community contexts. We aim to shift the location of pedagogical power out of the classroom and into the CBA, where we identify three key pedagogical opportunities: (1) to align the mission, vision, values, and practices of the CBA with naming practices; (2) to insist on intergenerational and multiple histories that engage the CBA as *stories so far*; and (3) to introduce *fingerweaving* as a method of unraveling and reweaving with decolonizing potential.[6]

The Power of Naming
Overview

In our research project, we convened four partner archives that represent a broad range of community-based archives, community initiatives, autonomous community archives, and their stakeholders to discuss archival production and naming practices. Partner archives include:

1. Arizona Queer Archives (AQA), Tucson, Arizona, which is a community-based LGBTQI archives that works *to queer* archival practices in and through its commitment to being an archival laboratory focused on storytelling;[7]

2.   South Asian American Digital Archive (SAADA), Philadelphia, Pennsylvania, which is an autonomous, nonprofit, post-custodial, digital archives that is attentive to the changing nature of its communities and the stories that they want to preserve and tell;[8]

3.   Chicano/a Research Collection's Community-Driven Archives Initiative (CDA), Arizona State University, Tempe, Arizona, which is a community-based archival project and university collection that centers the training of Latinx, Native American, and LGBTQ+ communities to collect and preserve their own records and collections;[9] and

4.   Houston Area Rainbow Collective History (Houston ARCH), a coalition of Houston archivists dedicated to preserving and documenting Houston's LGBTQ history, University of Houston, Houston, Texas, which encompasses a myriad of archival contexts from personal archives to community archives to institutional archives across the University of Houston and Rice University.[10]

We selected these partner archives because of their diverse stakeholders as well as their commitment to documenting, holding, and making accessible the histories of underrepresented communities. While some are connected to institutional and academic archival contexts and some are not, each has a distinct story of how it came to be and how it works closely with, in, and for its communities. Each emerges as a vital site not only for inquiry but also for teaching and learning.

In seeking to better understand naming practices across institutional and community contexts, we consider the relationships that each of our partner archives has with institutional archival contexts. Our research also considers the roles that communities can play in naming themselves.[11] We engage queer, feminist, and decolonial theories to acknowledge the social justice potential of CBA and of the community archivists. Archival scholar Jarrett M. Drake centers Michelle Caswell's words to offer insight into the role of the archivist:

> How we as members of local and global communities remember the past is wholly bound up with how we imagine what is possible in the future. In this light, archivists are not just memory activists, but visionaries whose work reconceives imagined worlds through space and time.[12]

Caswell's words woven through Drake's engagements are a reminder of the multiple roles of the archivist including as activist, visionary, and pedagogue. As "memory activists" and "visionaries," CBA and their archivists have a lot to teach about the multiple historical narratives from and about underrepresented communities.

Methods

Together with other members of our research team,[13] we employed a qualitative framework to conduct focus groups (ten stakeholders at each partner archives) and semi-structured individual interviews (three stakeholders at each partner archives). Through focus groups and interviews with a total of fifty-two community members at the partner archives sites across the US, we examined the distinct ways that each defines and deploys naming practices through their archives' descriptions as well as in their archival appraisal and description practices. From August 2020 to January 2021, we conducted focus groups and interviews through Zoom. We created preliminary transcripts and then imported transcripts into Dedoose,[14] reviewed, revised, and discussed emerging codes to establish our coding schema.

Focus Groups and Interviews

The first focus group took place on August 5, 2020, with community archivists, institutional and university archivists, personal archivists, and scholars who all participated in some distinct way with Houston ARCH as a coalition of people and groups committed to preserving LGBTQ+ histories in the Houston area. While we have facilitated four focus groups, we center that of Houston ARCH because it instantiates not only the diversity of the concept of community archives but also how, as a coalition, its members have creatively worked to align its early mission and vision with its values and practices to best support multiple constituents through coalitional efforts. Their attention to its mission, vision, values, and practices demonstrates our first key pedagogical opportunity. By naming it Houston ARCH, members have effectively opened up how it acknowledges the many different ways that its stakeholders name themselves, describe their collections, and participate in the greater coalition.

Houston ARCH was founded in early 2008 because of a community-wide meeting that Jo Collier, librarian, Houston Public Library, organized to bring together people who were working on collecting LGBTQ+ histories in the Houston area. In his individual interview conducted via Zoom on August 24, 2020,

Brian Reidel, Houston ARCH facilitator from 2009 to 2013, noted that Collier was "the person to blame/give credit to …who realized …that none of these people had ever been in a room together before." At that first meeting, there were a lot of different kinds of archives present, as Reidel described:

> Everything from, you know, I've got my shoebox full of videotapes that I've made at events to the Botts Collection, which was in the old locker room of a gym at a church at the time …to GCAM, which was in warehouses and never could have been visited…. And then something like, you know, University of Houston. All of them were visible in the room. So to (say) "Here's what an archive is," we made it visible to each other that there were lots of different kinds of archives. That was really valuable. (Reidel interview)

Houston ARCH demonstrates how its coalition is one that can be considered *stories so far.* By this we mean the emergent coalition is one that exists in a particular time in the history of the archives (now) and is a part of a larger historical narrative. The idea of stories so far is one that lends itself, too, to the multiplicity (in this case of many forms of archives and community stories) that can get erased or obscured by an emphasis on singularity. The coalitional approach that came into view through our focus group and individual interviews reveals how CBA change to meet the desires, needs, strengths, and experiences of their communities. Focus group participants offered intergenerational perspectives of how they came to the work of archiving and how they, in turn, identify and name themselves in the archival work that they do. One focus group participant, Don Kelly, introduced himself as "an eighty-year-old gay man. I think I am a nonprofessional archivist…. I was instrumental in building the collection at Texas A&M University, which is named in my honor. As of now, there's 28,000 volumes in it." Sara Fernandez, another focus group participant, introduced herself as "an accidental person here. I just love stories and history. I started off recording people's stories and recording presentations that people gave at meetings. That's how I was first invited to ARCH and then I went on to do the Banners Project." Temporally each member changes and, so, their relationship to their home communities' histories changes and their relationship to the greater Houston ARCH group changes. Community-based archives are not held captive by one earlier iteration of themselves; they are designed to change over time.

Each CBA offers distinct educational opportunities for how an archives comes to be and why. As a sort of microcosm that demonstrates the spectrum of archives across community and institutional contexts, Houston ARCH illuminates the roles people play to adequately represent, collect, and preserve LGBTQ+ histories and make them accessible. Houston ARCH's naming practices at the macro and micro levels since their inception demonstrate our key pedagogical opportunities to show how teaching and learning can take place across intergenerational histories and conversations.

A Return to and a Review of the Archival Studies Literatures

Kristen Suagee-Beauduy (Cherokee Nation), Phase 1 graduate research assistant, searched for scholarly publications that directly addressed *description* in CBA. She did this to identify gaps in the archival studies literatures. In what follows, Kristen narrates her experience conducting this literature review, including the search terms she used and the opportunity this inquiry gave her to propose an archival method and pedagogy that she introduces here as *fingerweaving*.

During early exploratory research, I (Kristen) used different tools, including the University of Arizona Library Search and the Library Literature and Information Science Full Text (H. W. Wilson) database to look for articles related to community archives and naming practices. I searched the following terms: "community archives," "appraise," "appraisal," "vocabulary," "descriptive," "description," "name," and "naming." I then looked more closely at the results for articles related to naming practices involved in appraisal and description. I found eighty-nine articles that identified the need for alternative description and naming practices. Reading through these articles, I found that naming practices that exist in libraries, archives, or museums are too limiting or otherwise insufficient. Importantly, the call for alternative practices presents an opportunity to draw from and center the perspectives of underrepresented people in CBA.

During my inquiry, I came to see that the Indigenous practice of fingerweaving, which I elaborate on below, could lend important insights into the need for relevant naming practices and decolonizing reading practices that could support underrepresented community members in finding themselves represented in the archival record. In the next section, I bring together my own situated perspective to consider the power to reweave description to be a better fit for underrepresented communities. If archival contexts—both community and institutional—shift their adherence from traditional archival practices intended to "fix" identities onto and into records to more dynamic practices that insist on revisiting description and naming, then records and collections can remain relevant and representative to those who exist within them and those who want to find them.

Fingerweaving: Method and Metaphor

In my inquiry, I called on my home knowledges, and on fingerweaving in particular. I started to think about traditional naming practices in archival appraisal
and description as a fingerwoven belt with hundreds of frayed threads. Their
organic composition has decayed over time. With some unraveling and reweaving with new threads sourced from underrepresented communities, we can make
the archival belt more durable.

Drawing on the previously mentioned focus group example, I notice that the
metaphor of fingerweaving, as I describe it, emerges in Houston ARCH's stories
about how it started and its distinct relationship across both community and
institutional archival contexts. The University of Houston (UH) Library and
Special Collections joined Houston ARCH in 2012 when Vince Lee came on
board as the archivist for the Carey C. Shuart Women's Archive and Research
Collection. He recognized that there were no LGBT collections at UH and
wanted to connect with communities to plant the seeds of creating an LGBT
collecting area. Today Vince Lee is archivist/librarian at the UH Libraries and
Special Collections and is the curator for the LGBT History Research Collections, which actively participates with Houston ARCH and in collaboration
with the variety of archives and archivists—community and institutional—to
ensure that any LGBTQ+ collections could have a long-term home at UH if
needed. Lee stated:

> Through my involvement, relationships, and friendships with many
> in the community, I feel my role more as the custodian because really
> the materials are their history. They know it backwards and forwards
> and can describe it in ways that, from my perspective, I could not.
> And as just a facilitator, I see how we can bring folks together and
> talk about things and see what their expectations are and what we
> can do together to make things happen. That's mutually beneficial.

Lee's role in the HoustonARCH embodies the third key pedagogical opportunity in that he practices a sort of fingerweaving to illuminate the multiplicities
of the many histories and collections that make up Houston ARCH. He recognizes and supports the bigger picture of the historical threading, connecting,
and networking that must happen to fully engage with the multiplicities and the
richness of the Houston area's LGBTQ+ collections. CBA are grappling with how
to name and describe these multiplicities. We (coauthors) found that naming
practices are under-engaged in the archival studies literature but that there are

emerging calls for alternatives to top-down naming practices and their re-pro-duced singularities.

Our preliminary inquiry into naming practices reinforced how institutions that educate graduate students to become archivists, librarians, and museum professionals often teach according to traditional theory and practice that accept singularity through ongoing, top-down description practices and stan-dards. Our research project questions the status quo, perfected over centuries through a Matrix of Domination, as the primary if not exclusive way of naming and seeing the world.[15] Imperialism, colonialism, and their contemporary itera-tions, especially in educational settings, continue to wield power over and about marginalized communities, including in archival contexts. The LIS literature that exists about naming practices attempts to raise the voices of underrepresented communities, most of which have been historically criminalized (the disabled, mentally ill, queer, gender nonbinary, Indigenous and People of Color, immi-grant). Activism in the archival studies discipline and profession has unraveled some threads in the dominant culture's fingerwoven belt, enough so that every-one can see where the record is threadbare and in need of revisiting, revising, and reweaving. For example, activists have been trying to unravel the "alien" and "illegal alien" threads in Library of Congress Subject Headings (LCSH) for decades because those terms dehumanize undocumented immigrants. Decolo-nization would have been the complete removal of both the "alien" and "illegal" threads, but for now the Library of Congress has rewoven "noncitizens" and "illegal immigration" in their place. While the American Library Association praises this decision, social justice and migrant rights advocates remind us that harm is still being done.[16]

Fingerweaving in the Archives

Emerging scholarship in LIS is enriching both the historical record and commu-nity-centered best practices within archival studies to incorporate perspectives and materials from communities previously unable to find themselves "suddenly existing" in the archives.[17] My early inquiry suggests that this is about access—*how* archivists make the search process more intuitive to those people who have historically been left out of the historical record. Relatedly, working groups have formed to focus on subjects related to Latin American and Indigenous Peoples of the Americas, such as the Subject Authority Cooperative Program, to coordinate efforts to change LCSH with implications for the ways the US categorizes information. Some archives, for example, have created thesauri to overlap LCSH subject headings (Pequot), and others have Indigenized their information retrieval systems by replacing the LCSH with their non-Western ontologies (Maori).[18] These moves started when people from underrepresented communities entered the field. Gene Joseph, the first Indigenous librarian in Canada at the X̱wi7x̱wa Library at the University of British Columbia,[19] started conversations about naming as a basic right and sign of respect. Practitioners like Joseph created room for the next generation, like librarian Shavonn Matsuda (Native Hawaiian) at the University of Hawaii Maui College, who has been able to collaborate with traditional-knowledge-bearing Elders to generate Indigenous language names and categorization systems as repositories of information that are more intuitively accessible to the Native Hawaiian community members.[20] Spending money on these kinds of renaming and reorganizing projects is social justice work because it is creating information equity. It also connects to my ideas of fingerweaving as a method of reweaving traditional knowledges with archival practice in meaningful ways that are relevant to community practices, needs, and desires. Drawing from the fingerwoven belt also helps one to read and understand the Houston ARCH as composed of multiple histories and historic actors with naming an integral practice that centers not only identity but also, importantly, ways of knowing. CBA, then, are rich sites of pedagogical possibility when we look closely at what is already being done there in and with underrepresented communities.

Interventions across LIS

Oppressive naming practices are being challenged at all levels, and information professionals are regularly creating more ethical and inclusive description practices.[21] Related to the pushback on the LCSH, people are producing toolkits, protocols, and policies to better serve underrepresented communities. Scholars are advocating for careful uses and expansion of colophons and finding aids that can allow for more nuanced and flexible description. Software programs, like Omeka and Mukurtu, support expanded fields of information that allow for more complex description that no longer relies on a hierarchy of metadata and no emphasis on a standard metadata above that which is derived from the community.[22] Local Contexts cofounders, Kimberly Christen and Jane Anderson, advocate for what they call "slow archiving,"[23] which engages the integrative capacity of Mukurtu to "provide the space for different ways of knowing, presenting, framing, and engaging with knowledge that allows for divergent temporal and spatial realities and relations."[24] Through Mukurtu, there are parallel and multiple sets of metadata with expanded fields based on local needs and vocabularies that include traditional knowledge and cultural narratives that allow for more elaborate and multiple sets of narrations, narrators, and attributions. These approaches relate to fingerweaving insofar as they engage spectrums and multiplicities to include different ways of doing, knowing, and telling and considers them through a slow/ed temporality.

Regarding the LCSH pushback, on one end of the spectrum is the Brian Deer Classification System in British Columbia, which replaces the LCSH. In the middle, some have created thesauri such as Pathways, the Mashantucket Pequot Thesaurus of American Indian Terminology Project, Archives for Black Lives in Philadelphia, and Maori Subject Headings website, among many others. On the other end of the spectrum are those who have lobbied and are lobbying for changes to the LCSH.

The Pathways thesauri are an online project of the Australian Institute for Aboriginal and Torres Strait Islander Studies first composed in 1997 as the Aboriginal and Torres Strait Islander Thesaurus. As of 2011, the Pathways thesauri now include one thesaurus for place names, another for language and peoples, and a third for subject areas. Cree-Métis librarian Deborah Lee writes that the "wide range of terminology preferences …[point] to the need for local thesauri (developed with input by Indigenous users) for each library."[25] To come to this conclusion, Lee collected more than fifty surveys from individuals in attendance at Indigenous-related conferences. Survey results revealed a clear consensus among survey participants that the LCSH were outdated and inappropriate.

Indigenous scholars are grappling with how to decolonize institutionalized information systems to make room for the dazzling specificities of our cultures. With thousands of distinct Indigenous communities using hundreds of heritage languages and the transliterations and translations that come with them, we have the raw materials needed to reweave Indigenized information retrieval in a way that actively makes space for diversity instead of oppressing it. For example, Cristina B. Villanueva presented a paper at the 2016 IFLA World Library and Information Congress to address the need for flexibility in subject access terms to increase the findability of Indigenous Cordillera language materials suppressed by an LCSH controlled vocabulary that lacked equivalent English terms. Villanueva also suggested solutions to solve issues involved with varying spelling and naming differences using the iLib cataloging system online.[26] This granular-level approach reveals that Indigenous ontologies cannot be expressed authentically within Eurocentric classification systems and indexing terminology.

The Subject Access and Classification bibliography put together by the American Indian Library Association traces conversations about the limitations of Eurocentric naming practices to the 1970s. The bibliography's description says:

"Collected here are works about Indigenous cataloging issues. The list is global in scope and includes American Indian, First Nations, Australian Aboriginal, Māori, and Sami resources."[27]

The Mashantucket Pequot Thesaurus of American Indian Terminology Project applied the Thesaurus to the Mashantucket Pequot Museum and Research Center. Under the guidance of Cheryl A. Metoyer (Eastern Band of Cherokee Indians), the project was launched because the existing controlled vocabularies did not reflect "Indigenous philosophies in the description of American Indian subjects.... By bringing together two systems of thought, the attending objective is the improvement of access for both Native and non-Native individuals conducting research on American Indian topics."[28] Existing subject headings

> have not been designed with the perspectives of Indigenous people in mind.... The cataloging language silences Native American history. It disregards the sovereignty of Native nations, as well as historicizes* and stereotypes Native people and cultures. Additionally, researchers have found that LCSH and other mainstream knowledge organization systems severely limit the retrieval of Native language materials and Native American topics.[29]

While some archivists have committed to creating and modifying thesauri to increase the ease of information retrieval for nondominant groups, other archivists are publishing tips for incorporating anti-oppressive strategies into their practice. The Archives for Black Lives in Philadelphia has published its own recommendations to humanize the lives it is archiving as opposed to upholding a false neutrality that obfuscates anti-Blackness. You can find these recommendations in the document *Anti-racist Description Resources* created by its Anti-racist Description Working Group.[30] Among dozens of recommendations for anti-oppressive practices, the authors of the document use one section to encourage archivists to transition away from descriptive practices that center enslavement as the most notable aspect of an individual's life and use another section to suggest reparative processing strategies that work against legacy descriptions that are racist. In the writing of this chapter, this Archives for Black Lives document

---

* Many Indigenous scholars critique how Native peoples are habitually relegated to the past, a move that does not acknowledge the accomplishments of our ancestors that ensured our contemporary survival, a move that hides the contemporary efforts to exercise our human rights as defined by the United Nations Declaration of the Rights of Indigenous Peoples.

was updated with notes added about how adopting new vocabularies is an iterative process.

The National Japanese American Citizens League represents another underrepresented community that is contributing to changes in descriptive language. League members have put together "The Power of Words" handbook, published in 2012 and updated in December 2020, to educate people about the "language euphemisms used to describe the Japanese American World War II experience and the preferred terminology that more accurately describes the dire realities of the experience."[31] They provide suggestions that clearly illuminate the actions of the federal American government through language that transitions away from, for example, the sterility of "relocation centers" toward the more accurate "American concentration camps."

CBA and the people who attend to them have the potential to lead conversations about naming practices that make collections more accessible to the underrepresented communities they represent. From participatory archiving projects to crowdsourcing folksonomy projects,[32] CBA are choosing which new materials to incorporate into their own *fingerwoven belts* and I'm here for this avant-garde experimentation (and thankful for those who are taking the time to document it).

Teaching and Learning in the Archives: A Call to Action

Our research demonstrates the importance of CBA to Critical Archival Studies (CAS) and its curricula. CAS is emancipatory in its goal of transforming archival practice. The interventions sketched above are instructive and can be taught as practice-based examples of work being accomplished by underrepresented community members and community archivists that challenge the singularity of top-down naming practices. As an academic subfield, CAS broadens the archival studies scope and builds a critical stance regarding the role of archives in the production of knowledge, history, and historic actors. Our collective efforts, including our literature review, together with our interviews, focus groups, and research meetings have confirmed the innovations CBA are imagining and undertaking with regard to naming themselves and their histories.

While we started this chapter in research, we end with not only research-relevant findings but also with teaching-relevant and action-oriented findings. By shifting the location of pedagogical power away from the traditional classroom and into CBA, students and teachers become teachers and learners in the midst of community archivists, volunteers, records creators, and visitors to the archives. The pedagogical milieu, therefore, is one situated in meaningful exchange and relationship, one that supports contextual relationality—those engaged methods of storytelling and relating to stories—in its fullness. Thinking temporally to engage CBA as *stories so far* means, for us, that records and their creators are not fixed in tiny boxes that identify them; rather, dynamic naming opens the nonlinear and disrupting potential to recognize peoples as multiply situated with many overlapping identity categories and stories that they get to determine and tell. Reading practices that inspire a decolonizing engagement through *fingerweaving* means, for us, that visitors to the archives, archivists, and community folks are invited to experience and contribute to these multiplicities in the CBA. We end with related action opportunities.

Action Opportunities for Teachers and Archivists

- Set up internships for students to work with CBA to build Omeka and Mukurtu systems so communities aren't beholden to LCSH hierarchies. Students can partner with CBA to codesign metadata that is relevant to underrepresented communities.

- Build glossaries and resource pages together to support future student career choices in CBA and with liberatory practices at the heart of their work.

- Identify community participation. Participatory archives are at the heart of the revolution. That's where advances in and adjustments to descriptive practices (the reweaving) must happen.

- Collaboratively build assignments for students to initiate documentation of how community archives are reweaving their description practices. Support students in sharing their findings at local, regional, and national LIS and archives conferences as well as to community archival contexts. We must keep learning from one another.

- Build CBA resource lists with documentation projects that demonstrate community participation. Collaboratively create community-centered activities that students can participate in. Ensure hands-on experiences along with the affective relationship building that can take place in CBA. Participatory work helps shift power. Archivists, students, and community members will see relevant and relational naming practices in action.

- Give students access to digital collections so that they can analyze and better understand how naming works, for whom, and with what consequences.

Learning in the CBA and reflecting upon this learning is pedagogical and archival theory in the making. Such community-centered theoretical understandings about everyday lives through archival storytelling means that the learning stays in community and is also incorporated back into the classrooms, where thinking about archives in, with, and on behalf of underrepresented communities becomes urgent as students graduate and take positions in institutional and community archival contexts. Hands-on work with living histories and those underrepresented historic actors changes the practice and discipline in ways to highlight the relational aspects of archival work where people can learn from one another. Students need to be in the community and prepared to learn from firsthand experiences that, in turn, make our classrooms and pedagogy more relevant, stronger, and more robust. In the classroom and in the community, teachers and archivists must emphasize the ongoing nature of archival work. We encourage teaching *fingerweaving* as method and metaphor with the potential paradigm shift for archival practice and naming.

Acknowledgments

The authors would like to thank Adela C. Licona for reviewing drafts and offering suggestions for critical pedagogical implications of community-based archives. Thanks, too, to our partner archives for sharing their histories with us and giving us permission to further tell your stories. We are grateful to be a part of this important collection.

Notes

1. For published research on community archives, see Michelle Caswell's Community Archives Lab UCLA, https://communityarchiveslab.ucla.edu/research/publications/; Andrew Flinn's research at University College, London; Sarah Welland and Amanda Cossham, "Defining the Undefinable: An Analysis of Definitions of Community Archives," *Global Knowledge, Memory and Communication* 68, no. 8/9 (2019): 617–35, https://doi.org/10.1108/GKMC-04-2019-0049.
2. Michelle Caswell, "Dusting for Fingerprints: Introducing Feminist Standpoint Appraisal," *Journal of Critical Library and Information Studies* 3, no. 2 (2021), https://doi.org/10.24242/jclis.v3i2.113.
3. IMLS Early Career Grant, LB21, RE-18-19-0049-19.
4. For more on contextual relationality, see Jamie A. Lee, *Producing the Archival Body* (London: Routledge 2021), 59.
5. Adela C. Licona, "'Mi'ja, Just Say You're a Feminist Like You Used to …': Pa/trolling and Performing Queer Rhetorics of the Everyday" (keynote address, Queering Spaces/Queering Borders Queer Studies Conference, University of North Carolina-Asheville, April 4–6, 2013).
6. In the context of this chapter, we use fingerweaving as a metaphor to talk about the ways informationists can decolonize (unravel) oppressive archival practices and reweave them to better fit nondominant

communities. The metaphor comes from Kristen's Cherokee culture, where off-loom, fingerwoven belts are part of a traditional outfit (popularized in the 1700s and still worn today).

7. Arizona Queer Archives, https://arizonaqueerarchives.com/.

8. SAADA: South Asian American Digital Archive, https://www.saada.org/.

9. Community-Driven Archives Initiative, Arizona State University Library, https://lib.asu.edu/communityarchives.

10. Houston ARCH Wiki, http://houstonarch.pbworks.com/w/page/19526143/FrontPage.

11. Jamie Ann Lee, "A Queer/ed Archival Methodology: Archival Bodies as Nomadic Subjects," *Journal of Critical Library and Information Studies* 1, no. 2 (2017): 7, https://doi.org/10.24242/jclis.v1i2.26.

12. Jarrett Drake, "Archivists without Archives: A Labor Day Reflection," Medium, September 2, 2016, https://medium.com/on-archivy/archivists-without-archives-a-labor-day-reflection-e120038848e. Drake cites Michelle Caswell, "Inventing New Archival Imaginaries: Theoretical Foundations for Identity-Based Community Archives," in Identity Palimpsests: Archiving Ethnicity in the U.S. and Canada, ed. Dominique Daniel and Amalia S. Levi (Sacramento, CA: Litwin Press, 2014), 49.

13. The Phase 2 research team includes aems emswiler, doctoral student, and Bianca Finley Alper, Knowledge River Scholar and MA LIS student at the University of Arizona.

14. Dedoose is a qualitative and quantitative research analysis application that is easy to use in a virtual research team capacity and allows for extensive coding and visualization tools.

15. The Matrix of Domination/Matrix of Oppression comes from Patricia Hill Collins's book *Black Feminist Thought: Knowledge, Consciousness, and the Politics of Empowerment* (New York: Routledge, 2000). While we do not explore the Matrix of Domination here, it might be helpful for one's understanding of intersectionality to look at it as Hill does, in a way that conceptualizes the matrix as composed of four "interrelated domains of power, namely, the structural, disciplinary, hegemonic, and interpersonal domains" (276).

16. American Library Association, "ALA Welcomes Removal of Offensive 'Illegal Aliens' Subject Headings," news release, ALA Member News, November 12, 2021, https://www.ala.org/news/member-news/2021/11/ala-welcomes-removal-offensive-illegal-aliens-subject-headings; Kelly Jensen, "Library of Congress Subject Heading Change Doesn't Address the Real Issue," Book Riot, November 15, 2021, https://bookriot.com/library-of-congress-subject-heading-change/.

17. Michelle Caswell, Marika Cifor, and Mario H. Ramirez. "'To Suddenly Discover Yourself Existing': Uncovering the Affective Impact of Community Archives," *American Archivist* 79, no. 1 (Spring/Summer 2016): 56–81. https://doi.org/10.17723/0360-9081.79.1.56.

18. Indigenization is a generative practice, whereas decolonization happens in response to colonization and works to undo the harmful effects of systemic oppression. Indigenization can happen only when Indigenous people are in control of the creation of their own tribally specific (in this case) systems.

19. X̱wi7x̱wa Library, University of British Columbia Library, https://xwi7xwa.library.ubc.ca/.

20. From the Nā Hawaiʻi ʻImi Loa, "Conversations on Hawaiian Librarianship" (presentation, Hoʻokele Naʻauao A Hawaiian Librarianship Symposium, online, November 9, 2020).

21. The Archives for Black Lives Philadelphia's Anti-racist Description Working Group credits the following groups: "La Tanya S. Autry, Curator of Art and Civil Rights at Mississippi Museum of Art created the Social Justice and Museums Resource List; many archival repositories are partnering with underrepresented communities to build collections like the Plateau Peoples' Web Portal and Project STAND; and communities and activists are creating their own collections using digital humanities tools like the Chicana por Mi Raza Digital Memory Collective, DocNow, A People's Archive of Police Violence in Cleveland, and the Borderlands Archives Cartography." Alexis A. Antracoli et al., *Archives for Black Lives in Philadelphia: Anti-racist Description Resources* (Philadelphia: Archives for Black Lives in Philadelphia, October 2019, upd. September 2020), 12, https://archivesforblacklives.files.wordpress.com/2019/10/ardr_final.pdf.

22. Kimberly Christen and Jane Anderson, "Toward Slow Archives," *Archival Science* 19 (2019): 102, https://doi.org/10.1007/s10502-019-09307-x.

23. Description from the Local Contexts website: "Local Contexts supports Indigenous communities to manage their intellectual and cultural property, cultural heritage, environmental data and genetic resources within digital environments. Local Contexts recognizes the inherent sovereignty that

Indigenous communities have over knowledge and data that comes from lands, territories, and waters." Local Contexts home page, https://localcontexts.org/.

24. Christen and Anderson, "Toward Slow Archives," 103.

25. Deborah Lee, "Indigenous Knowledge Organization: A Study of Concepts, Terminology, Structure, and (Mostly) Indigenous Voices," *Partnership: The Canadian Journal of Library and Information Practice and Research* 6, no. 1 (July 2011): 27, https://doi.org/10.21083/partnership.v6i1.1427.

26. Cristina B. Villanueva, "Classification and Indexing of Philippine Indigenous Materials with Emphasis on the Cordillera" (presentation, IFLA World Library and Information Congress 2016, Columbus, OH, August 2016), https://library.ifla.org/1335/.

27. AILA Subject Access and Classification Wiki, "Selected Bibliography," last updated November 28, 2011, http://ailasacc.pbworks.com/w/page/1597605/Selected%20 Bibliography?fbclid=IwAR2TkyMP_8pbs1Z-hhvT9aT3BRUutJcSQoqaxGxorelsuAqggLVSlcWhvgg.

28. Sandra Littletree and Cheryl A. Metoyer, "Knowledge Organization from an Indigenous Perspective: The Mashantucket Pequot Thesaurus of American Indian Terminology Project," *Cataloging and Classification Quarterly* 53, no. 5–6, (2015): 641, https://doi.org/10.1080/01639374.2015.1010113.

29. Littletree and Metoyer, "Knowledge Organization," 642.

30. Antracoli et al., "Anti-racist Description Resources."

31. National Japanese American Citizens League Power of Words Committee, "The Power of Words," accessed July 29, 2021, https://jacl.org/power-of-words.

32. On participatory archiving projects, see Ana Roeschley and Jeonghyun Kim, "'Something That Feels Like a Community': The Role of Personal Stories in Building Community-Based Participatory Archives," *Archival Science* 19 (2019); 30, https://doi.org/10.1007/s10502-019-09302-2.

Bibliography

AILA Subject Access and Classification Wiki. "Selected Bibliography." Last updated November 28, 2011. http://ailasacc.pbworks.com/w/page/1597605/Selected%20 Bibliography?fbclid=IwAR2TkyMP_8pbs1Z-hhvT9aT3BRUutJcSQoqaxGxorelsuAqggLVSlcWhvgg.

American Library Association. "ALA Welcomes Removal of Offensive 'Illegal Aliens' Subject Headings." News release, ALA Member News, November 12, 2021. https://www.ala.org/news/ member-news/2021/11/ala-welcomes-removal-offensive-illegal-aliens-subject-headings.

Antracoli, Alexis A., Annalise Berdini, Kelly Bolding, Faith Charlton, Amanda Ferrara, Valencia Johnson, and Katy Rawdon. *Archives for Black Lives in Philadelphia: Anti-racist Description Resources*. Philadelphia: Archives for Black Lives, October 2019, updated September 2020. https://archivesforblacklives. files.wordpress.com/2019/10/ardr_final.pdf.

Arizona Queer Archives. https://arizonaqueerarchives.com/.

Arizona State University Library. Community-Driven Archives Initiative. https://lib.asu.edu/ communityarchives.

Caswell, Michelle. "Dusting for Fingerprints: Introducing Feminist Standpoint Appraisal." *Journal of Critical Library and Information Studies* 3, no. 2 (2021). https://doi.org/10.24242/jclis.v3i2.113.

———, "Inventing New Archival Imaginaries: Theoretical Foundations for Identity-Based Community Archives." In *Identity Palimpsests: Archiving Ethnicity in the U.S. and Canada*, edited by Dominique Daniel and Amalia S. Levi, 35–58. Sacramento, CA: Litwin Press, 2014.

Caswell, Michelle, Marika Cifor, and Mario Ramírez. "'To Suddenly Discover Yourself Existing': Uncovering the Affective Impact of Community Archives." *American Archivist* 79, no. 1 (Spring/Summer 2016): 56–81. https://doi.org/10.17723/0360-9081.79.1.56.

Christen, Kimberly, and Jane Anderson. "Toward Slow Archives." *Archival Science* 19 (2019): 87–116. https://doi.org/10.1007/s10502-019-09307-x.

Collins, Patricia Hill. *Black Feminist Thought: Knowledge, Consciousness, and the Politics of Empowerment*. New York: Routledge, 2000.

Drake, Jarrett M. "Archivists without Archives: A Labor Day Reflection." Medium, September 2, 2016. https://medium.com/on-archivy/archivists-without-archives-a-labor-day-reflection-e120038848

Houston ARCH Wiki. http://houstonarch.pbworks.com/w/page/19526143/FrontPage.

Jensen, Kelly. "Library of Congress Subject Heading Change Doesn't Address the Real Issue." Book Riot, November 15, 2021. https://bookriot.com/library-of-congress-subject-heading-change/.

Lee, Deborah. "Indigenous Knowledge Organization: A Study of Concepts, Terminology, Structure, and (Mostly) Indigenous Voices." *Partnership: The Canadian Journal of Library and Information Practice and Research* 6, no. 1 (July 2011). https://doi.org/10.21083/partnership.v6i1.1427.

Lee, Jamie Ann. "Be/Longing in the Archival Body: Eros and the 'Endearing' Value of Material Lives." *Archival Science* 16 (2016): 33–51. https://doi.org/10.1007/s10502-016-9264-x.

———. *Producing the Archival Body*. London: Routledge, 2021.

Licona, Adela C. "'Mi'ja, Just Say You're a Feminist Like You Used to …': Pa/trolling and Performing Queer Rhetorics of the Everyday." Keynote address, Queering Spaces/Queering Borders Queer Studies Conference, University of North Carolina Asheville, April 4–6, 2013.

Littletree, Sandra, and Cheryl A. Metoyer. "Knowledge Organization from an Indigenous Perspective: The Mashantucket Pequot Thesaurus of American Indian Terminology Project." *Cataloging and Classification Quarterly* 53, no. 5–6 (2015): 640–57. https://doi.org/10.1080/01639374.2015.1010113.

Local Contexts home page. https://localcontexts.org/.

Nā Hawai'i 'Imi Loa. "Conversations on Hawaiian Librarianship." Presentation, Ho'okele Na'auao A Hawaiian Librarianship Symposium, online, November 9, 2020.

National Japanese American Citizens League Power of Words Committee. "The Power of Words." Accessed July 29, 2021. https://jacl.org/power-of-words.

Roeschley, Ana, and Jeonghyun Kim. "'Something That Feels Like a Community': The Role of Personal Stories in Building Community-Based Participatory Archives." *Archival Science* 19 (2019): 27–49. https://doi.org/10.1007/s10502-019-09302-2.

SAADA: South Asian American Digital Archive. https://www.saada.org/.

Villanueva, Cristina B. "Classification and Indexing of Philippine Indigenous Materials with Emphasis on the Cordillera." Presentation, IFLA WLIC 2016, Columbus, OH, August 2016. https://library.ifla.org/1335/.

Welland, Sarah, and Amanda Cossham. "Defining the Undefinable: An Analysis of Definitions of Community Archives." *Global Knowledge, Memory and Communication* 68, no. 8/9 (2019): 617–34. https://doi.org/10.1108/GKMC-04-2019-0049.

X̱wi7x̱wa Library. University of British Columbia Library. https://xwi7xwa.library.ubc.ca/.

Suggested Further Reading

Arnstein, Sherry R. "A Ladder of Citizenship Participation." *Journal of American Institute of Planners* 35, no. 4 (1969): 216–24. https://doi.org/10.1080/01944366908977225.

Bryson, Mary, and Suzanne de Castell. "Queer Pedagogy: Praxis Makes Im/Perfect." *Canadian Journal of Education* 18, no. 3 (Summer 1993): 285–305. https://doi.org/10.2307/1495388.

Carden, Kailah R., and Sabina E. Vaught with Arturo Muñoz, Vanessa Pinto, Cecilia Vaught, and Maya Zeigler. "A Critical Archival Pedagogy: The Lesbian Herstory Archives and a Course in Radical Lesbian Thought." *Radical Teacher* 105 (Summer 2016): 23–32. https://doi.org/10.5195/rt.2016.275.

Caswell, Michelle, Ricardo Punzalan, and T-Kay Sangwand. "Critical Archival Studies: An Introduction." Editors' note, *Journal of Critical Library and Information Studies* 1, no. 2 (2017). https://doi.org/10.24242/jclis.v1i2.50.

Cifor, Marika, and Stacy Wood. "Critical Feminism in the Archives." *Journal of Critical Library and Information Studies* 1, no. 2 (2017). https://doi.org/10.24242/jclis.v1i2.27.

Cook, Terry. "Evidence, Memory, Identity, and Community: Four Shifting Archival Paradigms." *Archival Science* 13 (2013): 95–120. https://doi.org/10.1007/s10502-012-9180-7.

Cook, Terry, and Joan M. Schwartz. "Archives, Records, and Power: From (Postmodern) Theory to (Archival) Performance." *Archival Science* 2 (2002): 171–85. https://doi.org/10.1007/BF02435620.

Daniel, Dominque. "Documenting the Immigrant and Ethnic Experience in American Archives." *American Archivist* 73, no. 1 (2010): 82–104. https://www.jstor.org/stable/27802716.

Day, Ronald E., and Ajit K. Pyati. "'We Must Now All Be Information Professionals': An Interview with Ron Day." *InterActions: UCLA Journal of Education and Information Studies* 1, no. 2 (2005). https://doi.org/10.5070/D412000554.

Drabinski, Emily. "Queering the Catalog: Queer Theory and the Politics of Correction." *Library Quarterly: Information, Community, Policy* 83, no. 2 (April 2013): 94–111. https://doi.org/10.1086/669547.

Duarte, Marisa Elena, and Miranda Belarde-Lewis. "Imagining: Creating Spaces for Indigenous Ontologies." *Cataloging and Classification Quarterly* 53, no. 5–6 (2015): 677–702. https://doi.org/10.1080/01639374.2015.1018396.

Flinn, Andrew, Mary Stevens, and Elizabeth Shepherd. "Whose Memories, Whose Archives? Independent Community Archives, Autonomy, and the Mainstream." *Archival Science* 9 (2009): article 71. https://doi.org/10.1007/s10502-009-9105-2.

Flinn, Andrew. "Archives and Their Communities: Collecting Histories, Challenging Heritage." *Memory, Narrative and Histories: Critical Debates, New Trajectories*, edited by Graham Dawson, 19–35. Working Papers on Memory, Narrative, and Histories no. 1. Brighton, UK: Centre for Research in Memory, Narrative and Histories, University of Brighton, 2012.

Ghaddar, J. J., and Michelle Caswell. "'To Go Beyond': Towards a Decolonial Archival Praxis." *Archival Science* 19 (2019): 71–85. https://doi.org/10.1007/s10502-019-09311-1.

Gilliland, Anne J. *Conceptualizing 21st-Century Archives*. Chicago: Society for American Archivists, 2014.

Gilliland, Anne J., and Kelvin White. "Perpetuating and Extending the Archival Paradigm: The Historical and Contemporary Roles of Professional Education and Pedagogy." *InterActions: UCLA Journal of Education and Information Studies* 5, no. 1 (2009). https://doi.org/10.5070/D451000648.

Gustafson, Melissa. "Critical Pedagogy in Libraries: A Unified Approach." *Journal of Critical Library and Information Studies* 1, no. 1 (2017). https://doi.org/10.24242/jclis.v1i1.15.

Hurley, Chris. "Parallel Provenance." *Archives and Manuscripts* 33, no. 1 (2005): 110–45. https://publications.archivists.org.au/index.php/asa/article/view/9765.

Hurley, David A., Sarah Kostelecky, and Lori Townsend. "Cultural Humility in Libraries." *Reference Services Review* 47, no. 4 (2019): 544–55. https://doi.org/10.1108/RSR-06-2019-0042.

Jules, Bergis. "Architecting Sustainable Futures: Exploring Funding Models in Community-Based Archives." *Medium*, June 19, 2018. https://medium.com/community-archives/architecting-sustainable-futures-exploring-funding-models-in-community-based-archives-da9a7a856cbe.

Lee, Jamie Ann. "Beyond Pillars of Evidence: Exploring the Shaky Ground of Queer/ed Archives and Their Methodologies." In *Research in the Archival Multiverse*, edited by Anne J. Gilliland, Sue McKemmish, and Andrew J. Lau, 324–51. Clayton, Australia: Monash University Press, 2016.

Lee, Jamie Ann. "A Queer/ed Archival Methodology: Archival Bodies as Nomadic Subjects." *Journal of Critical Library and Information Studies* 1, no. 2 (2017). https://doi.org/10.24242/jclis.v1i2.26.

Lyotard, Jean-François. *The Postmodern Condition: A Report on Knowledge*. Minneapolis: University of Minnesota Press, 1984.

Sheffield, Rebecka. "Community Archives." In *Currents of Archival Thinking*, 2nd ed., edited by Heather MacNeil and Terry Eastwood, 351–76. Santa Barbara, CA: Libraries Unlimited. 2017.

Shilton, Katie, and Ramesh Srinivasan. "Participatory Appraisal and Arrangement for Multicultural Archival Collections." *Archivaria* 63 (Spring 2007): 87–101. https://archivaria.ca/index.php/archivaria/article/view/13129.

Shildrick, Margrit. "Queering the Social Imaginaries of the Dead." *Australian Feminist Studies* 35, no. 104 (2020): 170–85. https://doi.org/10.1080/08164649.2020.1791690.

Tuck, Eve, and K. Wayne Yang. "Decolonization Is Not a Metaphor." *Decolonization: Indigeneity, Education and Society* 1, no. 1 (2012): 1–40.

Wurl, Joel. "Ethnicity as Provenance: In Search of Values and Principles for Documenting the Immigrant Experience." *Archival Issues* 29, no. 1 (2005): 65–76. https://www.jstor.org/stable/41102095.

About the Editors

Yvonne Mery, Associate Librarian, leads the Instructional Design and e-Learning unit at the University of Arizona Libraries. She is also adjunct professor in the iSchool at the University of Arizona where she teaches courses in research methods and e-learning. Ms. Mery has designed and implemented online courses in information literacy skills for undergraduate students and collaborated with departments across campus to support students and instructors in their research needs. She has authored several papers and a book on the integration of information literacy in online classes and presented at numerous national conferences on best practices for online information literacy instruction. Ms. Mery has also designed and delivered workshops and courses in instructional design and tutorial development. She is the co-founder of Sidecar Learning, an e-learning platform. In addition to her MLS, she also holds an MA in Teaching English as a Second Language and a BA in English Literature. She has extensive experience working with a diverse group of undergraduate and graduate students.

Anthony Sanchez is an Associate Librarian and lead for the Research Incubator unit at the University of Arizona Libraries. He is also a co-founder of the CATalyst Studios multidisciplinary makerspace sponsored by UAL. Anthony has previously held academic library positions at the University of California, Riverside and throughout the Maricopa County Community College District. He holds a BA in English literature and an MA in library and information science from the University of Arizona. His research interests include peer learning models, ethical approaches to archives, and inclusive digital literacy practices.

About the Authors

Veronica Arellano Douglas is head of teaching and learning at the University of Houston Libraries. She received her MLS from the University of North Texas and BA in English from Rice University. Her research interests include critical perspectives on information literacy and reflective pedagogy, relational-cultural theory and its application to feminist library work, and constructions of librarian identity in higher education. Veronica is a proud alumna of the ALA Spectrum Scholarship Program and the ARL Leadership and Career Development program. You can read her writing at https://veronicaarellanodouglas.com.

Scout Calvert is a research data librarian at University of Nebraska-Lincoln. She grew up on a cattle ranch in northern Arizona, a settler descendent of farmers, miners, ranchers, and schoolteachers. Scout earned an MA in information resources and library science from University of Arizona, then a PhD from the University of California, Santa Cruz, in History of Consciousness, a distinctive interdisciplinary graduate program, focusing on science and technology in society. Her current projects trace the social aspects of data-centric knowledge production among genealogists, cattle breeders, and citizen historians. Dr. Calvert also investigates data infrastructure and practice in libraries and among academic researchers, informing data policy issues in academic libraries.

Hannah Carlton (she/her) is a reference and instruction librarian at St. Ambrose University, where she primarily works with undergraduate students and teaches a for-credit information literacy course. She holds an MLIS from Dominican University, and her library work has included time in public, community college, and university libraries. Her research interests include feminist and critical pedagogy in libraries, media literacy and instruction, and outreach. Outside of the library, Hannah is a runner, a baker, and a podcaster and identifies as a white, cisgender, queer woman.

Anastasia Chiu (they/them/theirs) is a scholarly communications librarian at New York University. In this role, they promote barrier-free access to scholarly and educational resources and support students and faculty in sharing their scholarly work. Anastasia was formerly a cataloging and metadata librarian. Their research includes multiple topics, including rights and copyright in digital collections metadata, supporting early-career librarians, applying relational-cultural theory and critical race theory to librarianship, and identifying how white supremacy manifests in library institutional work cultures. Their MSLIS is from St. John's University. They are guided by the principles of the #Femifesto in their work.

Paige Crowl is a Teaching and Learning Librarian at Emory University's Oxford College. Her work focuses on bringing the principles of equity and justice into librarianship; she frequently presents at library conferences on making library instruction more inclusive and accessible. Paige graduated from Emory University with a BS in environmental science and earned her MS in library and information sciences from the iSchool at University of Illinois Urbana-Champaign. She lives near Atlanta, Georgia, with her partner Robin and an extremely adorable snake.

Emily Deal serves as researcher services librarian for special collections at the University of Houston Libraries. She previously worked as an English and instruction librarian.

Siân Evans is the online programs librarian at Johns Hopkins University and the cofounder of Art+Feminism, a global campaign to create meaningful changes to the body of knowledge available about feminism and the arts on Wikipedia. Her writing can be found in edited volumes from MIT Press and Litwin Press and in journals such as *Art Documentation* and the *Serials Librarian*. Her work with Art+Feminism has been covered by the *New York Times*, the *Wall Street Journal*, *ARTnews*, and more. She was named a Leading Global Thinker by *Foreign Policy* magazine and a Badass Woman by Buzzfeed.

Joanna Gadsby works as the instruction coordinator and a reference and instruction librarian at University of Maryland, Baltimore County. She holds an MEd from Loyola University Maryland and an MLIS from University of Maryland, and she has been working in education for over twenty years. Her research interests include relational practice, critical and constructivist pedagogies, and gendered labor in librarianship. She is coeditor, along with Veronica Arellano Douglas, of the book *Deconstructing Service in Libraries: Intersections of Identities and Expectations*.

Amy Gilgan (they/she/he) is the School of Education librarian at the University of San Francisco. They are a facilitator with Rise for Racial Justice, an organization that offers racial literacy training to K–12 teachers. As a certified mediator and volunteer conflict coach with SEEDS Community Resolution Center, they are passionate about transforming harm and the systemic conditions that cause it. Amy identifies as white, queer, and nonbinary and is also trained as a restorative justice facilitator.

Lua Gregory is the public services librarian at Riverside City College. She has an MLIS from University of California, Los Angeles. Her research interests include social justice issues in librarianship, capitalism and its deleterious effects, and critical information literacy. She has authored book chapters and articles on these subjects and is coeditor, along with Shana Higgins, of *Information Literacy and Social Justice: Radical Professional Praxis*. She can be contacted at lua.gregory@rcc.edu.

Martinique Hallerduff (she/her) is an associate professor and chair of the library department at Oakton College. Her research interests include feminism, feminist pedagogy, leadership, and anti-racism. She holds an MLIS in library and information science, an MA in English, and a graduate certificate in women's and gender studies. Her previous publications focus on feminism and library leadership and mentoring instruction librarians. Outside of her professional work, she is a company member, and storyteller with 2nd Story Chicago. Martinique's various identities include being a mother and a lesbian/queer cisgender white woman living in Chicago.

Carolina Hernandez is currently the student success librarian at the University of Houston. She received her MLIS from the University of Wisconsin-Madison, an MA in media studies from the University of Texas at Austin, and a BA in French from Rutgers University. Her current research interests include critical information literacy, inclusive pedagogy, and institutional racism in librarianship. Most recently, she cowrote the chapter "We're Not Libraries; We're People:

Identity and Emotional Labor in Providing Face-to-Face Services in Libraries," published in *Deconstructing Service in Libraries*.

Shana Higgins is the access services librarian at California State University, San Bernardino. Research interests include critical information literacy teaching and learning, social justice issues in librarianship, educational justice, and feminist leadership practices in higher education. Shana is the author and coauthor of book chapters and articles on these subjects, and coeditor with Lua Gregory of *Information Literacy and Social Justice: Radical Professional Praxis*. Shana is currently a doctoral candidate in the Leadership for Educational Justice program at University of Redlands.

Alana Kumbier is a research and instruction librarian at Amherst College and a member of the Relational Cultural Theory Community of Practice with Veronica Arellano Douglas, Anastasia Chiu, Joanna Gadsby, and Lalitha Nataraj. Alana is the author of *Ephemeral Material: Queering the Archive*, and they coedited, with Maria T. Accardi and Emily Drabinski, *Critical Library Instruction: Theories and Methods* along with a special issue of *Communications in Information Literacy* reflecting on the publication, its afterlives, and essential counternarratives contributors have articulated to its praxis.

Jamie A. Lee is associate professor in the School of Information at the University of Arizona, USA, where their research and teaching attend to critical archival theory and methodologies, multimodal media-making contexts, storytelling, and bodies. Lee's book, *Producing the Archival Body* (Routledge, 2021), interrogates how power circulates and is deployed in archival contexts in order to build critical understandings of how deeply archives influence and shape the production of knowledges and human subjectivities. Lee is an IMLS Early Career Grantee and an Agnese Nelms Haury Program in Environment and Social Justice Faculty Fellow. For more on their research: https://www.thestorytellinglab.io.

Amanda Meeks currently works at the Permanent Legacy Foundation, as the community and partnerships manager. Her practice as a librarian has focused on developing intentionally reflective, feminist, and critical programs and instruction in order to integrate information literacy, art/making, and social justice. As the former Diversity Committee chair for the Art Libraries Society of North America, she led the development of an annual forum centered on accessibility and disability justice (April 2020—cancelled due to COVID-19) and leading through an intersectional, anti-oppressive lens (March 2019). She served on the

Association of College and Research Libraries President's Program Committee, which facilitated a program around generous accountability in academic librarianship for the American Library Association annual conference (June 2020). Lastly, she is a regional ambassador for the international organization Art+Feminism, a grassroots collective that prioritizes brave, accountable, and transformative participation on Wikipedia worldwide.

Rafia Mirza is a Digital Scholarship librarian at Southern Methodist University. She helps provide research and instructional support for students and faculty who are interested in digital scholarship projects. Rafia holds an MSI from the University of Michigan School of Information and has done graduate coursework in American Studies from the University of Minnesota. Her research focuses on digital humanities, library pedagogy, project planning and infrastructure in libraries as well as race, gender, and labor in librarianship. She has published articles in the *Canadian Journal of Academic Librarianship*, *Library Trends*, *Journal of Radical Librarianship*, and *College and Undergraduate Libraries* and contributed chapters to *Topographies of Whiteness: Mapping Whiteness in Library and Information Science* (Library Juice Press, 2017) and the forthcoming *Debates in the Digital Humanities 2023* (University of Minnesota Press, 2023). More information can be found at https://librarianrafia.github.io/about, and she can be contacted at @librarianrafia on Twitter.

Samantha Montes was born and raised in Tucson, Arizona. As a Knowledge River Scholar, she earned her MA in library and information science in 2020 from the University of Arizona with a focus in archives and special collections. She holds a BA in English literature and religious studies, graduating with honors in 2018. She currently teaches at the University of Arizona's Worlds of Words: Center of Global Literacies and Literatures while pursuing graduate studies in teaching, learning, and sociocultural studies with a concentration in children's literature.

Lalitha Nataraj is the social sciences librarian at California State University, San Marcos. She holds an MLIS from UCLA and a BA in English and women's studies from UC Berkeley. Her research interests include feminist pedagogy, critical information literacy, South Asians in librarianship, relational-cultural theory in LIS, and scholarly inquiry and the research cycle.

Karen P. Nicholson is Associate Librarian at the University of Guelph and an instructor for the Faculty of Information and Media Studies at Western

University. Her research focuses on information literacy, academic libraries, and higher education. She has published in *Journal of Documentation*, *Library Quarterly*, *College & Research Libraries*, *Library Trends*, and *Journal of Critical Library and Information Studies*. Together with Maura Seale, she coedited *The Politics of Theory and the Practice of Critical Librarianship* (Library Juice Press, 2018). She obtained her PhD (LIS) from Western and holds an MLIS and MA from McGill.

Elizabeth Novosel (she/her) is a liaison librarian at the University of Colorado Boulder. Elizabeth's research interests are human-centered and wide-ranging: they include neurodiversity, librarian support of disabled students in information literacy instruction, and user experience in academic libraries. Elizabeth has previously worked as an academic advisor, university foreign language instructor, and massage therapist, and these experiences inform her current work as an academic librarian. She received an MLIS (2009) from the University of Wisconsin, Milwaukee, and an MA in German language and literature (2004) from the University of Colorado, Boulder.

Maura Seale is the history librarian at the University of Michigan, providing research and instructional support for students and faculty in the history department. Maura holds an MSI from the University of Michigan School of Information, an MA in American studies from the University of Minnesota, and a graduate certificate in digital public humanities from George Mason University. Her research focuses on critical librarianship, library pedagogy, political economy and labor in libraries, and race and gender in libraries. She is the coeditor, with Karen P. Nicholson, of *The Politics of Theory in the Practice of Critical Librarianship* (2018) and is also coediting the volume from ACRL Press, *Exploring Inclusive & Equitable Pedagogies: Creating Space for All Learners*. Her work can be found at http://mauraseale.org, and she welcomes comments via @mauraseale.

Kristen Suagee-Beauduy is an enrolled member of the Cherokee Nation in Oklahoma. She is a mixed blood settler living within the ancestral territory of the O'odham people in what is now called southern Arizona. Kristen has an undergraduate degree in creative writing from the University of Arizona, where she minored in American Indian studies, as well as a graduate certificate in Cherokee studies from Western Carolina University. As of this publication, Kristen is ten credits shy of a master's degree in library and information science. Kristen is most interested in working with Indigenous people and institutions to maintain cultural heritage resources for tribal communities.